Sunningdale, the Ulster Workers' Council strike and the struggle for democracy in Northern Ireland

MANCHESTER
1824

Manchester University Press

Sunningdale, the Ulster Workers' Council strike and the struggle for democracy in Northern Ireland

Edited by

David McCann and Cillian McGrattan

Manchester University Press

Published by Manchester University Press
Altrincham Street, Manchester M1 7JA

www.manchesteruniversitypress.co.uk

British Library Cataloguing-in-Publication Data
A catalogue record for this book is available from the British Library

Library of Congress Cataloging-in-Publication Data applied for

ISBN   978 0 7190 9951 9   hardback

First published 2017

Typeset
by Toppan Best-set Premedia Limited
Printed in Great Britain
by Lightning Source

Contents

Contributors

Arthur Aughey is Professor of Politics at Ulster University and Senior Fellow at the Centre for British Politics at the University of Hull. Recent publications on Irish politics include *The Politics of Northern Ireland: Beyond the Belfast Agreement* (Routledge, 2005); *The Anglo-Irish Agreement: Rethinking Its Legacy* edited with Cathy Gormley-Heenan (Manchester University Press, 2011); and *The British Question* (Manchester University Press, 2013).

Stuart Aveyard is an Irish Research Council post-doctoral fellow at the Centre for War Studies, University College Dublin. He previously held posts at Queen's University Belfast as a research fellow and lecturer in modern British history. His book *No Solution: The Labour Government and the Northern Ireland Conflict 1974–79* is forthcoming with Manchester University Press.

Sarah Campbell is a Lecturer of Modern British and Irish history at Newcastle University. She has published on Irish history and the Northern Ireland conflict and is the author of *Gerry Fitt and the SDLP: 'In a minority of one'* (Manchester University Press, 2015).

John Coakley, MRIA is a Professor of Politics in Queen's University Belfast and Professor Emeritus at University College Dublin. Recent publications include *Nationalism, Ethnicity and the State: Making and Breaking Nations* (Sage, 2012), *Breaking Patterns of Conflict: Britain, Ireland and the Northern Ireland Question* (Routledge, 2014) and *Non-Territorial Autonomy and the Government of Divided Societies* (Routledge, 2016).

Tony Craig is Associate Professor of Modern History at Staffordshire University. Whilst his research has previously focused on Anglo-Irish diplomatic relations, more recently he has published research on the use of political intelligence during both the Northern Ireland Troubles and throughout Britain's end of empire.

Aaron Edwards is a Senior Lecturer in Defence and International Affairs at the Royal Military Academy Sandhurst and author or editor of several books, including *Mad Mitch's Tribal Law: Aden and the End of Empire* (Transworld Books, 2014) and *UVF: Behind the Mask*, which will be published by Merrion Press in 2016.

Gordon Gillespie has taught Northern Ireland politics at both Queen's University Belfast and the University of Ulster. He is the author of a number of works on Loyalism, flag disputes, and reference works relating to Northern Ireland. He is currently writing a biography of the former Northern Ireland loyalist leader Glen Barr.

Thomas Hennessey is Professor of Modern Irish History at Canterbury Christ Church University. He is a co-author of *The Democratic Unionist Party: From Protest to Power* (Oxford University Press, 2014) and the author of *Hunger Strike: Mrs Thatcher's Battle with the IRA 1980–1981* (Irish Academic Press, 2013).

David McCann is a Lecturer in Politics at Ulster University. He is the author of *From Protest to Pragmatism: The Unionist Government and North–South Relations* (Palgrave, 2015) and completed his PhD on the approach of policymakers to relations between Northern Ireland and the Republic of Ireland from 1959 to 1972 at Ulster University.

Shaun McDaid is Research Fellow at the Centre for Research in the Social Sciences, University of Huddersfield. He is author of *Template for Peace: Northern Ireland, 1972–75* (Manchester University Press, 2013) and has published articles in journals such as *Terrorism and Political Violence*, *British Politics*, and Irish *Historical Studies*.

Cillian McGrattan is a Lecturer in Politics at the University of Ulster. His books include *Northern Ireland, 1968–2008: The Politics of Entrenchment* (Palgrave Macmillan, 2010) and *The Politics of Trauma and Peace-Building: Lessons from Northern Ireland* (Routledge, 2016).

Eamonn O'Kane is Reader in Conflict Studies at the University of Wolverhampton. He is author of *Britain, Ireland and Northern Ireland Since 1980* (Routledge, 2007) and co-author, with Paul Dixon, of *Northern Ireland Since 1969* (Longman, 2011). He is currently writing a book on the peace process, to be published by Manchester University Press.

Connal Parr studied Modern History at the University of Oxford and obtained his PhD at Queen's University Belfast in 2013. He was Irish Government Senior Scholar for 2014–15 at Hertford College, Oxford, and currently teaches twentieth-century European history at Fordham University's London Centre.

Henry Patterson is Emeritus Professor of Irish Politics at Ulster University. His *Ireland's Violent Frontier: The Border and Anglo-Irish Relations during the Troubles* will be published in a new paperback edition in 2016 (Palgrave Macmillan). At present he is working on a book on the ideology of the peace process that will examine the social forces and political and ideological currents which promote the empty idea of Northern Ireland as a society in transition to promote their own sectional and institutional interests whilst masking the profound absence of any significant structural changes in the conditions of its working class.

Acknowledgements

This book arose from a symposium held in May 2014 at the Public Records Office of Northern Ireland (PRONI). The event was funded by Ulster University's Institute for Research in the Social Sciences, and the editors wish to thank the Institute's Directors, Cathy Gormely-Heenan and Kris Lasslett, for their support. We also thank the staff at PRONI, in particular David Huddleston and Stephen Scarth.

The book is dedicated to Henry Patterson, who acted as a supervisor to both the editors, and to Christine and Steffi.

List of abbreviations
and Irish terms

AIA	Anglo-Irish Agreement
AIIC	Anglo-Irish Intergovernmental Conference
An Phoblacht	'The Republic', a republican newspaper supportive of Sinn Féin
Ard Chomhairle	the national executives of a political party
Ard Fheis	'High Assembly', the term used for party conferences in Ireland
BBC	British Broadcasting Corporation
B/GFA	Belfast/Good Friday Agreement (1998)
CAB	Cabinet Office
Dáil	Lower house of the Oireachtas
DFA	Department of Foreign Affairs
DT	Department of the Taoiseach
DUP	Democratic Unionist Party
EEC	European Economic Community
Éire Nua	'New Ieland', a proposal in the 1970s for a federal United Ireland
Fianna Fáil	'Soldiers of Destiny', one of the major political parties in Ireland, serving in government from 1957 to 1973
Fine Gael	'Family of Ireland', one of the major political parties in Ireland, leading a coalition government with the Labour Party from 1973 to 1977
GFA	Good Friday Agreement (1998)
HMG	Her Majesty's Government
IDU	Inter-Departmental Unit on the North of Ireland

IRA	Irish Republican Army
LAW	Loyalist Association of Workers
MP	Member of Parliament
NAI	National Archives of Ireland
NICRA	Northern Ireland Civil Rights Association
NILP	Northern Ireland Labour Party
NIO	Northern Ireland Office
NIPC	Northern Ireland Political Collection
OE	Office of the Executive
OIRA	Official Irish Republican Army
Oireachtas	Combined name for the Lower house (Dáil) and the Upper house (Seanad) of the Irish Parliament
PIRA	Provisional Irish Republican Army
PRONI	Public Records Office of Northern Ireland
RTÉ	Raidió Teilifís Éireann
RUC	Royal Ulster Constabulary
SDLP	Social Democratic and Labour Party
Seanad	Upper house of the Oireachtas
Sinn Féin (Provisional)	'We Ourselves', a party supportive of the Provisional IRA during the Troubles
SIS	Secret Intelligence Service
Tánaiste	the Office of Deputy Prime Minister of Ireland
Taoiseach	'Chieftain', used for the office of Prime Minister of Ireland
TD	Teachta Dála, Member of the Dáil
TNA	The National Archives (UK)
UAC	Ulster Army Council
UDA	Ulster Defence Association
UK	United Kingdom
UN	United Nations
UPNI	Unionist Party of Northern Ireland
UUAC	United Ulster Action Campaign
UUC	Ulster Unionist Council
UUP	Ulster Unionist Party
UUUC	United Ulster Unionist Council
UUUM	United Ulster Unionist Movement
UVF	Ulster Volunteer Force
UWC	Ulster Workers' Council
WBLC	West Belfast Loyalist Coalition

Chronology

1920	Government of Ireland Act partitions Ireland.
1963	Terence O'Neill becomes Prime Minister of Northern Ireland, promising to 'transform the face of Ulster'.
1965	The Ulster Volunteer Force (UVF) is formed in November. The paramilitary grouping was established to destabilise O'Neill. The group carries out three sectarian murders the following year.
1967	The Northern Ireland Civil Rights Association (NICRA) is formed in January.
1968	A civil rights march is violently broken up by police in Derry in October. The television pictures create outrage across the UK and Ireland. O'Neill promises a series of reforms that meet nearly all of NICRA's agenda.
1969	O'Neill resigns from office in April, following a series of bombings carried out by the UVF, which were initially reputed to be the responsibility of the Irish Republican Army (IRA). He is succeeded by James Chichester Clark. Following a summer of disturbances, in August British troops are sent to maintain law and order and provide relief to the police in Northern Ireland. The Republican movement splits in December between those who favour political agitation and those who prefer armed struggle. The IRA splits between the more Marxian and Southern-based Officials and the more Northern-based and sectarian Provisionals.

1970   Alliance Party formed in April. Social Democratic and Labour Party (SDLP) formed in August.

1971   Brian Faulkner assumes premiership of Northern Ireland in March. The SDLP walkout of the Northern Ireland Parliament in June following the killings of two Catholics in Derry by the British Army. A deteriorating security situation convinces Faulkner of the necessity of introducing internment without trial in August – a critical decision that alienates large sections of the minority, Catholic community. The Democratic Unionist Party (DUP) is founded in September.

1972   In January, an anti-internment march in Derry is attacked by soldiers of the First Battalion, the Parachute Regiment, resulting in the deaths of 14 people. The Northern Ireland Parliament is prorogued in March and direct rule of the province is assumed by Edward Heath's government in Westminster. William ('Willie') Whitelaw is appointed Secretary of State for Northern Ireland. A conference bringing together Northern Irish parties is held in Darlington in September to discuss restoring devolution based on a form of power sharing. The year sees the greatest loss of life as a result of violence in the history of the Troubles with almost fivr hundred killings.

1973   Britain and Ireland join the European Economic Community in January. An Irish General Election in February results in a Fine Gael–Labour coalition, headed by Liam Cosgrave. In March a White Paper is published outlining proposals for restored devolution based on power sharing. The Unionist Party's ruling body, the Ulster Unionist Council (UUC), authorises Faulkner to negotiate on the basis of the White Paper's proposals. Faulkner pledges to not share power with anyone 'whose primary object is to break the link with Britain' in May. Elections to a new Northern Ireland Assembly are held in June. In October, inter-party talks involving the Ulster Unionists, the SDLP and the Alliance Party are convened at Stormont with the object of establishing a power-sharing executive. In November the Unionist Party's ruling Council agrees in principle to power sharing. The Sunningdale Communiqué of December that year provides for the institutionalisation of the Irish dimension through a 'Council of Ireland'. The Irish government's position is challenged by Kevin Boland, TD, in the courts, which prevents the coalition government from clarifying its stance and adds to the pressure on Faulkner from within Ulster unionism regarding the Council of Ireland.

1974   A power-sharing executive takes its seats in January. Faulkner is defeated on a motion on the Council of Ireland at a UUC meeting. He resigns as leader of the Unionist Party but remains as head of the new Executive with the support of pro-Faulknerite Unionists in the Assembly. A British General Election in February sees a rout of pro-Sunningdale forces, with only Gerry Fitt of the SDLP being returned. The anti-Sunningdale forces in the United Ulster Unionist Coalition campaign under the slogan 'Dublin is only a Sunningdale away'. Harold Wilson's Labour Party replaces Edward Heath's Conservative government. In March Merlyn Rees is named as the new Secretary of State for Northern Ireland. In May the pro-Faulknerite Unionists begin to organise a new party, the Unionist Party of Northern Ireland. An Assembly motion in favour of the power-sharing Executive is passed with 44 votes to 38. The vote leads the loyalist-backed Ulster Workers' Council (UWC) to call a strike that begins on 14 May. Lasting until 28 May, the UWC strike precipitates the collapse of the 'Sunningdale experiment'; direct rule is reassumed by Westminster.

1975   A 'Constitutional Convention' is established within Northern Ireland to deliberate on the possibilities of political progress. A Provisional IRA (PIRA) ceasefire (begun in December 1974 but formally announced in February 1975) enables Republicans to hold secret talks with the British government. The ceasefire and talks break down in August.

1976   The Constitutional Convention ends. The Convention's Report rejects power sharing in favour of majority rule and an Irish dimension. The Report is repudiated by the SDLP.

1980–81 Republicans hold two hunger strikes to press for 'political status' for prisoners. The first hunger-striker to die was Bobby Sands in May 1981. He had been elected to the House of Commons in a by-election in Fermanagh-South Tyrone in April 1981. The hunger strikes are called off in October after nine other prisoners have died.

1982   Sinn Féin contests elections for a new Northern Ireland Assembly, winning ten per cent of the vote (or around one-in-three Catholic votes). Nationalists boycott the Assembly.

1985	The Anglo-Irish Agreement is signed by Margaret Thatcher and Garret FitzGerald in November. The Agreement causes outrage among the Ulster Unionist population, particularly due to it providing a consultative role for Dublin governments in Northern Ireland (which could be reduced if devolved power sharing were to be established); around a hundred thousand unionists gather at Belfast City Hall to protest against the Agreement.
1987	In November French authorities intercept a ship bearing a large consignment of weapons and explosives from Libya to the PIRA. A PIRA bomb kills 11 people at a Remembrance Day ceremony in Enniskillen.
1988	Gerry Adams and John Hume begin a series of secret talks, which last, intermittently into the 1990s.
1990	Secretary of State Peter Brooke states that Britain has 'no selfish strategic or economic interest' in Northern Ireland.
1991	Brooke announces a 'three-stranded approach' to political talks that would take into account relationships between Northern Ireland and London, between Northern Ireland and the Irish Republic, and between the Republic and the UK.
1993	The Downing Street Declaration is published in December. The document, which was agreed between the two governments, reiterates the 'principle of consent' – namely, the need for a democratic vote on any constitutional change in Northern Ireland's status – and calls on Republicans to renounce violence.
1994	The PIRA announces a 'complete cessation' of its armed campaign in August. Loyalists announce a ceasefire in October. In December, President Bill Clinton appoints Senator George Mitchell as his economic envoy to Northern Ireland.
1995	The two governments appoint Mitchell to head a commission to propose a way of decommissioning paramilitary arms as a precondition for entry by their political representatives into talks.
1996	In January, the Mitchell Commission recommends that decommissioning should occur in tandem with the talks process. In February, the PIRA ceasefire ends with a massive explosion in London's Canary Wharf. A summer of unrest follows the stand-off between Orangemen and residents' coalitions in Belfast and Derry; the most serious stand-off occurs in Portadown where the Orange Order is prevented,

for the second year, from walking along the mainly nationalist/ Catholic Garvaghy Road.

1997   Tony Blair's New Labour wins a landslide victory in the May General Election. In July the PIRA announces another ceasefire. Sinn Féin sign up to the Mitchell Principles of non-violence and enters political talks in September.

1998   The Belfast/Good Friday Agreement is signed by all parties to the talks except for the DUP in April.

Part I

Introduction and overview of the Sunningdale Agreement

1

Introduction

David McCann and Cillian McGrattan

Conceptions of democracy and ideas about democratic practice lie at the heart of debates on and about Northern Ireland. They have inspired violence and continue to precipitate division, confounding those who seek to explore non-conflictual ways of filtering antagonism. In this regard, Richard Bourke has argued that '[t]he case of Northern Ireland highlights the existence of a shortfall between our basic political aspirations and what in actual fact transpires in the world we have inherited' (2003: 7). *Sunningdale, the Ulster Workers' Council Strike and the Struggle for Democracy in Northern Ireland* aims to explore this disconnect by focusing on the first attempt to implement a power-sharing democratic framework in Northern Ireland and analysing, from a number of perspectives, reactions to that framework at the time and in subsequent years. Those reactions spoke to foundational ideas about democracy including how we think about and implement notions of inclusion, transparency, justice, fairness, accountability and plurality. The aim of this book, then, is to examine how the lessons that actors took from the 1973–74 'experiment' of these notions impacted upon the experiment itself and later attempts at trying to reach a political settlement.

The arguments and ideals that characterised the Sunningdale era, of course, continue to resonate in contemporary Northern Ireland – often in violent and aggressive ways. For example, Loyalist protestors besieged Belfast city centre in early December 2012 to vent their anger at the removal of the Union Flag from the top of the city hall. The issue had been debated within the council chamber and on the streets for a number of weeks beforehand. The city's Unionist community, who tend to favour maintaining the constitutional link with the United Kingdom, held that the question represented the crystallisation of their fears that their identity was being eroded in the public sphere. On the other hand, the city's Nationalist population, who tend to favour a reunification with the Irish Republic, believed that the flag should be removed completely since it represented for them an alienating presence in their city. In actuality, the 3 December decision by Belfast city council's elected representatives was to curtail the flying of the flag to 'designated days' of historic and symbolic importance. This option was suggested by the cross-community, middle-ground Alliance Party, as a compromise between removal and having the flag flying every day. Despite a decade and a half of peaceful politics, the flags protest spiralled into violence: politicians (particularly from the Alliance Party) and journalists were issued death threats and their homes and party offices were targeted with nail bombs and shooting; the police were subject to attack from petrol bombs and by the New Year the rioting and road blocks that brought the city to a standstill had resulted in over a hundred arrests and had been estimated at costing up to £15 million in lost revenue, police time and clean-up operations.

While it criticised the violence, the protests were immediately framed by the Belfast *News Letter* (a daily whose readership is mainly Protestant and Unionist) as being about a battle over democracy. Thus, its editorial argued that '[t]he current crisis over the Union Flag has its origins in nationalist intransigence. The consent principle recognises Northern Ireland's place in the UK, yet Britain's flag is objectionable' (*News Letter*, 10 December 2012). While the *News Letter's* allusion to the consent principle spoke to the idea that a majority within Northern Ireland advocate maintaining the constitutional link with Great Britain, the allusion itself speaks to and brings to light (even if by way of deferral) distinctions in how democracy is conceptualised and practised in Northern Ireland. This point about distinctions in thought and practice was evident in a series of short position pieces by Belfast city councillors that had appeared in the same paper the previous day. Tim Attwood of the moderate Nationalist Social Democratic and Labour Party (SDLP), for example, pointed out that while his party favoured a policy of flying no flags, the idea of restricting the Union Flag to flying on designated days represented 'an honourable and reasonable way forward'. Consensual politics, he said, were possible in a divided city like Belfast, pointing to agreements reached between Nationalist and Unionist councillors about how to commemorate events from the critical period 1912–22; however, people needed to focus on important issues that effected everyone such as economic regeneration. Attwood's message was reiterated by the Alliance councillor Máire Hendron, who argued that 'instead of sending out a message to the world that yet again Northern Ireland has retreated to traditional tribal positions, we should demonstrate clearly that we can act in a mature manner on such a sensitive issue' (*News Letter*, 10 December 2012). A contrary view was offered in a retrospective analysis by the Ulster Unionist Party counsellor Alderman Jim Rodgers who accused Alliance and the Nationalist parties of the SDLP and Sinn Féin of betraying the people of Belfast. The restriction of the flying of the flag, he argued, 'was a blow against consensus politics and very much represented the politics of the past ... [The] decision created untold anger and impacted community relations in a way that hasn't been seen for years ... the out-workings of which continue right up until today' (*News Letter*, 3 December 2013). In such ways are differences over ideas about consent and voice often masked by or worked through attributions and allegations of blame and responsibility: the lessons taken from events therefore often reaffirm pre-existing ideological and ethnic sentiments.

Linked in with these battles over symbolism was a sense of illegitimacy that was linked to a similar concept that loyalists used in 1974. Despite the fact that the flags' decision was taken by democratically elected councillors, the protestors argued that the Loyalist community has stopped voting and is effectively disenfranchised from the political process. Since 1998, turnout in elections has steadily fallen from around 70 per cent to 54.5 per cent at the 2011 Assembly election. In recent elections despite the tendency for people from working-class communities to vote there are proportionately around 10 per cent more Catholics voting than Protestants (Garry, 2011). This in effect bolsters Sinn Féin while eroding support for Loyalist parties like the Progressive Unionist Party (PUP). The declining turnout and demographic shifts have turned what used to be a solid Unionist majority into a hung council with Nationalists holding a slight edge. This loss of a majority and the removal of the Union Flag fuelled the narrative of a culture war against the Loyalist community by what they perceived as an illegitimate decision. This sense of disengagement was in large part what gave the protestors justification to adopt similar methods to the Ulster Workers' Council (UWC) of blocking roads at peak times during the day. A mural in East Belfast showing Loyalists celebrating the collapse of the 1974 power-sharing Executive illustrates the resonance of these lessons of alienation, disenfranchisement and contested legitimacy that continue to underpin Loyalist claims-making today.

Agreeing to disagree?

This politics of claims-making often circles around feelings of justified grievance and the allocation of blame. As Alvin Jackson has pointed out, the
problems of causation and blame intersect with analysis and explanation,
giving rise to a central question 'why did the power sharing executive fall, and
who carried the responsibility?' (2003: 268). The Sunningdale Communiqué of December 1973 has often been described as an 'agreement to disagree'
– resolution of key issues surrounding the establishment of cross-border
bodies and police and justice reform was postponed and instead devolved
power sharing was established. The parallels with the Belfast/Good Friday
Agreement are not simply in the fact that the latter covered much of the
same ground (hence its description as 'Sunningdale Mark II' or, more infamously, by Seamus Mallon of the SDLP and a former Deputy First Minister,
as 'Sunningdale for slow learners'). Several contributors to this book explore
the implications of Mallon's somewhat scathing remark – targeted, as it
seemed to have been, against republicans – and the logic that lines of thought
and policy can be drawn across time (see, for instance, Aughey, Campbell,
O'Kane and Hennessey). Parallels might also be found in the political cho-
reography in which 'wicked' questions concerning constitutional frameworks, policing, prisoner release and victims' rights were dealt with, fudged
or left aside; certainly, as several contributors point out, the ambiguities surrounding what was actually agreed and what was left to be agreed or ratified
at a later date helped to establish power sharing but also worked to undermine its legitimacy – particularly in the eyes of the unionist community (see,
for instance, Gillespie and Aveyard and McDaid). Indeed, the 'Agreement'
that was reached in December 1973 between the two governments, the
Ulster Unionists, the SDLP and the Alliance Party, was actually a 'communiqué' that, in effect, noted a consensus on the fundamentals but deferred
full implementation.

The sudden fall of the power-sharing Assembly in May 1974 amidst a
general strike organised by the paramilitary-backed UWC has tended to
overshadow consideration of what might be called the democratic lessons
contained in the 'Sunningdale experiment'. Instead, historical and political
debate has centred on questions of blame and counter-factuals surrounding
Sunningdale as some kind of tragic missed opportunity. A populist history
by McKittrick and McVea, for example, ambles around the question of
whether Sunningdale was a 'new beginning' had it not been for the 'schizo-
phrenic Unionist attitude towards law and order and legitimate protests'
(2001: 108). As Aughey points out, the notion of missed opportunity was
at the core of debate in the immediate aftermath of the fall of the executive.

It is, as McKittrick and McVea's reflections demonstrate, ultimately tautological as it is derived from an idea that Sunningdale was was an idea before its time. The politically toxic atmosphere that existed over bodies such as the Council of Ireland and North–South ministerial meetings was nearly erased by 2007 as the then First Minister and leading opponent of the Sunningdale Agreement, Ian Paisley, gave a warm public embrace of the Taoiseach, Bertie Ahern. Speaking about the event Paisley spoke about the 'release' of emotions that had built up over time. Likewise, O'Donnell points out how it was politically difficult for the then party leader, Jack Lynch, to get the Fianna Fáil party to give its support to Sunningdale due to concerns over constitutional recognition (2007a: 12). Yet in 1998, with a great deal of ease, Ahern managed to remove the territorial claim on Northern Ireland from the Irish constitution but also reform the party's policy platform on Northern Ireland.

Seemingly, the lesson of this is that legitimacy is linked to, or defined by, what is politically viable. The point is arguably underscored by Sir Kenneth Bloomfield, a senior civil servant at the time of Sunningdale and adviser to the Unionist leader, Brian Faulkner. Bloomfield pointed out that the actual text of the Communiqué was especially formatted so as to have one side of the page devoted to the Irish government's position on the agreement and the other to the British government (1994: 193). This failure to agree on some of the most fundamental issues such as the constitutional position of Northern Ireland is the first thing that becomes apparent within the Communiqué as the first three substantive paragraphs set out the failure to agree a common policy, instead recognising the right of the Irish government and the SDLP to aspire to Irish unity alongside the Unionists' desire to remain British. What was a selling point for the Irish government, to say that no compromises had occurred in relation to ideological aspirations, was in reality detrimental for Faulkner as fears around the border and security issues were the main drivers of opposition within the Unionist community from 1970 onwards.

While the Agreement fudged the issue of constitutional recognition; it none the less made provision for the establishment of a Council of Ireland, which would facilitate the harmonisation and consultation of joint initiatives in areas such as tourism and electricity. The Council would be run by a Council of Ministers (seven members from each government) with a consultative assembly for advisory and review functions. In reality, the Council had very limited scope or real power. Maurice Hayes, a Northern Irish official, for example, recalled that trying to assign tasks to the new body in 1974 was a particularly slow process as government departments were reluctant to cede too much power or control (1995: 174).

On the critical issue of border security, the Communiqué recorded the concerns of the Unionist and Alliance parties that those who were committed to violence be brought to trial. The Irish government shared a similar concern and agreed to undertake legal steps to ensure that people who had been accused of murder in Northern Ireland would stand trial. The Communiqué noted that 'problems of considerable legal complexity' were involved in this area. All that was agreed, however, was that a commission set up by the British and Irish governments would examine proposals from all parties and recommend the most effective way of dealing with those who had committed crimes. Gillespie notes the early failure of this approach as the Irish Justice Minister, Patrick Cooney, just three days after the signing of the agreement, promised only limited changes to the Irish Republic's existing laws (1998: 104).

Recriminations over the collapse of the executive began immediately. The *Irish News* (a nationalist daily), for example, argued that 'Power-sharing was possibly the last hope for the Six Counties [Northern Ireland] of political survival ... Inevitably now, this area [Northern Ireland] would seem to be facing a lengthy period of direct rule. At the end of it – what?' The paper's editorial set out a number of options – try again with power-sharing, integrate Northern Ireland into the rest of the UK or reunification. While its preferred option was the latter, it was in no doubt where the blame for the failure of power sharing lay: 'The truth is now out in the open. Protestants do not want power-sharing with Catholics. They have shown that they have little feeling for reconciliation ... they persist in believing themselves to be superior and separate from the United Kingdom, although they bray about their Britishness, their loyalty and their belief that the sundered six counties of Ireland possess the mythical autonomy of a province of Britain' (*Irish News*, 1974).

The *Belfast Telegraph* meanwhile was concerned with Northern Ireland's reputation within the United Kingdom ('[t]he British Government has its responsibilities here but if Northern Ireland consistently forgets its responsibilities to Britain, it will be pushed increasingly out into the cold'), but argued that the failure of power sharing was due to overreach:

> Power-sharing is a hazardous and difficult operation, and there must be disappointment, but not despair that the first experiment has failed. Next time, politicians on both sides may be prepared to lower their sights, and settle for a lot less, to achieve a better consensus. (*Belfast Telegraph*, 1974)

Of course, the question remained as to why overreach occurred and why it proved to be so detrimental to fostering consensus. For unionist politicians, it was the insistence on the Council of Ireland as an evolutionary body that scuppered the possibility of power sharing working within Northern Ireland. One example of this thinking is contained in the memoires of Basil McIvor, a Faulknerite and member of the Assembly. It was, in McIvor's opinion, the attachment of the SDLP and in particular its key personality, John Hume, to the Council of Ireland that was at fault for the collapse:

> [Hume's] part in the Sunningdale Agreement spelt disaster for the survival of power-sharing. To me, he was the man who, at Sunningdale, blew out the light at the end of the tunnel. His insistence on the promise of a Council of Ireland, which he must surely have anticipated would arouse fierce opposition amongst the majority of Protestants, wrecked the prospects of an otherwise excellent and hopeful power-sharing arrangement. (McIvor, 1998: 104)

However, Robert Ramsey, one of Faulkner's closest advisers, believed that the failure of Sunningdale came in part from serious miscalculations by Faulkner during negotiations about the level of opposition that could be aroused within the Unionist community over the Council of Ireland. Faulkner, who was always in favour of cross-border co-operation, viewed the creation of a North–South body as a natural part to facilitate good governance between the two Irish states. This slightly detached view and the underestimation of Unionist opposition is recalled in Ramsay's memoirs as a key reason for the agreement's failure:

> I think that he under estimated the fear of the Council of Ireland provisions would engender in the wider unionist community. He was personally relaxed about enhanced cross-border co-operation, not believing it to be a constitutional threat, but the slogan 'Dublin is only a Sunningdale away', coined by opponents within his own party, proved to have a far greater resonance within unionism than he had expected. (2009: 123)

On the other hand, Merlyn Rees, the then Secretary of State for Northern Ireland, believed that the blame should be shared among unionist and nationalist politicians. Alluding to the idea of a 'missed opportunity', Rees commented in his memoir that:

> it may be that the executive could have worked if it had been given the time. It was what I had hoped. Even so, many of its members did not behave sensibly: too many of Faulkner's men wasted time in tittle-tattle against their leader; and too many of the SDLP members spent too much time in Dublin, thus reinforcing the distrust of loyalists. The adverse reaction of loyalists to the Council of Ireland might have been overcome if the SDLP in general had acted with more flexibility, and if its elected members had recognised earlier that the concept could not be proceeded with until there had been another assembly election. By the time it was realised and accepted, it looked like a victory for UWC pressure. (Rees, 1985: 89)

Rees had settled early on this narrative at an early stage during the aftermath of the UWC strike, for example, writing to Wilson on 31 May about his perceptions of an emerging 'Ulster nationalism' and concluding that since 'the British [Government] cannot solve the Irish problem ... it would be better to let them have a shot at it themselves' (The National Achives (UK) (TNA) 1974 PREM 16/148). The point resonated in Whitehall; Wilson's press secretary, Joe Haines, for instance, later remarked that

> The strike had demonstrated that the government's writ did not run in Ulster if the Protestant workers decided they were not going to man the power stations. It put a permanent, recognisable limit on the power of the British government. From then on, we were not even refereeing the fight, only holding the coats while the religious factions go on with it. We could only do such things in Ireland as the organised Protestant population were prepared to agree with, acquiesce in, or tolerate with reluctance and grumbles. (Haines, 1977: 133)

Arguably, the fallout precipitated a process of withdrawal from Northern Ireland by both governments but also from the idea of a co-ordinated governmental approach (see also Coakely and O'Kane's chapters below). Thus, the Northern Ireland Office began exploring a policy of what it called 'distancing', by which it meant 'the reduction of our commitments in Northern Ireland ... and the relegation of the Northern Ireland problem to a place of lesser importance than it currently occupies on the British political scene' (cited in McGrattan, 2010: 110). Perhaps the most radical expression of this sentiment was to be found in Harold Wilson's so-called 'Apocalyptic note' of January 1976 – a memorandum with limited circulation to senior civil servants and cabinet members outlining options for withdrawal from the province (see McGrattan, 2010: 108–9). In his autobiography Garret FitzGerald speculates about whether the 'uncertainty' that this kind of thinking generated was either deliberate or the product of 'confusion and muddle' (1991: 268). Certainly, it sowed something like panic in Dublin and, he asserts, 'for a period at least, a greater degree of trust and confidence existed between many of the leaders of both communities in the North and our Government than existed between any of these politicians and the British government at that time' (1991: 267). However, Sunningdale marked a degree of maturation of governmental relations – particularly surrounding security (see Craig, 2010, and chapters by Coakley, Edwards and Hennessey in this volume). It would, however, arguably, take years – until the 1980s and the 1985 Anglo-Irish Agreement, in fact, and gradually after that into the peace process of the 1990s – for a similar coming-together would occur (Aughey and Gormley-Heenan, 2011).

Paddy Devlin emblematises the SDLP's belief that it was the British government's failure to confront the UWC that led to the breakdown of the power-sharing experiment. He argued that the Northern Irish pro-Sunningdale parties had emphasised the rule of law and the inability of

Britain to face-down the Loyalists represented a betrayal of the democratically elected Executive:

> We reckoned that the loyalists were largely the products of a law and order community
> and would not operate outside the law once it was established that they were in breach
> of it. This was never really understood by Rees or Wilson at any time during the stop-
> page. (Devlin, 1975: 21)

The SDLP struggled to come to terms with the fall of the executive. A
depressed atmosphere lingered throughout much of the later 1970s, a trace
of which may be found in the choice of 'Nadir' as a chapter title for the period
in Austin Currie's autobiography. Currie alluded to the prevailing sentiment,
claiming that 'whatever might be said about how successful the Power-
Sharing Executive had been, the harsh reality was that it took two to tango,
and there was now no group on the unionist side willing, or able, to share
power with the SDLP. Nor was there likely to be for the foreseeable future'
(2004: 281). The mood was captured at the time in a civil service memorandum prepared by Maurice Hayes that argued that Catholics were 'gloomy ...
disillusioned [and] frightened'; they felt 'bitter' about the collapse of the
executive, about the extent to which 'employment in heavy industries was
dominated by Protestants', and about the 'reluctance of the British army to
face the situation'. Hayes went on to warn that the lack of trust in the British
government together with the 'severe psychological blow [dealt] by the
apparent withdrawal of Dublin support' could produce 'total alienation',
leading Catholics to abandon the SDLP for 'abstention or Sinn Féin' (cited
in McGrattan, 2010: 94).

Within the Irish government, disillusionment about the SDLP's approach
towards the agreement, particularly John Hume's, was led by the Minister
for Posts and Telegraphs, Conor Cruise O'Brien. O'Brien believed that
Hume had overplayed his hand in the negotiations which effectively pushed
Faulkner into an unworkable deal. He later argued that the fall of the Executive and the Irish government's support of the SDLP during the talks were
all based on this notion that Hume simply got the politics and tactics 'spec-
tacularly wrong'; however, Hume was, he explained, 'in no way discredited
in the eyes of public opinion in the Republic by having got it all wrong,
and having misled others, including the Dublin government' (O'Brien,
1998: 352).

For O'Brien, the SDLP narrative of blaming a weak, indifferent British
government for not standing up to the UWC Strike was a 'grotesque version
of the facts'. The then Minister for Foreign Affairs, Garret FitzGerald, admitted that in hindsight O'Brien judged the Unionist reaction to the agreement
much better than he and others (1991: 198). Yet, this narrative of the failure

of Wilson and Rees to take action against the UWC is perhaps the dominant one in memoirs of the period. For example Hayes has delivered a scathing representation of British betrayal:

> Wilson was a gnomic figure, Rees, the new secretary of state, was a haverer who found it hard to make up his mind on anything. From their point of view, Sunningdale had been designed to bring peace, it had not done so. The Provo's were still active, and now the Protestants were up in arms. The new government's attitude was at best *laisser faire*, if the executive survived, well and good, if not, there would be no great effort to provide a lifeline. (Hayes, 1995: 176)

For Paul Bew, the Faulknerite Unionists were the biggest losers from the failure of power sharing – under pressure to compromise on constitutional and security issues from all sides, the loss of confidence from middle, liberal Unionism in Faulkner was devastating, contributing as it did to the backlash of Loyalist mobilisation in May 1974 and to Faulkner's sudden fall from power (2007: 512). Arguably, Unionism had to wait two decades before it had another leader who was articulate enough to tackle the theoretical and practical issues involved in building institutions to support a movement away from violence into a form of democratic peace. For Bew, the key lesson that the British government took from Sunningdale was the need for disengagement – intervention, it seemed, only enabled Nationalism and Unionism to indulge their worst fears and maximalist hopes. This trend of thinking was elaborated by the Prime Minister himself, who, against the continued advice of his officials and ministers, continued to entertain thoughts of an outright withdrawal. The effect of which was, in some ways, similar to intervention – fears and suspicions were raised on all sides, not least among the Dublin political establishment and the Provisional Irish Republican Army (PIRA) who seemed to believe that their 1974–75 ceasefire was a prelude to the British Army withdrawing.

Evaluating Sunningdale

Academic appraisals of the Sunningdale experiment are still somewhat divided over the nuances of what ideas or whose actions (or omissions) should be emphasised. Gordon Gillespie has tackled the idea that the power-sharing experiment might have worked had it not been for an adverse and unpredictable series of events:

> the Sunningdale package has, wrongly, been described as a missed opportunity for the long-term settlement of the Northern Ireland conflict. In 1974, however, neither unionists nor nationalists at large were prepared to make the compromises necessary to make such a political settlement work. (2004: 141)

The stress put on the Council of Ireland has led some commentators to argue that consent was being assumed rather than requested by Dublin and the SDLP (Farrington, 2007; McGrattan, 2009). A recent survey of the period has suggested that this thesis depends on too much congruence between the two Nationalist groupings, which did not in fact exist. Indeed, writes Shaun McDaid, there was no unanimity within the Irish government to use the Council of Ireland as a stepping stone to reunification:

> The Department of Foreign Affairs (DFA) sought a strong Council with the potential to become an all-Ireland government. The DFA, however, was isolated and to a large extent ignored by the other Irish departments. The evidence also suggests that the proposed Council was not a particular divisive issue for the power-sharing administration, and that the executive was in no danger of collapsing because of it. (2013: 74)

Several authors in this book refer to the (in)famous remarks of a prominent SDLP Assembly member, Hugh Logue, to the effect that Nationalists believed that the Council of Ireland would 'trundle' unionism into a reunited state. Coakley qualifies the remarks by referring to McLoughlin's research on Hume in which he points out that the quotation did not appear in any of the main Dublin newspapers the day after it was supposed to have been made. The quotation nevertheless quickly became entrenched in the Unionist imagination and acted as fuel for the anti-Sunningdale sentiments, for example appearing prominently on the United Ulster Unionist Council's General Election advertisements (see *News Letter* 22 February 1974).

The Sunningdale period has been reimagined as a first or prototype peace process (Dixon, 2001; Kerr, 2011). Typically, this reasoning reads Sunningdale as preparing the way, or setting out a framework that was more substantially and successfully completed in the Belfast/Good Friday Agreement of 1998. As Wolff argues:

> The Sunningdale agreement was not a treaty between two states, but an agreement reached between two states and a selected number of political parties.In order to work, it would have required substantial support for those partners in the agreement who were most volatile to pressures from within their own communities: the pro-agreement parties in both blocs who were vulnerable to outflanking by extremists. That this support for pro-agreement politicians was not forthcoming was one of the major reasons for the failure of this early attempt to resolve the Northern Ireland conflict. (2003: 7–8)

Of course, there is an unfathomable condescension at play in this kind of logic that sees the majority of the Unionist electorate as somehow mystified or duped by 'extremists' – a logic that Aughey, in his chapter, relates to the traditional Nationalist view of Unionism and describes as Rousseauean. However, it can be acknowledged that the language is imprecise: Wolff could also be read as claiming that Unionist majority were themselves extremists. A clarification to these arguments is found in the work of Tonge, who states that

> Most accounts, not unreasonably, concentrate upon the role played by unionists in ensuring the demise of the agreement. Nonetheless, it should be noted that even if greater unionist support had been forthcoming, continued republican violence would have placed the agreement under great strain. (2000: 43)

Indeed, although 1972 was the high watermark for killings (496), 1973 and 1974 were also extremely violent (263 and 303 deaths respectively (McKittrick et al., 1999: 1473)). The rise in Republican violence had an important impact on how the moderate SDLP sold the agreement. McLoughlin argues that the radicalisation of the Nationalist people due to events like internment and Bloody Sunday caused the SDLP to 'adopt a more dynamic language, which portrayed the negotiation of a new political settlement as an incontrovertible process towards a united Ireland' (2007: 17). He goes further, arguing that the environment at that time led the party away from its founding principles to misrepresent the agreement which, in effect, debased it within Unionist opinion. Like O'Brien above, McLoughlin suggests a certain degree of ignorance of Unionist opinion as he notes that for a time it appeared that constitutional Nationalism believed that Unionism had no right to hold back moves towards reunification (2007: 18).

Outside of the Irish government forces were conspiring within Irish Nationalism that would place a great deal of pressure on the agreement and Faulkner's position at the head of the executive. A former Fianna Fáil minister, Kevin Boland, in January 1974 began proceedings to have the Sunningdale Agreement and the government's recognition of Northern Ireland declared unconstitutional. Boland's actions forced the Irish government into a position where it had to declare that its earlier declaration that the constitutional position of Northern Ireland could not be changed without the consent of the population was not a part of the agreement. Furthermore, the government argued that the declaration was merely a statement of policy about how a united Ireland might come about rather than a substantive change in a country's constitutional outlook. The damaging aspects of this on Faulkner's position have been noted by FitzGerald, who recalled that 'the subtle legal arguments used to defend the agreement were not merely lost on Unionists; they totally destroyed the value of the declaration, undermining Faulkner's already shaky position' (1991: 226). The total divergence in political priorities for Unionism, Nationalism and the British and Irish governments confirms McLoughlin's thesis of the inability for big compromises to be made in such a politically toxic environment.

Sunningdale and Northern Ireland's struggle for democracy

While the 'blame game' surrounding the collapse of the Sunningdale executive can be summarised, what is more difficult to assess is the ramifications
of those recriminations. It is that effort at assessment that this book takes as
its starting point. This book attempts to fill the gap in the market regarding
a seminal period in Northern Irish history and its implications for the struggle to achieve a peaceful, stable, democratic settlement in the region. While
there have been a number of history books that examine the 1970s in Northern Ireland, this is the first attempt to look at the ideas behind the 1973–74
power-sharing experiment (the so-called 'Sunningdale' Assembly and/or
Executive) and its collapse amidst the May 1974 UWC strike. It isalso the
first attempt to analyse systematically what became of those ideas.

The questions that surround the power-sharing experiment continue to
resonate within Northern Ireland today. As the flag protest continues to
demonstrate, issues to do with inclusion and exclusion of voice and experience remain central to debates in Northern Ireland; discussions over procedures and trust lie at the core of studies and commentaries surrounding
increasing voter apathy; and differing perceptions over what exactly consti-
tutes 'agreement' abound in contemporary arguments over political
developments.

The 'blame game' might, arguably, be seen to work against clarity in terms
of placing Sunningdale in a political context. As alluded to above, the 'blame
game' speaks implicitly to this context along the logic that according to a
particular version or image of democracy a decision made by another person
or group is read as damaging democracy. Where that damage is seen as fundamental and irrevocable then a radical fissure between the contending
parties (and, ultimately, their images of legitimacy) occurs. Those fissures and
images are underpinned by ideas about what actually occurred and are given
effect in the lessons that politicians 'take'. The importance of this process of
lesson learning for politics and efforts towards democratization has been
elucidated by Bermeo:

> What are the ideas that must be affected by political learning if democracy is to be
> reconstructed? At the most basic level, critical elites must change their assessments of
> the relative effectiveness of democratic institutions for the fulfilment of group goals.
> In order for this to happen, at least one of four subsidiary changes must take place.
> Elites must change their evaluations of the alternatives to democratic rule; they must
> change their evaluations of democracy itself; they must change the ordering or nature
> of group goals; or they must change their perceptions of one another. (1992: 274)

The key seems to be what kind of lessons are taken from a particular event.
If, following Wolff, the key lesson from Sunningdale was that power sharing

was the only option and that the Belfast/Good Friday Agreement squared the circle about how to achieve it, then an immediate follow-up question relates to why it took so long. Was it simply a case that Sunningdale was too little too late? If it is the case that ending violent conflict requires a fundamental repositioning of state 'orientations, prioritisations and policies' (Todd, 2013: 1), was Sunningdale simply too 'internalist', too much focused on Northern Ireland? A related question might be: why did it take the political leaders in Northern Ireland so long to recognise the necessity for power sharing (Dixon, 2001: 157)? One answer might be that there were different ways to achieve power sharing and different ways to conceive of it and put it into practice; yet the context in which those became salient and congruent did not emerge until the 1990s. Yet, this in turn, gives rise to queries relating to causality and chronology – in other words, what happened to the first ideas that they took so long to return, and what happened to them in between that caused them to be more palatable at the later date? What changed? And how and why did the change occur? The reason for the time-lag might be down to the fact that, as Aguilar argues, within political learning and decision-making,

> the kind of decision that led to failure tends to be avoided, without considering the consequences that would have ensued if a different policy had been implemented. Nevertheless, what is certainly true is that those who take political decisions tend to place excessive emphasis on the lessons which derive from their own personal experience and undervalue the lessons which derive from the experience of others. (2002: 21–2)

Another answer might be that the 'ripe moment' had not been reached – that it took three decades and countless suffering to build up an urgency for peace (see O'Kane, 2006, for a critique of this form of argument). Another answer might be to avoid answering and instead warn of the dangers of an overly teleological approach to history that sees processes in terms of pieces of a jigsaw puzzle that can slowly be worked into place: The process cannot be predetermined, is the logic of this position. As Bermeo, again, explains: '[u] nless the range of negotiable issues expands, the divisions that produced the breakdown of democracy in the first place will simply emerge again. This is why the change of mind intrinsic to political learning is so important' (1992: 277). Whether or not a 'change of mind', or what Bermeo goes on to refer to as a 'discrediting' of old ideas, occurred in Northern Ireland between 1973 and 1998 is, again, a matter for debate.

A final point might be raised as regards the light that Sunningdale throws on Northern Irish politics: namely, that the 'blame game' can, arguably, be seen as deferring consideration of the *type* or *quality* of democracy that is

conceptualised and practised. While power-sharing and institutional inno-
vations such as the Council of Ireland (or its later reinvention as the 1998
Agreement's Strand Two and Strand Three provisions for cross-border and
inter-archipelagic bodies) may improve the breadth and variety of democratic practice, they may not necessarily lead to increased access to the
decision-making apparatus, improved transparency of how decisions are
made and/or implemented, or greater ease of accountability. The distinctions over how the flag protests are framed and the blame game over Sunningdale point to the same under-researched topic: namely, the confusion
between the *width* and the *depth* of democracy (Papadopoulos, 2013). The
idea of congruence between representatives and their voters as constituting
a test of democratic practice (Stoker, 2006) does not really apply to an eth-
nically divided society such as Northern Ireland's (unless a quasi-Marxist
notion of false consciousness is deployed) where 'elites' and the ordinary
population often share similar political, social and religious or normative
beliefs. The necessity for switching from procedural notions of democracy
to more substantive ones then becomes clear – and, arguably, it is this
impulse that lies at the heart of the efforts to facilitate and restore power
sharing in Northern Ireland: that is to say, a basic desire to cultivate ways
and means of doing politics that are not filtered through the violence that
marred the society for so long. Extrapolating from this point can bring us
back to the sanguinity necessary for avoiding a 'direct-line' teleological
approach to history: the best of motivations may not always result in optimal
products – or, more simply, the best of intentions may merely be paving the
road to hell.

Conclusion

Sunningdale therefore poses unsettling and unsettled historical and political
questions; the contributors in this book seek to tackle these head-on from a
number of perspectives. Frequently debate over the past in general in Northern Ireland is emotive and personal, and as a result history might be seen as
some kind of Rorschach blot into which individuals can read whatever occurs
to them. A key aim of this book is to explore alternative ways of working
within and through a divisive event by focusing on the interpretations, the
available evidence and the divided and progressive legacies that Sunningdale
bequeathed, but what the chapters, taken together, suggest is that the period
represented no kind of 'missed opportunity'. Indeed, if any kind of straight
line can be discerned in the historical analyses that follow, it must relate to
the seeming inevitability of power sharing coming up short – unable, as the

policy proved, to square the demands of Nationalist overreach, Unionist division against the backdrop of a grave and bloody campaign of violence.

Mallon's aphorism about slow learning raises the missed opportunity counterfactual. As such, a question continues to linger over the period that relates to whether Sunningdale was indeed an honourable compromise that had the potential to win consent (Fisk, 1975); and whether, over a period of time, and without the February 1974 Westminster General Election (in which anti-Sunningdale Unionist forces won 51 per cent of the vote), the new arrangements might have taken root. This may, indeed, be a useful way to conceptualise political developments. However, the chapters also broaden the analysis beyond this somewhat restricted historical vision to taken into account the implications of the context that Northern Ireland was facing: namely, a range of problems, some of which lay outwith the remit of the Sunningdale framework but which nevertheless had the potential to impact upon political negotiations.

The point of departure, then, for this book is to try to situate Sunningdale in this broad historical context and, in so doing, to try to draw out what lessons, if any, the period offers for Northern Ireland today and for peace-building and the deepening and widening of democracy in general. These lessons may, arguably, be seen to fall under the following questions:

- An aim of Sunningdale was to widen democracy through power sharing: to what extent did it fail to deepen democracy?

- To what extent did the differing lessons that protagonists took from Sunningdale regarding what they saw as legitimate political behaviour colour later policy agendas for Northern Ireland and shape attitudes towards political dialogue?

- What, if anything, can we learn from the Sunningdale period about how to deal with groups who feel alienated from mainstream politics and/or who believe that violence remains an option for remedying those sentiments?

The book tries to deliver an overview of the findings of political historians and political scientists working on Northern Ireland and on the Sunningdale era. In so doing, it hopes to offer some preliminary answers to the above questions. Gordon Gillespie, for example, provides a detailed overview of the historical context, which places events in Northern Ireland against the background of international unrest. Teasing out the intricacies of the development of the anti-Sunningdale movement, he argues that it was the combination of national, local and international factors that combined to create a 'perfect storm' for peaceful power sharing in Northern Ireland in 1974. Arthur Aughey, meanwhile, in the third chapter, addresses the interpretative legacies of Sunningdale. Referring to Scott's notion of a 'fantasy echo', he explains that historical references seem to echo present concerns and experiences as the past continues to impact on contemporary decision-making. Aughey traces how these echoes resonated throughout Nationalist and Unionist thinking during the ensuing conflict and turmoil in Northern Ireland and cites Gillespie's argument that a reality of 1974 that has been hard to come to terms with is that it 'would have taken miracle for the Sunningdale deal to have survived'. Other 'lessons' persisted, however, and Aughey asserts that the rhetorical interventions made by Nationalism in 1974 regarding Unionist obduracy worked to limit the seriousness in which subsequent Unionist concerns and arguments were received by other political actors.

The series of chapters beginning with John Coakley's addresses the role of different groups of actors in the period. Coakley's own chapter on the Irish governments' role(s), for example, traces the 'policy shifts and learning' that took place in Dublin's approach to Northern Ireland. Drawing on a wide range of theoretical and empirical sources, Coakley's conclusions point to the importance of what might be termed bureaucratic politics in shaping outcomes: in this case, the resistance by Irish civil servants to cede powers to the putative Council of Ireland. Eamonn O'Kane, meanwhile, engages with the ongoing debates over what exactly the British government 'learned' from Sunningdale that it applied in its later approach to Northern Ireland. He argues that clear British objectives developed but that Britain was often constrained by the complex and changing nature of events in Northern Ireland when trying to put those into practice. As such, O'Kane suggests that it was not the case of 'slow learning' on the part of the British that prevented the development of peaceful politics until into the 1990s, but rather a process of policy adaptation and construction. Aaron Edwards's chapter on security responses to Sunningdale also argues for looking at subterranean political dynamics in tracing the development of lesson-drawing by political elites. He points out that, while discussion about Sunningdale tends to circle around issues to do with power sharing and the Irish dimension, the agreement actually reflected the British government's concern with the deteriorating security situation – evidenced in the fact that it included nine clauses relating to security policy.

Stuart Aveyard and Shaun McDaid examine the dynamics within Ulster Unionism during the Sunningdale era. 'The failure of unionism to compromise', in 1974, they argue, 'only served to reinforce Westminster's reluctant acceptance of direct rule'. Aveyard and McDaid map Unionist responses to

Sunningdale and its collapse with careful attention to the primary sources and suggest that a key problem that Unionist leaders faced was how to avoid being seen as a type of second Faulkner: namely, a figure so predisposed to compromise that he lost the backing of his own electorate. Tony Craig addresses the forces that lined up against Faulkner in 1974 and charts the history of the Labour MP Stanley Orme and his negotiations with Loyalism to try to build a newly politicised Protestant working class in Belfast to try to direct workers away from Loyalist terror organisations. Again, echoing Gillespie's arguments in his earlier chapter, Craig suggests that a range of national and international factors – the collapse of the IRA's 1975 ceasefire and the decline of shipbuilding in Belfast, for example – stymied these attempts to address the underrepresentation of fringe politics in Northern Ireland.

Sarah Campbell's and Henry Patterson's chapters look at Northern Irish nationalism. For her part, Campbell draws on extensive primary archival material to appraise the position of the SDLP. She argues that the '1974 deal was a pivotal turning point for the party and saw it move from being a party of repudiation to a party willing to participate in the Northern Ireland state'. The reason for this transition was, as Campbell explains, that the Sunningdale agreement was emblematic of the SDLP's two policy goals of power sharing within Northern Ireland and a strong place for the Irish government in the administration of the country. One major dividing line within Northern Irish nationalism has been over the question of violence – the 'constitutional nationalism' of the SDLP versus the 'physical force' nationalism of the republican movement. Patterson's chapter explores the somewhat underresearched dimension of the responses within Republicanism to the Sunningdale period. Patterson argues that one aspect of the IRA's violence and its capacity for destroying political progress was the unintended consequence of forcing a 'reconstruction' of the 'British connection and a resigned acceptance that the British state was in for a long haul'.

The final two chapters provide overviews of the enduring ramifications of the Sunningdale experiment on Northern Irish society, politics and culture. Connal Parr, for instance, uses Stuart Parker's 1987 play about the strike, *Pentecost* (Parker, 1989), to reflect on the issues that the strike brought to the fore in terms of violence, democracy and political participation. In the concluding chapter, Thomas Hennessey looks at the legacy of the central ideas behind the Sunningdale agreement and maps their progress and development throughout later Northern Irish political discussions.

Individually, then, the chapters in this book focus on particular aspects of the Sunningdale experiment and its ongoing legacies for Northern Irish politics. Points of divergence appear surrounding the emphasis placed on particular events and/or actors by the individual chapters but a picture emerges of detailed complexity. Many of the chapters are based on hitherto unpublished research and archival evidence and draw on a wide range of sources and interpretations. The governmental papers for this period have been open to researchers for a number of years and the authors present their findings. In addition, several authors draw on private collections of individuals and parties that supplement existing understandings. However, taken as a whole, the book aims for breadth and depth: contributors complement and challenge existing accounts – academic, journalistic and autobiographical. The goal of the book is to draw together lessons from different academics, different viewpoints and different sources to begin to tackle in a serious, informed and even-handed fashion the important and enduring questions that the Sunningdale period posed for peace-building, democratisation and division in Northern Ireland.

2

The Ulster Workers' Council strike: the perfect storm

Gordon Gillespie

From the outbreak of the Troubles in 1968 up to 1974 Unionists believed that they had suffered a series of political defeats which included the abolition of the B Specials and the failure of security forces to defeat the Irish Republican Army (IRA), culminating in the suspension (effectively the abolition) of the Northern Ireland Parliament in March 1972. British government plans for a new administration for Northern Ireland suggested the inclusion of individuals like Gerry Fitt and John Hume of the Social Democratic and Labour Party (SDLP) who, Unionists believed, had been instrumental in destroying the democratically elected Northern Ireland government and who were now making political gains on the back of the IRA's campaign of terror. For Unionists the belief was that they were being edged into a united Ireland. This process had to be stopped; the only question was, how?

In March 1973 the United Kingdom (UK) government had issued the White Paper *Northern Ireland Constitutional Proposals* which included plans for a Northern Ireland Assembly elected by proportional representation, the stipulation that the Executive should have 'widespread support' and, crucially, given how events developed, a Council of Ireland which, the paper stated, 'must operate with the consent of both majority and minority opinion in Northern Ireland who have a right to prior consultation and involvement in the process of determining its form, functions and procedures' (NIO, 1973: Para. 111).

The Castle Talks between the Ulster Unionist Party (UUP), Alliance and SDLP in October and November 1973 concluded on 22 November with the announcement that a power-sharing executive would be formed – provided that North–South structural arrangements could also be agreed. It was at approximately this time that William (Bill) Craig, leader of the anti-White Paper Vanguard Unionist Party (which had grown from a ginger group of the Unionist Party to a party in its own right; see Aveyard and McDaid below), wrote to his party members stating, 'If the Executive can't be prevented from getting off the ground as a credible institution it will survive long enough to bring the unification of Ireland meaningfully closer' (William Craig undated letter, Glen Barr papers). Craig believed that Unionist opposition in the Assembly would be ineffective as it could be ignored by the Secretary of State for Northern Ireland (then William Whitelaw) and that 'the campaign will be won or lost in the country.' Significantly he added,

> The form of organisation is all important – it must provide a coming together and it must be free of the personality cult. People must be able to identify without feeling disloyal to existing commitments and without having to join an already identifiable organisation. A Loyalist Action Council or Central Body to which constituency associations of political parties could affiliate seems a necessary starting point to be followed by Action Groups in every county, town, village and factory and suitable work place. (Ibid., Glen Barr papers)

This suggested a possible framework which was similar in many respects to that which emerged in May 1974.

One form of opposition which was clearly on the loyalist agenda was an industrial stoppage. This had worked well for Vanguard in March 1972 at the time of the suspension of Stormont but had proved disastrous in February 1973 when a loyalist protest strike against the internment of Ulster Defence Association (UDA) members had been characterised by widespread violence.[1] Another consequence of the February 1973 strike was the effective collapse of the Loyalist Association of Workers (LAW) and now attempts were made to create a new loyalist workers' organisation. An early indication of this came on 2 November when the *Belfast Telegraph* reported on the formation of a group called East Antrim Loyalist Workers which had split from LAW and which included Ballylumford power station workers.

Developments in Northern Ireland took place against a background of political instability both in Britain and Ireland and internationally. In October 1973 Egypt and Syria attacked Israel, thus beginning the Yom Kippur War. Crucially for the Western world, Arab oil-producing states began increasing prices and cutting back production in protest at American support for Israel. Western Europe depended on Arab producers for 80 per cent of its oil and the rapid price increase precipitated an economic crisis in the West.

As a result of the oil price increases the UK government announced on 26 November that it was printing and issuing 16 million petrol rationing books. By this time some two hundred petrol stations in England alone had closed because of shortage of petrol. Special arrangements were planned for essential business use and others considered priority users including doctors, vets, nurses, ministers and undertakers.

The oil crisis was exacerbated by an overtime ban by coalminers which reduced coal supplies to power stations by 40 per cent. As a result industry and commerce were restricted to using five days' electricity a week until the end of the year and three days a week from the New Year. The issue came to a head with the February 1974 General Election which was held on the question of 'Who Governs Britain?'; however, the result failed to produce a clear winner. The Conservative Prime Minister Edward Heath's subsequent attempts to reach an agreement with the Liberal Party to remain in office failed and, on 5 March, a minority Labour government led by Harold Wilson took power.

The incoming Labour government faced a number of serious problems: dealing with industrial relations including ending the miners' strike (the strike ended on 6 March after the miners were awarded a 35 per cent pay increase), the impact of the Yom Kippur War and the quadrupling of crude oil prices. Besides this there were also internal disputes between members of Wilson's 'kitchen cabinet' and rumours of MI5 conspiracies to undermine Wilson.

By 20 November the implementation of the government's plans for Northern Ireland, outlined in the March 1973 White Paper, appeared to be progressing satisfactorily when the UUP's governing body, the Ulster Unionist Council (UUC), narrowly voted not to reject a power-sharing administration. However, late November also saw the first meeting, at Vanguard party headquarters, of the group that would eventually become the Ulster Workers' Council (UWC). The loyalist trade Unionist and shipyard worker Harry Murray had been invited to the meeting to represent Harland and Wolff and agreed to participate in a new loyalist workers' organisation provided politicians and paramilitaries were not part of it. Although Murray's proviso was agreed to by those present, the reality was that politicians and paramilitaries remained close to the workings of the new group and even arguably an integral part of it. One of Murray's closest allies in the following months, for example, Bob Pagels, was also a UDA member. What emerged therefore was a situation in which there was a rough compromise between workers and paramilitary and political groups as to who was to lead, or play the primary role in, the campaign against Sunningdale. In the longer term this would also lead to competing claims from the various elements as to who was the real force behind the UWC strike (Gillespie, 2004).

Unionist opposition

As the Sunningdale process progressed, so Unionist opposition to it also coalesced with the formation of both a political umbrella body, the United Ulster Unionist Council (or Coalition) (UUUC) and the paramilitary equivalent, the Ulster Army Council (UAC).

Although the Sunningdale Communiqué, outlining the provisions for a Council of Ireland, was signed by the British and Irish governments and Executive parties on 9 December, attempts to sell it to Unionists were arguably already a lost cause by 16 December when Austin Currie told the Irish broadcaster RTÉ that it 'fulfilled Wolfe Tone's desire to break the connection with England' and the Taoiseach Liam Cosgrave told the *Sunday Press* that there was no question of the Republic changing its territorial claim to Northern Ireland – something which was crucial to selling the deal to Unionists. The trend of growing Unionist opposition to Sunningdale became even clearer on 18 December when the North Tyrone Unionist Association, which was viewed as a weathervane of UUP opinion, voted by a ratio of 2 to 1 to support anti-Sunningdale candidates. Even the pro-Faulkner *Belfast Telegraph* was now predicting that he would be defeated on the issue of Sunningdale when the party's ruling body, the UUC, met in early January 1974 (Gillespie, 1998).

Despite this, anti-Sunningdale opposition was still not focused on the single objective of opposing Sunningdale – on 22 December, for example, the UDA blocked roads in protest against the treatment of loyalist prisoners. In mid-February 1974 meanwhile two UDA men were shot dead by the army and a third wounded during riots in East Belfast.

On 4 January 1974, three days after the Northern Ireland Executive took office, Faulkner lost the UUC vote on the 'proposed all-Ireland Council settlement' and resigned as party leader three days later (though continuing to lead the Executive and the pro-Faulkner Unionists therein). Alarm bells were now ringing in Belfast and London government circles, and the precarious nature of the settlement became even more apparent on 16 January when the Dublin High Court ruled on a case brought by the former TD Kevin Boland that the Sunningdale Agreement statement on Northern Ireland did not conflict with Articles 2 and 3 of the Irish constitution claiming jurisdiction over the North and that the statement included in the Sunningdale Agreement was therefore 'no more than a statement of policy'.

Faulkner subsequently met Cosgrave at Baldonnel Airport, Dublin, for talks and told Cosgrave that his position had been eroded since Sunningdale, first by Cosgrave's *Sunday Press* interview and then by the Irish government's defence position on the Boland case which had 'robbed him of all credibility' on the question of the status of Northern Ireland'. Faulkner added,

> It had to be realised that it was much more difficult to sell the Council of Ireland than the concept of power-sharing, which was now, Faulkner felt, widely accepted. Unionists saw a Council of Ireland as a half-way house to unity, or a form of all-Ireland Parliament. Therefore, the proposition could only be sold on the basis of a positive assurance about status. (Public Record Office of Northern Ireland (hereinafter PRONI) OE/1/29 CAIN website)

He concluded that 'there was not a hope of proceeding to the formal conference and ratifying Sunningdale, including the proposals for a Council of Ireland, unless the status issue could be cleared up. It would also be necessary to see real action on the anti-terrorist front.'

On 17 January Kenneth Bloomfield, Permanent Secretary to the Northern Ireland Executive, in a political brief for Faulkner, warned that, unless Sunningdale could be ratified with the consent of the majority of the Protestant community, 'it may not long survive on any useful basis'. Later that same day, however, the SDLP Assembly Member Hugh Logue told a Dublin audience that the Council of Ireland was 'the vehicle that would trundle Unionists into a united Ireland' – confirming many Unionists' suspicions of what Sunningdale meant. The public decision on Sunningdale was delivered on 28 February in the UK General Election when the UUUC, running under the slogan 'Dublin is just a Sunningdale away', won 11 of the 12 Northern Ireland seats with 51 per cent of the vote. The incoming minority Labour government was well aware that, at a minimum, the early implementation of the Council was a difficult proposition but was unable to convince either the SDLP or the Irish government of this hard reality and Faulkner's position continued to erode.

On 7 March 1974 the *News Letter* mentioned the UWC for the first time when the organisation challenged the new Northern Ireland Secretary of State, Merlyn Rees, to attend a victory rally to be held at Stormont on Saturday afternoon for the 11 successful UUUC candidates in the General Election. Five days later anti-Sunningdale Unionists tabled a motion in the Assembly calling for the re-negotiation of the Sunningdale Agreement. It would be the conclusion of this debate, on 14 May, which would provide the pretext for the calling of the UWC strike.

On 23 March the UWC issued a statement threatening widespread civil disobedience unless fresh Assembly elections were called. Elsewhere tensions were further heightened by a renewed IRA bombing offensive, and March saw the greatest number of security incidents (921) of any month in 1974 as well as the greatest number of explosions (*Chief Constable's Report*, 1975). Two weeks later, against this background, the Northern Ireland Office (NIO) ministers Merlyn Rees and Stanley Orme met UWC representatives at Stormont in what deteriorated into an angry shouting match (Rees, 1985: 58–9).

Divisions within the anti-Sunningdale camp still continued, however, and paramilitaries were angry at being excluded from a UUUC conference held in Portrush between 24 and 26 April. Significantly, however, this conference saw Harry Murray and Billy Kelly of the power workers being included as members of a UUUC study group set up to devise a blueprint for 'selective sanctions' as a means of 'implementing the will of the people' (*Irish Times* 14 May 1974).

The question of a strike in opposition to Sunningdale was by now becoming more urgent. Over the winter Billy Kelly had repeatedly pushed for an immediate strike while Harry Murray wanted to wait until the spring in an attempt to win further support and reduce the hardship a strike might cause. By May the weather had improved while it also appeared that the success of the UUUC candidates in the General Election had had no impact in halting Sunningdale and that other actions might now be required.

The strike

On 8 May, when UWC members met the UDA to ask for its tacit support for the strike, the Vanguard Assembly Member and UDA spokesman Glen Barr suggested linking the outcome of the Sunningdale motion at Stormont with the launch of an all-out strike (Transcript of Glen Barr interview with Peter Taylor, July 1974, Glen Barr papers). Events were now moving quickly and, on 10 May, the UWC issued a statement calling for fresh Assembly elections and two days later warned of an all-out strike if the Assembly voted to continue with Sunningdale.

By the eve of the strike Harry Murray was still concerned about whether the UWC 'constitutional stoppage' had the full backing of loyalist politicians and paramilitaries. When Murray and other UWC members travelled to Larne to meet UUUC politicians on 13 May to again ask them to support the strike, however, they received a somewhat lukewarm response. Murray was later to recall that it was only through the auspices of the Vanguard

Deputy Leader Ernie Baird that they were able to talk to the politicians at all (Gillespie, 1994).

On 14 May the Assembly voted by 44 to 28 not to re-negotiate the Sunningdale package, leading Harry Murray to announce an open-ended 'constitutional stoppage' and a reduction in electricity generation from 725 to 400 megawatts. He then went to meet the UDA leader Andy Tyrie to confirm the UDA's support for the strike. Tyrie responded by telling Murray, 'I'll see you in the morning'. Murray took this as a sign of support although the comment was somewhat open to interpretation.

Tactically one of the major difficulties for the strike leaders appears to have been the different attitudes taken by the UWC and the paramilitaries as to how quickly industry should be brought to a halt. A UWC spokesman of the time took the view that the strike would be entirely passive, merely asking people not to go to work (Gillespie, 1994).

The paramilitary view, however, was that the strike would not work without a show of force on the ground, and this view was strengthened when industry did not come to a halt on the first day. Although orders to erect road blocks and threaten or use intimidation were not given by the Strike Co-ordinating Committee (and the UWC itself appears to have had no plans for enforcing the strike on the ground), the paramilitaries did plan such action on their own. The UWC spokesman was certain that the paramilitaries were following their own agenda in this area:

> What actually happened was that the [Strike Co-ordinating] Committee would sit and would say, 'Here's what is happening', and they would issue a statement. Other people would go off to their secret rendezvous, they would sit down and they would say, 'what are we going to do?' because these guys were geared up to do something else, they were geared up to break legs and skulls and worse. How are they going to harness the people who are in their organisations, how are they going to say to these people, 'Now sit at home don't do anything and that is your contribution'. (Ibid.)

Although the UWC spokesman recognised that the strike could not work without the support of the politicians and paramilitaries he stressed that all that was ever asked of the paramilitaries was tacit support. The paramilitaries rejected this view, however, and claimed that the UWC was left in no doubt as to what each group's role in the strike was to be. Glen Barr commented:

> What we said to the Workers was, 'You go away and organise and you keep continually reporting back to us'. They were allowed to organise it, it was the paramilitaries they were going to do the work. The power workers would pull the plug basically but it was up to the paramilitaries to instruct all their people to come out and we were then to man the barricades ... If they wanted paramilitary support it was on that basis, and that basis alone, that they were going to get it. (Quoted in Gillespie, 1994: 118–19)

On the morning of 15 May the strike began with power cuts and factory closures. Many workers, including those in Harland and Wolff shipyard, went on strike but there were also threats to burn workers' cars in order to coerce some to leave.

By that evening factories had closed due to lack of power supplies while others had shut down because workers had failed to turn up. Businesses in Larne, Co. Antrim, had shut down and men in combat jackets and carrying wooden clubs told businesses to close. The ferry from Stranraer in Scotland to Larne turned back when reports of trouble were sent to the ferry captain. Sirocco works in Belfast was partially closed, more than a thousand men left Harland and Wolff but there was a low degree of absenteeism at Shorts aircraft factory in Belfast. STC at Monkstown, Co. Antrim, closed completely. Fifteen hundred men stopped work at ICI Kilroot. At Maydown in Derry and Limavady, Co. Londonderry, most employees were working. Power was also off in Enniskillen, Co. Fermanagh. In Portadown, Co. Armagh, industry had almost shut down – most workers showed up but had to be sent home due to a lack of power. There were also power cuts in Dungannon, Co. Tyrone, and in parts of County Down (*Belfast Telegraph* 15 May 1974).

Later that day Harry Murray, Harry Patterson and Bob Pagels of the UWC accompanied by Bill Craig, the Democratic Unionist Party (DUP) leader Ian Paisley, the UUP member John Laird and three 'armed observers' met Stan Orme at Stormont Castle. The UWC view of this meeting was less than positive, the delegation was kept waiting for an hour and then:

> as soon as they met Mr Orme and before they could utter one word, the Minister of State subjected them to a stream of verbal abuse. The epithets used were: bigots, sectarian extremists, and other similar remarks. When he had spewed out all his hatred of the loyalist people of Northern Ireland he then said that he believed in, and would always devote his energies to, a united Ireland. (UWC Press statement. Meeting with Minister of State: Stanley Orme – venue Stormont Castle, Glen Barr papers)

The UWC members in turn complained that the Sunningdale system was unrepresentative and undemocratic. In order to alleviate distress, however, they said they would continue to supply 60 per cent of the electricity normally used in Northern Ireland. The UWC statement claimed that Orme instructed the civil servant Frank Cooper to see that the electricity supplied was used for essential services only. Subsequently, however, the UWC discovered that electricity was being used by industrial complexes in Londonderry.

The UWC statement also highlighted the inconsistent position of the Labour administration by saying, 'The constitutional stoppage was described as a political strike. Rees stated that he could not negotiate with political strikers nor was he prepared to submit to political blackmail. Despite the fact that the Labour Party when in Opposition had supported the miners' strike which was a strike against the Industrial Relations Act – a Constitutional Bill' (UWC Press statement. Meeting with Minister of State: Stanley Orme – venue Stormont Castle, Glen Barr papers).

When Rees spoke on the telephone to Wilson, at 10.30 pm that evening he was bullish about the situation. Rees believed the strike was 'a last fling by the Protestants' and that 'the Government's policies were closer to success than they had ever been; if the Government stood up to this Protestant action then he would be in a position very shortly to make proposals to the Prime Minister about a date for ratifying the Sunningdale Agreement at a meeting somewhere in Britain'. Rees had also put on standby troops he believed were capable of running power stations and sewage plants.

A sign that the paramilitaries were preparing to ramp up the pressure, however, came late on 15 May when a spokesman for the UAC (significantly, not the UWC) said that those on strike would be 'prominent' on the streets the following day and that non-essential workers would be advised to go home (*Irish Times* 16 May 1974). This marked the beginning of a campaign of roadblocks in Belfast and across many parts of Northern Ireland.

By 16 May it was estimated that the strike had already cost over £1 million in lost production (*Daily Express* 16 May 1974). However, this was put into context later in the day when the Minister of State Stan Orme told the House of Commons that, from 1 January to 30 April 1974, 74 people had been killed and that claims for compensation for damage to property had amounted to £102 million.

Among the strike leadership an attempt was now made to streamline the decision-making process with representatives of the various workers, political and paramilitary interests being represented in a Strike Co-ordinating Committee. The committee was chaired by Glen Barr, who bridged all three elements of the strike coalition.

The *News Letter* meanwhile reflected the Unionist discontent which had led to the strike and accused Faulkner and his colleagues of trying to 'gull the public' by pressing ahead with Sunningdale:

> No one in his right senses wishes to see industry disrupted or their wage packet put in jeopardy by a protest of this kind. No reasonable person deliberately goes out of his way to embark on a destructive course unless all other options have been closed. And in Ulster the options have been closed. The voice that sounded so loudly and so clearly last February fell on deaf ears. Today it is being raised again, and it was inevitable this time that it should be accompanied by protest of a different form. (*News Letter* 16 May 1974)

The pro-Faulkner *Belfast Telegraph* meanwhile reported that the shut-down was almost total and estimated that 90 per cent of engineering workers had now joined the stoppage (*Belfast Telegraph* 16 May 1974).

In the House of Commons meanwhile a frustrated Merlyn Rees told the South Down Unionist MP Lawrence (Willie) Orr that Loyalists in Northern Ireland might soon have to face the question of whether their Loyalism would lead them into confrontation with British troops. Rees's comments were badly received in Unionist and Loyalist circles and provided a forewarning of how similar comments were likely to be taken within Unionism.

By the morning of 17 May Rees's mood had become much more pessimistic. He told Wilson that electricity supply was getting 'extremely difficult' and that although about three hundred naval and air force personnel had been prepared to come to Northern Ireland to run the power stations they would not be able to operate all of them because 'the Belfast ones are firmly under the control of this man [Billy] Kelly, who is in league with Craig'.

Rees later met a Loyalist deputation that included Craig, the Rev. William Beattie, Harry West and Glen Barr. Craig warned Rees that while the UWC was willing to reach an arrangement to resolve the crisis the government's continued refusal to negotiate would destroy the Executive and lead to a return to direct rule (Kerr, 2011: 209).

Somewhat inaccurately the *News Letter* reported, 'there were no representatives from the strike organisers' and Rees was adamant that 'he would not be negotiating with people involved in a political strike'. Rees confirmed that contingency plans might include the use of troops in power stations. Craig, however, told reporters after the meeting that troops would be unable to maintain power without the assistance of electricity workers. Although work at Belfast East and West power plants had started again there were now reports that petrol supplies were running low and some filling stations were introducing their own rationing system (*News Letter* 18 May 1974).

The *Irish Independent* reported on 18 May that contingency plans had been made to deal with the situation where electricity supplies were completely cut off. A decision had been made the previous day by the coal and ash squads at the two Belfast power stations to walk out, while maintenance men were already on strike. The UWC in turn responded to threats by the Labour government to use troops in power stations by saying that 'If it was acceptable to the British Labour Party that the miners' strike could be used to bring about political change in Britain, then they must equally accept the rights of the Ulster workers to pursue their legitimate demands using similar tactics.'

The *News Letter* made it clear who it believed had brought the strike about. On 18 May the newspaper's editorial, 'In this week of Protest', stated:

> The unrest that has made life so difficult in Northern Ireland this week is to be deplored, but no more than – if as much as – the course taken by those misguided politicians who brought it all about. It was apparent for weeks and months that if they would not hear the voice of the people, if they would not attempt to listen to the people, then the people would protest ... The form of the present protest must obviously be open to criticism – all strike action is injurious – but how do you start to convey a message from the public to members of parties who are prepared to go as far as to ignore the results of a general election. (*News Letter* 18 May 1974)

Loyalist paramilitaries meanwhile continued to tighten their grip on industry and on 18 May 1974 the *Irish Times* reported that workplaces which had refused to close on Thursday did so when threatened. These included the government training centre in East Belfast, the Ulster Museum and Berkshire hosiery factory in Newtownards, Co. Down. The following day the Defence Secretary Roy Mason authorised the dispatch of the Spearhead Battalion from Britain to Northern Ireland (the 1st Battalion The Light Infantry) in response to a request from the British Army's General Officer Commanding (GOC) Northern Ireland. Rees, meanwhile, announced a State of Emergency under section 40 of the Northern Ireland I Constitution Act (1973).

When the Northern Ireland Executive met to assess the situation on 20 May, Maurice Hayes, a senior civil servant, reported that in the event of a complete breakdown of power supplies essential services could be maintained for two to four days without serious danger to public health but at some risk to life among the elderly and the sick. Despite this, Executive Ministers were generally agreed that there should be no deal with the strikers but that the Executive should urgently try to reach agreement on Sunningdale (PRONI, Exmin 74/72).

This view was, however, at odds with the facts on the ground and a further sign of the gathering support for the strike came on the morning of 20 May when Unionist politicians publicly called for support for the strike in a half-page advertisement in the *News Letter*.

On 21 May a back to work march led by the Trades Union Congress General Secretary Len Murray attracted only two hundred participants and the marchers were pelted with eggs and tomatoes by supporters of the strike. A UWC press statement scathingly commented that 'large numbers of security forces can be spared to protect the "Duke of York" parade by Len Murray and his communist supporters' and then added that 'Due to inexcusable statements from senior politicians in Westminster' there would be a complete embargo on oil and petrol supplies forthwith.

That same day the Northern Ireland Executive Minister of Health and Social Services, Paddy Devlin, introduced an Emergency Benefits Payments scheme. The emergency system made it difficult to distinguish between those unable to get to work or laid off due to the lack of electricity or intimidation, who were entitled to payment, and those on strike voluntarily, who were not. The system also meant that those unable to work may well have received more than they were officially entitled to. In effect any distinction between the 'deserving' and 'undeserving' poor evaporated during the strike. *Fortnight* magazine subsequently estimated that around £4 million was paid out by the Department of Health and Social Security during the strike while, in a written answer in the House of Commons on 25 July, the NIO minister Don Concannon estimated £5 million had been paid out.

On 22 May the Executive agreed to the Council of Ireland being introduced in stages. SDLP members initially voted by 11 to 8 against the revised plan but after talks with Stan Orme agreed to accept the changes. By this time, however, the political initiative increasingly lay with loyalist and Unionist opponents of the Sunningdale Agreement, and the decision to introduce the Council of Ireland in stages was little more than the proverbial rearranging of deckchairs on the *Titanic* after the iceberg had hit.

Despite its success some anti-Sunningdale elements were now clearly worried about the impact the strike would have if it continued. The *News Letter* called for an end to the stoppage, saying,

> To-day the strikers are at the apex of their success. Now it is time to go back to work – and to consider what more is required of them. They have won this battle: they have shown their determination to win the war. Downing Street would be foolish to put that determination to the test yet again. (*News Letter* 22 May 1974)

The report of the Anglo-Irish Law Enforcement Commission, released on 23 May, confirmed previous rumours and recommended an 'extra-territorial' method of bringing terrorist suspects to trial in the part of Ireland where they were arrested, no matter where the offence had been committed. This again fell far short of the extradition system that Faulkner had promised Unionists would result from the Sunningdale Agreement.

When Wilson held talks with Faulkner, Fitt and Oliver Napier at Chequers on 24 May, Faulkner was now more pessimistic about the situation and said that:

> With every hour that passed the Secretary of State and the British Government on the one hand, and he and the Northern Ireland Executive on the other enjoyed less support and credibility, as it became increasingly evident that the administration of the country was in fact in the hands of the Ulster Workers Council. In his view, however, this erosion of support for duly constituted authority could be put right quickly by the assertion of authority on the ground. (PREM 16/147 CAIN website)

Faulkner was, however, still opposed to any negotiation with the strike leaders, arguing that

> those who were responsible for the strike action had failed to realise that the situation was now out of the control of Mr West and Mr Paisley. Control had passed to other and more dangerous hands. The issue was not now whether the Sunningdale Agreement would or would not survive. The outcome which the Protestant extremists sought was without question an independent, neo-fascist Northern Ireland. (Ibid.)

Faulkner said that although the strikers were in control he felt the situation could still be saved by strong government action. Wilson said the army could play a role in petrol distribution but feared that military intervention in the power stations might lead middle management to leave (Ibid.).

The *News Letter* editorial of 25 May, 'No one will listen', accurately reflected broader Unionist attitudes towards the strike at this time by commenting:

> There are thousands upon thousands from all walks of life in Northern Ireland who are thoroughly unhappy about the great protest strike but who are in complete understanding of, and sympathy with, the reasons behind it. This, presumably, is something that few British politicians could be expected to appreciate.
>
> It poses the question that so many people were asking for so long:- Is there nothing we can do to make the Government realise that we cannot and will not be forced on to a road that is not of our choosing?
>
> The Workers' Council provided the answer to that question and who is to say there could have been any better? What else were they to do, what else were we all to do when deaf ears at Westminster were being turned consistently on democratic cries from the country? A government that refuses to listen to the majority of the people – and that is still the case – embellishes a recipe for revolution and anarchy. (*News Letter* 25 May 1974)

That evening Wilson made a radio and television broadcast in which he said that the strike was being run by 'thugs and bullies'. He continued, 'We recognise that behind this situation lie many genuine and deeply held fears, I have to say that these fears are unfounded: that they are being deliberately fostered by people in search of power.' In fact, despite Wilson's public assurances the fears were far from being unfounded for, on 20 May, Wilson had considered the possibilities of British withdrawal from Northern Ireland, repartition or 'a sort of dominion status' (Donoughue, 2004: 124).

In what was widely perceived in Northern Ireland as an anti-Unionist rant, Wilson accused those who opposed the Sunningdale deal of 'sponging on Westminster and British democracy'. The comments caused outrage and anger across the Unionist community and further increased support for the strike.

In a final role of the dice, on 27 May the army took over 21 petrol stations throughout Northern Ireland. In response the UWC stepped up strike action by threatening further power cuts. Glen Barr, as strike co-ordinating committee chairman, announced that power workers would leave Ballylumford power station at midnight on 28 May.

In a memo to Wilson on 27 May Rees noted that gas supplies had stopped, electricity supply was less than half capacity and food supplies were seriously disrupted. Rees commented, 'Those who have supported the strike, whatever they may say, will have nothing to do with real power-sharing and an election is likely to be no more than a precursor to pressure for a Protestant state for a Protestant people'. He continued:

> If the UWC can maintain the strike – and there is every indication that they can – it will not be easy to resist their demands. We have done everything we can to support the Northern Ireland Executive by committing troops to maintain essential services (although there is a definite limit to what they can be expected to do). While the Northern Ireland Executive remain in being, there can be no real movement. But the situation changes if they go. From our point of view the most desirable situation now is that they should go of their [own] accord. (PREM 16/148 CAIN website)

By the morning of 28 May the Strike Co-ordinating Committee was planning to shut down the electricity grid by 6.00 pm. The crisis appeared to be coming to a head with the grid on the verge of collapse and pumping stations then being unable to pump sewage. Faulkner appealed to Rees to negotiate with the strike leaders but Rees refused and at 1.00 pm Faulkner and the Unionist Ministers resigned from the Executive. Announcing his resignation, Faulkner noted that it was, 'apparent to us from the extent of support for the present stoppage that the degree of consent needed to sustain the Executive does not at present exist. Nor, as Ulstermen, are we prepared to see our country undergo, for any political reason, the catastrophe which now confronts it' (quoted in Bew and Gillespie, 1999: 88–9). In response the strike leaders stepped back from the brink and began to increase electricity production again.

Conclusion

With the perceived threat of a Council of Ireland removed, Protestant support for the strike quickly began to evaporate and people quickly began returning to work. Despite protests from many of their followers, UWC leaders announced an end to the stoppage on 29 May, without having achieved the goal of fresh Assembly elections. On 21 May 1974

Harold Wilson spoke of the UWC strike in the House of Commons and said:

> This is not only a political strike; it is a sectarian strike which is aimed at destroying decisions taken by this House of Commons, both as regards power-sharing, and by the elected Assembly. It is being done for sectarian purposes, having no relation to this century but only to the seventeenth century. (quoted in Bew and Gillespie, 1999: 86)

Wilson was correct in calling the UWC strike a political strike taken in opposition to the decisions of Parliament and the Assembly and there were undoubtedly sectarian undertones to the strike; however, he was entirely wrong to compare it to the seventeenth-century wars of religion. In many respects the UWC strike bore a greater resemblance to the miners' strike and poll tax riots of the Thatcher era where a government came into conflict with particular communities by attempting to enforce deeply unpopular policies on those communities. It might also be noted that while the UWC strike merely succeeded in bringing about the collapse of an already unstable, and unrepresentative, local administration. the poll tax riots of 1990 played a significant role in forcing the resignation of a Prime Minister – Margaret Thatcher.

Fundamentally the Sunningdale settlement did not operate with the 'widespread support' of the electorate of Northern Ireland nor did North–South structures 'operate with the prior consent of both majority and minority opinion', representatives of which were not given 'a right to prior consultation and involvement in the process of determining its form, functions and procedures'. Matched against the criteria set out in the White Paper of 1973, the Sunningdale Agreement was a failure in its own terms.

Beyond this, the wider national and international factors, which provided the background to the UWC strike, have often ignored as an element in the failure of the Sunningdale deal. The coalminers' strikes and the impact of the Yom Kippur War led to petrol rationing and power cuts, and the public, to some extent at least, became accustomed to the inconveniences which these created. Thus, many of the disruptions which people faced during the UWC strike were not new and the impact of the strike was less of a shock than might have been the case in a more economically stable period.

In the arena of national and international politics the British, Irish (and United States) governments were largely concerned with dealing with economic problems, making Northern Ireland even less of a priority. The irritation of the British government in 1974 might also be partly attributed to the view that Northern Ireland had been 'solved' at Sunningdale and the government could now move on to more pressing matters. In the event this view proved to be entirely wrong. At the centre of the political turbulence in

Northern Ireland sat the power-sharing Executive which, with its insecure political foundations, was unable to survive the combination of local, national and international economic and political factors which provided the perfect storm which destroyed the Sunningdale Agreement.

Note

1   Formed in 1971, the Ulster Defence Association was a vigilante organisation that would conduct sectarian attacks under the *nom de guerre* Ulster Volunteer Force (UVF). The UDA was not proscribed until 1982.

3

Understanding aspiration, anxiety, assumption and ambiguity: the anatomy of Sunningdale

Arthur Aughey

In his magisterial history, *Ireland: The Politics of Enmity* (2007: 511–13), Lord Bew argues that the failure of the power-sharing Executive in 1973–74 – and especially of the proposal for a Council of Ireland – was largely the product of three intersecting, mutually re-enforcing and politically destructive factors. Together they constitute what could be called the three 'As' of Sunningdale. The first factor that Bew identifies is Nationalist anticipation about the course of events, anticipation which was at odds with the scope of the proposed institutional structures. This was immortalised by the passing remark of the Social Democratic and Labour Party (SDLP)'s Hugh Logue to a Dublin audience that the Council of Ireland was to be 'the vehicle that would trundle unionists into a united Ireland' (see editorss' introduction and Coakley below). This anticipation encouraged, secondly, heightened Unionist anxiety about what was being established, not only regarding the Council of Ireland but also the implications of power sharing within Northern Ireland. Unionist anxiety has been equally immortalised in the words of one United Ulster Unionist Council (UUUC) poster during the February 1974 General Election which proclaimed that 'Dublin is just a Sunningdale away'. And thirdly, Bew thinks that nationalist anticipation and Unionist anxiety were responding to exaggerated official assumptions in both British and Irish governments about what was achievable. In London, it was thought that the

Secretary of State for Northern Ireland, William Whitelaw, had delivered the basis of a solution to the Irish problem and that all that remained for the Prime Minister Edward Heath to do at Sunningdale was to complete the embellishment and detail. Dublin, pushing for advantage on the role of the Council of Ireland while conceding little on Unionist concerns, raised few doubts initially about the stability of arrangements.

To these three 'As' perhaps a fourth should be added – ambiguity. There was a fatal ambiguity in the commitments which had been arrived at that made the goal of political accommodation within Northern Ireland and between North and South highly unlikely, if only because they encouraged anxiety and anticipation in equal measure. This was captured best by the Irish Attorney General's insistence that, irrespective of any declaration made at Sunningdale, no one could doubt that the Irish constitutional claim to 'the Six Counties' remained unchanged. Together, these four 'As' constituted a likely scenario for institutional failure. And the sustained terrorist campaigns of Republicans and Loyalists – both of whom, albeit in their very different ways, understood Sunningdale as an exercise in neo-colonialism – made it a perfect template for collapse. And, of course, it did collapse.

Although we know that to have been the case, it is important to be inter-pretatively cautious. As an event of 'contemporary history', Sunningdale is both contemporary in the sense that it is still within the living memory of many people and its undoing is a familiar story; but it is also history, and even those who did live through those events may find that scholarly studies do not correspond with 'how it appeared at the time'. There are three matters which are worth distinguishing. The first may be called the 'Chinese whisper' syndrome. This involves the intergenerational transmission of communal memory or the mediation by narrative of immediate experience. Joan Scott (2001: 285–7) coined the phrase 'fantasy echo' to describe the complexities of this intergenerational transmission. Thus, historical references appear to echo the past directly in terms of present experience. Scott thought that this is the basis of collective memory and, when a person or a community claims a historical identity, the 'echo is a fantasy, the fantasy an echo; the two are inextricably intertwined'. Here, the past is not a foreign country. It shapes daily practices and physical spaces as well as relationships between and within communities. For those who lived through events the ghosts of the past whisper strongly in the present. New generation(s) are 'guests' of that past and are invited to adopt those memories as their own as social and political actors (see also Aughey and Barnes, 2006). Sunningdale confirms distinct readings of the past and the present which constitute Unionist and National-ist narratives of politics.

If the first syndrome involves a 'bottom-up' transmission of ideas about the past, the second involves a 'top-down', considered, reinterpretation of events. This, following Michael Oakeshott, may be called the 'crow flies' syndrome (1991: 59). Oakeshott was critical of the sort of ideological histories which consider events 'as the crow flies' or which ignore inconvenient complexities about the past. Two relevant narratives can be identified. In each case, the flight path of the crow is backwards, albeit by different possible routes, as the attempt is made to reconfigure past events in the light of contemporary experience or of current political needs. The first is a narrative of return, the view that the institutional shape of the Belfast Agreement which was concluded 25 years later had been always inherent at Sunningdale in 1973. What was necessary to a just accommodation of interests and aspirations was always obvious to right-thinking people. This judgement very rapidly became accepted wisdom and one can find it in the immediate recollection of Brian Faulkner (1978: 279–80). It is back to the future. It is most succinctly expressed in the saying, coined by Seamus Mallon, that the 1998 Belfast Agreement was 'Sunningdale for slow learners'. In other words, the meaning of all subsequent initiatives was to return to where it all began and to understand its necessity for the first time. According to Michael Lillis, the key official responsible for Anglo-Irish policy, how much suffering could have been avoided if republicans and Unionists had only settled for 'the 1973 Sunningdale terms'. Even Danny Kennedy, Deputy Leader of the Ulster Unionist Party (UUP), has argued that, had 'Sunningdale not been wrecked by Ian Paisley and company, constitutional nationalism would have been the order of the day, rather than the violent republicanism that wrecked so many lives over the troubled years' (cited in Gordon, 2010). This is a 'wasted years' thesis. It is a narrative which is persuasive to many Nationalists and Unionists for whom the details of any particular initiative are irrelevant to that narrative's moral force.

The second is a narrative of transcendence, the view that the 1998 Agreement – and, for the Democratic Unionist Party (DUP), its modification by the St Andrews Agreement of 2006 – went beyond all previous attempts to resolve the Troubles. Rather than this representing a return to the lesson of 1973–74, today's institutions represent a new beginning. Sunningdale is either registered as a failure by going too far towards Irish unity (the DUP version) or by reproducing the dead-end of a 'Northern Free State' (the Sinn Féin version). Of course, it also has a general appeal, not only for those who have a partisan political investment in the present, but also for those seeking to make sense of a complicated past and perhaps their own inglorious part in it, thus conveniently addressing both the Lillis and Kennedy criticisms. It differs from the first narrative because what needed to be learned from

Sunningdale was the importance of 'inclusiveness' – could people not see that in 1973? What both narratives share is an interpretation of the past with (at least) one eye upon the present which, as Herbert Butterfield (1931: 31) taught us all those years ago, 'is the source of all sins and sophistries in history'.

The interpretative question remains: how do we do justice to the contemporary – Sunningdale in its own time – and to the historical – disciplined thinking about that time in relation to subsequent events? To which one can add a further question: how does one avoid as far as possible the sin and sophistry of the political manipulation of narratives? In this context it is worth reflecting on a remark by G.K. Chesterton in his popular *A Short History of England*. He noted a familiar paradox: the paradox is that the past is always present but what people remember may not be, for the historian, their real history. Chesterton put it this way (1917: 2): 'We may find men wrong in what they thought they were, but we cannot find them wrong in what they thought they thought'. This anticipated E.P. Thompson's (1991: 3) more celebrated and succinct remark that it is important to be wary of the 'enormous condescension of posterity'. Chesterton's formulation provides a way to reflect seriously on the interpretative challenge of Sunningdale. When we consider an event like Sunningdale, we have to accept that what people thought they thought is a matter of record – their anticipations, their anxieties and their assumptions in a period of profound ambiguity. That moment has an integrity which requires respect, because these four 'As' characterise our own time as well. What historians bring to those accounts is knowledge of what those at the time could *not* know. They have a fuller perspective because they are conscious of the echoes and the fantasies and they have access to evidence other than the momentary. For example, to take Bew's assessment, they may argue according to the record and subsequent events that official assumptions were exaggerated, that Nationalist anticipation was inflated and that Unionist anxiety was often misplaced. That is a considered judgement based on what the evidence obliges Bew to believe – not as a past remembered but a past understood according to what is revealed by the archives. However, those involved in those events did not believe that either their anticipations were inflated or their anxieties were misplaced; otherwise they would not have acted as they did.

There is certainly some comfort in the belief that the recent history of Northern Ireland between Sunningdale and the Belfast Agreement was a process of slow learning by those who came to recognise that they had been wrong in what they thought. The comfort lies in a notion of progress from misunderstanding to knowledge. One must accept the possibility, however, that this is an illusion. It may be that, in what they thought they thought, there was little misunderstanding at all. As the historian A.T.Q. Stewart (2001) has argued, underneath changing events the fundamentals of Irish history can look very familiar. In his view there is little room for misunderstanding between Nationalists and Unionists in Northern Ireland. 'Nor do they need to get to know each other better. They know each other only too well, having lived alongside each other for four centuries' (2001: 185). In short, the division at the heart of the modern Irish question 'is not just a clash of cultures; it is a culture in itself, a point overlooked by most observers'. To think otherwise falls into that category of an error of intelligence of the sort pointed to by T.W. Rolleston (1975: 21) in his introduction to the reprint of Shelley's *Address to the Irish People*. For all his very good intentions, the English poet's liberal radicalism never had a hope of success because, though he desired the emancipation of Catholics, 'he avowedly desired still more their emancipation from Catholicism, the creed for which the nation had fought and suffered for three centuries'. Perhaps one can suggest that the radicalism of Sunningdale was of a similar character. It announced itself to the world as the emancipation of Unionists and Nationalists in Northern Ireland from those self-defeating aspects of their creeds but ignored not only the tenacity of those creeds but also the unwillingness of those who held them to abjure their fundamentals. As one prominent member of the SDLP accepted (Farren, 2007: 1):

> As in all conflict resolution situations Sunningdale was an agreement that demanded significant compromises from all its signatories. However, despite the language of compromise, few if any of the parties to the agreement were ready to move as far or as speedily as the agreement required in order for it to take root. This I believe to have been the case whether we are talking about the British or the Irish governments, or more immediately the Northern Irish parties.

Farren's insight is worth examining in more detail.

Nationalist anticipation

The knowledge of which Stewart writes, especially in its political form, is not the kind of subtle understanding which would impress the historian. It is not the kind of knowledge, in other words, which is an end in itself. It is instrumental knowledge and concerned with means to an end. There were two aspects of this means-to-end thinking when nationalists considered the problem of Unionism in 1973. The first involved imagining Unionists according to the requirements of Nationalist ideological purpose and according to the wished-for end of Irish unity. It was expressed positively in terms of the need for reconciliation between traditions on the island of Ireland.

There was a large degree of Shelley-like emancipation to this imagining, and specifically it involved imagining Unionists out of their Britishness. There was a Rousseauean inflection as well since nationalists felt that the British connection acted as an external impediment preventing Unionist recognition of their real interests and their potential to act according to their real will. For example, as early as 1971 John Hume was convinced that most Unionists believed that a united Ireland was inevitable and that this private admission just needed proper political expression. He thought that the search for agreement on unity should begin as soon as possible since there was 'little point in evading any further the inevitability on which all are agreed' (McLoughlin, 2010: 34). The practical question concerned the process by which Unionists would come to see reason, a process which might be taken less benignly as code for 'educating the Prods' (Patterson, 2006: 254). The second involved the brute acceptance that 'political' Unionism was an obstacle to progress and would have to be manoeuvred to see reason. For example, Hume was opposed to what he believed to be 'the false liberalism of placating' Unionists in the negotiation of Sunningdale or any subsequent amendment of its terms (Patterson, 2006: 239); or, to put that otherwise, they needed to be forced to be free. This must be by 'persuasion', of course, and not by the brutal militarism of the IRA. However, the line dividing persuasion and political coercion was a fine one. At Sunningdale, according to even a sympathetic account of northern nationalism (McLoughlin, 2010: 218), 'Hume and his colleagues lost sight of the SDLP's founding principles: they appeared to assume that Irish unity could be achieved through unionists' acquiescence rather than their active assent.'

And yet, why would the SDLP not assume that the purpose of Sunningdale was to 'educate the Prods'? Why would it settle for less if it believed that more was on offer? Northern nationalists had been confined by a political system not of their choosing and one which had seemed, until very recently, unchanging. In short measure, Stormont had gone, the Unionist 'monolith' had fragmented and there was every possibility of moving rapidly towards Irish unity. After all, the SDLP believed that Northern Ireland was an unstable political entity and unable to secure for Unionists what they most required of it, security. The Irish Republican Army (IRA) campaign, while it could not be condoned, only served to illustrate that truth. Moreover, was not the leader of the UUP prepared to negotiate a new deal with Irish Nationalism and was not the British government prepared to push him towards a settlement congenial to the SDLP's analysis of the problem? In Chestertonian terms, they had little reason to think they were wrong in what they thought and every reason to think that they were right: that history was in their favour and that the moment was there to be seized. This reading corresponds with McGrattan's archival research (2009: 72) which shows that, apart from its leader Gerry Fitt, the SDLP generally held a 'maximalist vision' of what was possible. To use a Faulknerite expression, it looked upon the power-sharing Executive as a 'necessary nonsense' in order to achieve its larger end of Irish unity. It was 'caught up in the pursuit of opening consti-tutional and political opportunities' and this process of thinking influenced what was thought possible, downplaying its own role in provoking Unionist anxiety. Indeed, McGrattan's conclusion illustrates in the language of social science that fine balance which Chesterton attempted to capture, namely the 'paradox of rational decisions creating sub-optimal outcomes' (1917: 73). And he believed that it is a historical sensibility which delivers the appropri-ate explanation since 'the policy decisions and direction established in the early 1970s not only effectively ruled out the possibility of changing course and "settling" for mid-range goals – it actually proved self-defeating in that it contributed to the undermining of the Sunningdale project' (McGrattan, 2009: 73). Politicians were not wrong in failing to see these facts if only because the evidence available to the historian was not present to them.

McGrattan (2009: 71–2) is equally critical and for good reason of existing interpretations of the disposition of the Irish government at this time. Those accounts fail to estimate adequately the traditional Nationalist aspiration of Dublin, as well as the political constraints upon any serious modification of that aspiration. The official mood was captured brilliantly by a series of Dublin 'letters' or reports by the *Irish Times* correspondent Dennis Kennedy which were published in the Belfast journal *Fortnight*. Kennedy regularly criticised the insouciance of Irish governments, insouciance at ideological odds with its constitution's claim to sovereignty over the six counties of Northern Ireland. Events were read simplistically just as wished-for outcomes were read into the attitudes of others; for example, Faulkner's transformation from the unacceptable face of incorrigible Unionism into an aspiring United Irishman, an attitude as superficial, thought Kennedy, as most political judge-ments in Dublin about Northern affairs. He summed up the political con-sensus on the eve of Sunningdale thus: 'A Council of Ireland is on the way, the SDLP, meaning the Catholics, are on their way to sharing power inside Northern Ireland. This, it is taken, is progress in an "Irish" direction, that is away from the basic "Ulster is British" or "Northern Ireland is an integral part etc. etc." stance.' Therefore, it must mean a significant move in the direc-tion of a united Ireland. Certainly, Kennedy added, 'very few people would see power-sharing and a new North–South understanding in a Council of Ireland as arrangements designed to make partition workable'. Or if that few did, they did not feel obliged to say so openly (*Fortnight*, 74, 14 December 1973: 9–10). After Sunningdale, Kennedy argued that there was little willingness on the part of the Irish government to make the agreement more sellable to Unionists. The attitude was legalistic – an agreement had been entered into by all parties and two sovereign states and so must stand as it was. There was no doubt that the package was fair and Unionists had to accept it. If there was a party consensus it was on that point. And here it is possible to detect again those two aspects of nationalist means to end thinking. 'In mind too, although, not spelled out now as much as it was in Fianna Fáil days, is the view that if they do not want to accept it, Britain, as the sovereign government of the second part, ought to make them accept it.' Though, as Kennedy remarked, quite how London was expected to make Unionists accept it without 'forcing' them to be free was left unspecified (*Fortnight*, 79, 8 March 1974: 14). Certainly, the spectre of Fianna Fáil keeping the government up to the mark in its obligations to the 'people' of Ireland could not be ignored either and this had immediate implications for any movement on Articles 2 and 3 of the constitution (even if the Fine Gael–Labour coalition had any intention of moving on those articles). As Fianna Fáil's Des O'Malley put it, the national aspirations of the great majority of the Irish nation must be respected and could not be put asunder by the 'anti-national semantics' of the likes of Conor Cruise O'Brien or Garret FitzGerald. The opposition presented itself, ably assisted by the SDLP, as the conscience of the nation's destiny, reaffirming that no section of the Irish people could opt out of that destiny (O'Donnell 2007b: 8–9).

So there was little incentive for the Irish government to assume that it had not succeeded in negotiating the appropriate solution to the crisis in Northern Ireland, ending both Unionist 'supremacy' and the Nationalist 'nightmare'. Why should it be concerned with Unionist sensitivities if the British government was willing to sign up for Sunningdale? And had not Faulkner as the leader of Unionism seen reason at last? Reconciliation with Unionists did not mean confirming partition, for to do so would have meant reconciling northern Nationalists to a fate its constitution forbade. 'To frame the Council of Ireland as a means of reconciliation belies its importance for northern nationalists and misrepresents the terms on which Unionists agreed to its establishment.' Indeed, as Farrington argues, the Irish government was tied into an ideologically motivated strategic game of outmanoeuvring Unionists rather than taking seriously the policy of national reconciliation (2007: 101–3). This may be put otherwise: the very assumption of 'reconciliation' as understood by both the Irish government and the SDLP meant that Unionists had to confront 'reality' whether they liked that reality or not, which is not to argue that they were engaged in bad faith. Farrington's conclusion is well made: 'The point is not that revisionist nationalism had no purchase on the idea of reconciliation; Irish civil servants and politicians were, without doubt, sincere about creating the conditions whereby unionists would consent to a united Ireland. The problem is that the Irish government misunderstood the conditions necessary for unionists to consent to a united Ireland' (Farrington, 2007).

The fantasy echo in the collective memory of Nationalism repeated the story of British perfidy and Unionist reaction, and the Chinese whispers from 1974 replay in contemporary politics. However, it is worth considering in this regard Gillespie's conclusion to an important history of this period (1998: 112): 'in our present era of "facing realities" we should perhaps consider that it would have taken a miracle for the Sunningdale deal to have survived. Clearly the "slow learners" in 1974 included the SDLP and Irish Government as well as the British Government, the unionists and loyalists.'

Unionist anxiety

The publication of Albert O. Hirschman's *Exit, Voice and Loyalty: Responses to Decline in Firms, Organisations, and States* (1970) coincided with those profound challenges within Unionism, and between Unionism and the state, which posed similar choices. Hirschman examined options which are appropriate not only to consumer behaviour and business strategy but also to the experience of political organisations. Discontent with the performance of leadership or the direction of policy provokes 'voice' or protest which is designed to make leaders either to be responsive to criticism or to change policy. The exercise of voice, however, may not have the desired effect and this raises the potential of 'exit'. Hirschman thought that the possibility of exit was an option which often made the exercise of voice more effective, putting pressure on leaders either to accede more readily to criticism or to compromise on policy. However, exit for members of a political party, for example, is likely to be costly and is generally avoided, especially if a split may threaten careers and the prospect of power. Loyalty often brings its own rewards of security and stability. Since it is an allegiance based on affinities of sentiment and purpose, loyalty is a profoundly conservative force, relying, as it often does, on appeals to trust. Severely abridging the experience of Unionist politics before and after Sunningdale, one can understand it as a debate between the options of exit, voice and loyalty, organisationally and ideologically. Indeed, one can take the analogy somewhat further and suggest that these choices found distinct political expression in the roles played by the Faulkner Unionists (loyalty), the United Ulster Unionist Council (UUUC) (voice) and loyalist paramilitaries (exit). The drama of this debate played itself out in the fevered circumstance of intense IRA violence and communal turmoil.

Once convinced of the rightness of his chosen course, Faulkner's appeal was to loyalty and trust – that the UUP was stronger as a united organisation and that it was important to confirm its reliability as a partner to the British government. Of course, this involved significant risks: that the party could be held together on an appeal to trust and that the British government would reciprocate such loyalty by helping to sustain Faulkner's leadership. We know that neither party unity was maintained nor sufficient support delivered but it was not entirely evident at the time such that Faulkner's strategy was ordained to fail. Its rational basis was an extension of the Unionist tradition of government and an appeal to a broad electoral constituency expecting responsible leadership. The message was that the dissenting voice was legitimate but that simple rejectionism would undermine and not strengthen the Unionist cause. Influence could be sustained only by being inside and not outside the governing consensus on power sharing and an Irish dimension. The real 'loyalists', in other words, were those Unionists who were prepared to adapt to the new, emerging, dispensation but adapting it to serve their own interests. Pragmatism and principle met here and were mutually supporting, an ironic restatement of O'Neill's *Ulster at the Crossroads* speech a few years earlier. This did not appear an impossible prospectus. Opinion polls shortly after the publication of William Whitelaw's White Paper suggested that it tapped a public mood which now desired moderation. Moreover, Faulkner had been able to bring his party and his electorate quite a distance down the road of adjustment to the prospect of power sharing and some form of Irish dimension. Even when the results of the local council and Assembly elections in May and June 1973 respectively showed that Unionist opinion was deeply divided and not as complaisant as London assumed, it was still possible to believe that investing in loyalty would continue to deliver (Dixon, 1997: 5–6).

Faulkner's memoirs reveal that he thought that Unionists 'had come off best at Sunningdale'. Indeed, he recounted that one member of his delegation was convinced that Sunningdale would go down in history as a Unionist victory. Faulkner's rather convoluted reflection on that thought was (1978: 236–7): 'I do not think if one examines the balance-sheet our conclusions can be shown to have been poorly judged'. His view of the disloyal rejection by a majority of the Unionist Council of the deal with which he returned from Sunningdale was that it was simply a result of 'fear and misunderstanding' which would resolve itself in time. There is no sense in that record of events that his resignation as leader of the Ulster Unionists meant that the very foundation of any deal had been undermined. Despite the General Election result of February 1974 delivering the fatal blow to Faulkner's hopes, some thought the investment in loyalty still might bring returns. For example, the 'Calvin Macnee' column in the eternally optimistic *Fortnight* magazine captured well that hopeful expectation. There was considerable force in the argument, it proposed, 'that as soon as people see what little there is to fear from Sunningdale Council of Ireland, with those famous executive powers pared down to the bare minimum, they'll begin to come round, just as they have begun to come round' to power sharing (*Fortnight*, 80, 22 March 1974). Loyalty, in other words, would be vital because it brings long-term pay-offs for Unionist compliance. The echo of this experience became fixed in some Unionist minds as an opportunity missed and, as Danny Kennedy believes, arrangements subsequently have not been as favourable as they were in 1974.

It may seem an outrageous suggestion that, by simply holding on to office irrespective of the lack of popular support amongst Unionists, the outcome might have been different. We are obliged to believe that all the historical evidence points to the necessary collapse of the Executive. Or, to put that otherwise, Unionist 'voice' in the form of Faulkner's opponents was destined to succeed. Yet, Unionist protest since the end of Stormont had not been particularly successful and time might indeed have healed many Unionist wounds. This was a slim hope, a Micawberish policy, highly unlikely, and the gap between the promised political dividend for Unionists and their immediate expenditure seemed disastrous. This gave not only energy but also legitimacy to Unionist voice. In their eyes, the deal was not a compromise. It was fatally compromised at a number of levels. First, they were not convinced of the bona fides of the SDLP and the seriousness of that party in trying to make Northern Ireland work. This has been put down normally to the narrowness of the 'dismal vision' of Unionism and to the failings of Unionist imagination. There is some truth in this judgement but it tends to replay the same explanation that Unionist concerns were exclusively psychological (fearful and uncertain) and not based on rational political calculations (even if one happens to think they were exaggerated). Even Faulkner identified the problem himself, noting (1978: 189) the difficulty of accepting into government a party which considered that Northern Ireland had 'no right to exist'. The underlying assumption of Nationalist thinking was that Unionists 'were a constituent part of the Irish people' and so, despite the effort of the SDLP 'to accept the authenticity of unionists' British identity', the assumption undermined the intention (McLoughlin, 2010: 229). Moreover, the rapid transition from fifty years of Unionist dominance to sharing power with such uncertain partners promised little and threatened much, especially when the SDLP in 1974 continued to withhold support from the police. An interesting Unionist aside on the SDLP's position after the fall of the Executive stated the position simply (Macnee, *Fortnight*, 93, 15 November 1974): 'it sounds insane that any politicians who show so little commitment to the whole concept of Northern Ireland should have the nerve to want to order its affairs'. Though that aside reveals much about the assumption of those Unionists opposed to Sunningdale, namely that Ulster was theirs to decide who should participate in the ordering of its affairs, it also involves a justifiable political grievance which Farren admits (2007: 7): from the moment of the agreement's signing it began losing Unionist support 'because unionist representatives were the only ones seen to have moved'. This point helps to contextualise arguments about the details of Sunningdale in terms of its democratic legitimacy.

For instance, in a review of Robert Fisk's influential account of the Ulster Workers' Council (UWC) strike, David Trimble emphasised one point: 'Sunningdale lacked consent' (*Fortnight*, 115, 21 November 1975: 13–14). Only massive self-deception encouraged its supporters to believe otherwise. The majority of Unionist elected representatives did not support it. Neither did the majority of the Unionist electorate. If this was 'consent', it seemed very like imposition (Tonge, 2000: 44). The exercise of 'voice' had sent a clear message. If self-deception there was, Trimble thought that it was to be found in those who turned a deaf ear. They had heard the message but the political misjudgement by supporters of Sunningdale was that the Unionist opposition could do little to change things. Gillespie (1998: 109) states the democratic deficit which had opened up: here was a 'dangerous position in which the views of the majority of unionists, let alone loyalists, were unrepresented in a supposedly "widely accepted" administration'. This only fed the suspicion that nationalists were indifferent anyway to the principle of Unionist consent and that, when the opportunity presented itself, were prepared to rely on coercion. And if, for the SDLP and the Irish government, coercion meant either the persuasion of the new 'reality' or imposition by the sovereign will of Westminster, unsubtle, literal Unionists might see little difference between the politics of Sunningdale and the terror campaign of the IRA if the common aim was a united Ireland. Where was the promised recognition of Northern Ireland's status? Where was co-operation on cross-border terrorism? Where was the commitment to deal effectively with extradition? From this perspective it was all one-way traffic. This may have been a misreading of the potential of Sunningdale but it was not an unintelligent or perverse reflection on it. It returns us to Bew's assessment with which the chapter began. By failing to define clearly not only the status of Northern Ireland but also the powers of the Council of Ireland, Sunningdale succeeded in inflating nationalist aspirations while raising Unionist fears that it was a means to force them into a united Ireland. 'But, of course, such a failure had its roots in the underlying pro-Irish unity rationale' of the original documentation (2007: 512). If voice – in the shape of the UWC strike – proved successful in bringing down the power-sharing Executive it was strikingly ineffective at delivering an alternative to satisfy Unionist demands. This ineffectiveness provoked widespread consideration of 'exit' amongst academics and journalists and commitment to negotiated independence by some loyalist paramilitaries, in particular those in the Ulster Defence Association (UDA).

The very idea of exit to an independent Ulster now seems fantastic and yet at the time it was discussed seriously for it corresponded with diverse agendas. And it also had a historical pedigree in the periodic Unionist interest in 'dominion status'. There was, first, a heady sensation of a Protestant working class emancipating itself from the thrall of Unionist political control and the false consciousness of British imperialism. Even the editor of *Fortnight* (84, 7 June 1974: 5) was seduced by the concept of autonomy, chosen to reflect what was thought to be the new spirit of 'Ulster nationalism which has been engendered by the strike and the British reaction to it'. In the 1970s one could speak sensibly of an identifiable Protestant industrial working class worthy of that name. However within a short period, as a result of deindustrialisation in Northern Ireland as in the rest of the United Kingdom, this working-class identity was demolished. With the benefit of hindsight, one can understand May 1974 to be not a beginning but the beginning of the end of that working-class Protestant idea of Ulster. Secondly, some Republicans had welcomed the UWC strike as evidence of Loyalists moving into the progressive and socialist camp, though as Tonge pointed out the strike was 'designed to collapse the prospect of either greater Irish unity or limited power-sharing' (2000: 44). Thirdly, the idea also corresponded with the sudden interest in Ulster nationalism of Labour's Secretary of State, Merlyn Rees, along with the musings of the new Prime Minister, Harold Wilson, about the possibility of British withdrawal from Northern Ireland. Whenever the New Ulster Political Research Group, under the direction of one of the leaders of the UWC strike Glen Barr, finally published its considered proposals for independence in 1978, the moment – if there ever was one – had definitely passed.

Conclusion

There appeared to be one immediate and obvious conclusion from the failure of Sunningdale and it was that there could be no stable institutional settlement without the active or passive consent of a majority of Unionists. If the Suez fiasco in 1956, as claimed, had been 'no end of a lesson' for British policy, then 1973–74 intimated another lesson on the limits of the possible.

However, it was equally clear that no stable settlement was now possible without the active or passive consent of a majority of Nationalists. Yet what would deliver that consent seemed mutually exclusive and politically unattainable. The Unionist position was that there should be no first step if it was a step towards Irish unity. Faulkner's loyalty to the requirements of London was believed to have put in place arrangements for the undoing of the Union. There were two responses. First, those Unionists who believed in the necessity of devolved government for the protection of their interests would only agree to a form of devolution, like that in the Convention Report of 1975, which not only the SDLP but also the British and Irish governments found unacceptable. Second, others thought that the lesson of Sunningdale was that devolution now required of Unionists too high a price. Why should they get involved in political initiatives the only object of which was their own undoing? Though his leadership has been subjected to relentless criticism, this judgement about what was on offer constituted the rational core of James Molyneaux's policy. He assumed that these initiatives were unacceptable politically and unsellable electorally.

The Nationalist position was that there should be no first step unless it was a step towards Irish unity. The lesson which the SDLP learnt at Sunningdale was that there did not seem to be much point in negotiating with Unionists. Their only principle, as Hume (1997: 121) later argued, is 'exclusivism'. Unionists never produce a single new idea or proposal. 'Where else in the world', he asked, 'would a powerful and influential government, such as the British, have tied the whole basis of their policy to such a pathetic and leaderless bunch of politicians?' He concluded by asking: 'Did anyone need to look any further for the roots of violence?' Here was a reading of the past which proposed that the British government lacked the proper will to impose a settlement or to use its political and economic resources to ensure Unionist compliance. Yet, as Dennis Kennedy had observed in 1973, how the British were supposed to deliver the 'consent' of Unionists was never thought through. Here is the Chinese whisper about Unionist intransigence passed down the years, intimating not only the Anglo-Irish Agreement of 1985 but also the Hume–Adams initiative of 1993. It is possible to argue that, after Sunningdale, the flow of interpretative sympathy was in favour of this argument. As Frank Millar (2008: 199) admitted, Unionists had lost the propaganda battle very early on in the Troubles and they found themselves invariably cast as the 'guilty party'. In short, Nationalism gained rhetorical advantage in 1974, putting Unionists consistently on the back foot. It proved to be effective politics of manoeuvre but was as incapable of securing 'agreement' in practice as was Sunningdale. Whether 1998 is such an agreement, as Zhou Enlai might say, is too early to tell.

Part II

The lessons of Sunningdale: the key protagonists

4

Sunningdale and the Irish dimension: a step too far?

John Coakley

Few episodes in the pursuit of a constitutional settlement in Northern Ireland have attracted as much academic controversy as the Sunningdale Agreement of December 1973 and its central institutional feature, the Council of Ireland. Analysts are divided as to its content (was it essentially the same as the later Good Friday Agreement of 1998, or was it radically different?), as to the motivations of the parties to it (did they see it as a final blueprint or as a step towards other ultimate goals?), and as to the circumstances leading to its demise (was collapse a consequence of a combination of determined unionist resistance and lukewarm British government support, or was it inevitable?).[1] Rather than revisiting these debates, this chapter focuses on a narrower question: the role of the Irish government in the Sunningdale process and, in particular, the extent to which this was marked by policy shift and political learning – not just in remoulding ideology and policy to match new political realities but also in respect of matters of strategy and tactics. In addressing this question, the chapter begins by exploring a potentially promising framework from which valuable theoretical insights into the relationship between the two Irish jurisdictions might be derived – the literature on the European integration process. It then analyses in turn the background planning conducted by the Irish government as it moved from abstract consideration of partition to the challenge of institutionalising a new North–South relationship, the process by which agreement in principle was reached between governments and parties at Sunningdale, and the unpicking and ultimate demise of the Council of Ireland. It concludes by generalising about the broad thrust of the government's position by reference to the theoretical perspectives mentioned above.

Interpreting the Council of Ireland

Hayward (2009) has argued that much of the process of political and ideological change that took place in Ireland in the late twentieth century drew on concepts and insights associated with the process of European integration. Indeed, Tannam (1999: 12–37) has demonstrated the value of theoretical perspectives designed to explain interaction between the EU and its member states in shedding light on the smaller stage of North–South relations in Ireland. While there are different ways of classifying and labelling such theories, they may be grouped into three approaches which correspond broadly (perhaps after a certain amount of shoe-horning) with three judgements on the Sunningdale Agreement and on its central feature, the Council of Ireland. Since these approaches (see, for example, Mitrany, 1965; Haas, 1970) were current in the academic literature in the run-up to Sunningdale, it is indeed possible that they may have leaked out into the world of policy-making.

First, the process of construction of a European political entity could, it was argued, proceed in a 'top down', federalist manner, with the creation of political structures at European level trumping the reservations of potential opponents, as advocated by such figures as the German diplomat Walter Hallstein (Krosigk, 1971). This corresponded to the fears and hopes of Unionists and Nationalists, respectively, that the Council of Ireland represented a decisive step down the path towards Irish unity. Thus, the Democratic Unionist Party Leader the Rev. Ian Paisley denounced the Sunningdale arrangements as 'machinery to force the pace towards a united Ireland' and as representing 'blatant treachery' on the part of Ulster Unionist leader Brian Faulkner (*Irish Times* 11 December 1973). Apparently sharing a similar view of its significance, the Social Democratic and Labour Party (SDLP) Assembly Member Hugh Logue reportedly praised it as 'the vehicle that would trundle Unionists into a united Ireland' (McLoughlin, 2010: 91).[2]

Second, and less ambitiously, momentum for European unity could be built from the bottom up, with functional co-operation expanding incrementally and creating a favourable climate for further political co-operation, along the lines proposed by the French diplomat Jean Monnet (Haas, 1958;

1967). To this corresponded the image of the Council of Ireland as an evolving and expanding organism rather than as a fully formed entity: it was seen by some as having long-term potential for persuading the reluctant of the benefits of Irish unity. As a Department of Foreign Affairs official put it when the idea was first raised, 'a Council of Ireland may be a premier means of working towards the growth of reconciliation, trust and friendship within Northern Ireland and between North and South; it should also be an embryo and symbol of our working towards unity based on consent' (National Archives of Ireland (NAI), Department of the Taoiseach (TSCH), 2004/21/624, Memo, Department of Foreign Affairs, 24 May 1973, p. 4). But this approach could also be seen as entirely objectionable. As a prominent Ulster Unionist MP, Harold McCusker, put it,

> the Sunningdale Agreement was designed not to kick us out of the United Kingdom, but to change our attitudes, to swing our gaze slowly from the centre of power we have always recognised as London towards Dublin and, by a slow process, to change the attitude of the Loyalist people so that one day they might believe the myth of Irish unity which so bedevils many people in Northern Ireland. I did not threaten the electorate with a united Ireland. I said that the Sunningdale Agreement was an insidious way of bringing our people eventually to agreeing that it was a solution. (*House of Commons Debates* (Hansard), 4 June 1974, Vol. 874, Col. 1108)

Third, the initiative in Europe could continue to rest with the existing nation states, whose leaders would pragmatically agree on specific domains of co-operation but who would retain political sovereignty, in the manner of the French President Charles de Gaulle's redefinition of the decision-making mechanisms of the European Economic Community (EEC) in the 1960s (Hoffmann, 1966). A corresponding interpretation of the Sunningdale Agreement sees the provisions for a Council of Ireland as vacuous, in effect leaving the constitutional status quo undisturbed, or even strengthening it. Thus, Brian Faulkner later described the provisions for a Council of Ireland as 'essentially propaganda' and as 'necessary nonsense' designed to placate the SDLP; he noted that the proposed equal representation of the Northern and Southern jurisdictions amounted to an acceptance of partition, contrasting with the Irish government's rejection (precisely for this reason) of the first Council of Ireland in 1925 (Faulkner, 1978: 229, 237). Sharing this analysis but not the perspective from which it emerged, the Independent Fianna Fáil TD Neil Blaney denounced the Council as powerless and as 'window dressing', and the agreement as 'the greatest sell-out in our history', since in his view it formally recognised partition (*Dáil Debates*, 13 December 1973, Vol. 269, Cols 1834–6).

These three approaches to interstate relations in Europe, which may be designated respectively federalist, neofunctionalist and intergovernmentalist, have remained central in the literature (though with federalism attracting declining attention) since the 1960s (see, for example, Hooghe and Marks, 2009; Webber, 2014). They offer a valuable framework for tracking the evolution of Irish government policy in the years around the Sunningdale Agreement.

Adjusting to political change

In the decades preceding the outbreak of civil conflict, the official Irish government position on Northern Ireland remained substantially unaltered. To the extent that there was cross-party agreement, it converged in the analysis elaborated by the All-Party Anti-Partition Conference in 1949, which described partition as a 'denial of the right to self-determination' – a refusal, imposed and supported by the British government, to accept the will of a majority of the people of Ireland (All-Party Anti-Partition Conference, 1949: 16). This departed from the traditional Sinn Féin position only in stopping short, on pragmatic rather than moral grounds, of advocating physical force to bring about unity. There is little evidence of sustained engagement with mechanisms for ending partition on the part of the dominant party, Fianna Fáil (Ó Beacháin, 2010), of its party organisation (Kelly, 2013) or of its founding leader (Bowman, 1982), though as civil unrest deepened in the 1970s and 1980s the party was forced to undertake a fundamental re-evaluation of its policy (O'Donnell, 2007a).[3]

Although Fine Gael and Labour had not developed an explicit policy in this area either, they had been moving gradually from coercive towards persuasive approaches, acknowledging that unity could only come about by agreement (Ivory, 1999: 89–90; McDermott, 2014: 102). In the early 1970s, this viewpoint was given particular intellectual weight in the respective parties by the contributions of two Dáil deputies elected in 1969, Dr Garret FitzGerald and Dr Conor Cruise O'Brien, each of whom also produced a major piece of analysis in book form that was highly influential both within and outside their parties. Offering a radical and carefully considered critique of traditional irredentist Nationalism, these works advocated a more conciliatory and less politically ambitious approach to the question of unity (FitzGerald, 1972; O'Brien, 1972).

An immediate consequence of the introduction of direct rule in Northern Ireland was the need to devise an alternative framework of government that would receive wide support. The Darlington conference of 25–7 September 1972, planned by the British government to promote agreement between the Northern Ireland parties, considered not just structures of domestic government within Northern Ireland but also the 'Irish dimension'. The Ulster Unionist Party and the Northern Ireland Labour Party each proposed a North–South consultative council, though making this conditional on Southern recognition of Northern Ireland's status. The Alliance Party proposed a different structure – an advisory inter-parliamentary Anglo-Irish Council with representatives from Westminster, the proposed Northern Ireland Assembly and the Dáil.[4] The SDLP, which, like the anti-power-sharing Unionist parties, did not attend the conference, proposed joint British–Irish rule over Northern Ireland, with a 50-member National Senate drawn equally from North and South exercising important powers in EEC-related regional planning, electricity and power, tourism and certain other areas (SDLP, 1972).

Following the conference, a 'Green Paper' or discussion document issued by the British government on 30 October 1972 recognised the 'Irish dimension' and proposed a three-stranded strategy: securing recognition of the status of Northern Ireland and of 'the principle of consent' to any change in this; making possible 'effective consultation and cooperation' between North and South; and concerted action against political violence (NIO, 1972: Para. 78). In the subsequent 'White Paper' or policy document issued on 20 March 1973, this was translated into a commitment to host a conference between Northern and Southern representatives to discuss how these concerns might best be addressed (NIO, 1973: Para. 112). The outcome was the Sunningdale conference of 6–9 December 1973.

Given its new role as a potential partner in the pursuit of a settlement, the Irish government sought to develop its expertise in respect of Northern Ireland in advance of this conference. It had quietly established an 'Inter-Departmental Unit on the North of Ireland' (IDU) on 27 May 1970, to gather and analyse information and offer advice on 'all aspects of Anglo-Irish relations having a bearing on the Six Counties', and to undertake the 'study in depth of possible long-term solutions (e.g., the federal solution), as well as short-term problems' (NAI, TSCH/2001/6/549, N.S. Ó Nualláin, Secretary to the Government, to J. McColgan, Department of External Affairs, 28 May 1970). It was made up of representatives of the departments of the Taoiseach, Foreign Affairs and Finance, and it co-ordinated a great deal of the research into possible structures and functions of a Council of Ireland.[5] Official thinking (apparently strongly influenced by EEC models) evolved through three broad, overlapping stages: formulating the fundamental objectives of the Council of Ireland, exploring its practical implications, and finalising the blueprint to be negotiated with the British and the Northern Ireland parties.

By 19 December 1972, barely three months after the Darlington conference, the IDU identified two scenarios for a Council of Ireland: a 'minimum' one (in which the Council would provide only a nominal link between North and South, and would be little more than a gesture to Nationalists), and a 'maximum' one (in which the Council would have real powers – perhaps exclusive ones – and growth potential) (NAI, DFA/2003/13/18, Brief for ministers: C: Council of Ireland, 19 December 1972). One of the officials most closely involved elaborated these positions further, identifying also an intermediate position. He saw them as corresponding to three different types of goal:

(a) to provide for harmonious common action in certain limited matters where the interests of North and South overlap – solely in order to promote these interests more efficiently and rationally

(b) to act as a symbolic North–South link sufficient to induce the bulk of the minority in the North to accept, work and live for the moment under new political structures which are now to be created in the area; and sufficient in consequence to allow Dublin to accept the new settlement

(c) to involve the common interests of North and South in pragmatic projects of mutual benefit – preferably projects with an in-built probability of growth – to such an extent as to encourage and accustom them to working together over a period; and in this way to promote reconciliation and set both parts of the island on a converging path without necessarily specifying the ultimate shape or timetable for possible unity between them. (NAI, DFA/2013/27/1620, Noel Dorr, Council of Ireland, 16 April 1973)

The nature of the Council of Ireland would thus depend on its underlying objective, with unionists likely to prefer (a) and nationalists (c), but with (b) representing a viable compromise.

The IDU proposed discussions with the appropriate government departments to identify functions for transfer to the Council of Ireland and to assess the administrative, staffing, financial and legislative implications, and these began on 1 June 1973 (D. Ó Súilleabháin, Secretary, Department of the Taoiseach, to the secretaries of all departments, 1 June 1973). The discussions highlighted a sharp gap between the idealistic thinking of Foreign Affairs officials and the conservative perspectives of other government departments. Although most departments had pre-1922, all-Ireland roots, the big impact of the border was clear half a century later: some departments failed to identify any area for possible transfer to the Council of Ireland, and others were prepared to part only with certain minor agencies (NAI, TSCH/2004/21/624, IDU Interim report (final version), June 1973, appendix 2: responses from departments). The Foreign Affairs Minister, Garret FitzGerald, was later to criticise this reluctance, suggesting that departments seemed to see the

Council of Ireland as 'some kind of external threat to the institutions of the state', and that 'partition had struck very deep roots in the South!' (FitzGerald, 1991: 203).[6]

The discussions highlighted diverging policy paths between North and South in certain areas (including local government, health, agriculture and electricity generation), and big gaps in service provision (notably in housing, social welfare, health and education). The IDU warned that the creation of a Council of Ireland with significant scope was likely to draw further attention to this, creating pressure on the government of the Republic to match Northern Ireland standards (IDU Interim report, p. 14, and appendix 2: responses from departments). Using two different methods, it estimated the cost of upgrading services in the Republic in the major service provision areas to Northern Ireland levels at £260–280 million (representing a massive expenditure increase of 41–4 per cent) (IDU Interim report, appendix 5: finances).

Nevertheless, an ambitious institutional model for a North–South council gradually emerged, and was endorsed by the government:

- a ministerial-executive body comprising equal representation from North and South, with a core of 'permanent' members and others added as the agenda required, operating on a basis of unanimity, meeting at least monthly, alternately in Northern Ireland and the Republic, and with a rotating chair
- a consultative Assembly of about 60 paid members nominated initially on a proportional basis by the Dáil and the Northern Ireland Assembly but possibly directly elected later; it would have power to make decisions by agreed majority about the future evolution of the Council
- a secretariat comprising permanent and full-time directly employed staff, headed by a secretary-general with powers of initiative
- an economic and social committee to advise on any matters affecting the economic or social wellbeing of Ireland or its regions. (NAI, TSCH/2004/21/627, Council of Ireland: structures, 28 November 1973)

The functions proposed for transfer to the Council were extensive, and were spread over three categories: executive, harmonising and consultative. It was estimated that the total number of Southern staff proposed by the government for transfer to the Council of Ireland would be just under six thousand, at a cost of almost £17 million. The more expensive items in the package included various agricultural services (2,080 staff, £5 million); forestry (1,000 staff, almost £3 million); social welfare administration (800 staff, £2.5 million); and three areas of similar size (with about 300 staff and a cost of about £1 million in each case) – the meteorological service, the housing area of local government, and health service administration.[7] It was proposed that the Council would be funded initially by the two administrations, but that in the longer term it would raise its own resources; the existing British grant would continue to fund activities on the Northern side (NAI, TSCH/2004/21/627, Council of Ireland: financing, 28 November 1973).

Negotiating the Council of Ireland

Parallel to developments in the Republic, consideration was being given in Northern Ireland to the form that a Council of Ireland might take. A 'Future Policy Group' comprising permanent heads of department had been established in Belfast shortly after the introduction of direct rule to explore constitutional alternatives (Bloomfield, 2007: 30–1). Its thinking was quite radical. One of its reports, completed in September 1972, considered the 'Irish dimension', and contemplated a bold gesture: a balance between recognition by the Republic of Northern Ireland's status within the UK and acceptance by Northern Ireland of 'a joint Council for cooperation and consultation', a mechanism that might lead towards Irish unity 'in stages, *subject to consent at each stage*' (Public Record Office of Northern Ireland (PRONI), Department of Community Relations (DCR) 1/126, H. Black, Political settlement: the 'Irish dimension', 8 September 1972).

Mainstream Unionist reactions were pragmatic, with many seeing the Council as a buttress for the union rather than as a path to Irish unity (NAI, DFA/2004/7/2599, Unionist Party views on a Council of Ireland, 24 October 1973). The Unionist leader Brian Faulkner disclosed privately to Irish civil servants in October 1973 his willingness to accept a North–South council with executive powers and a small secretariat, but expressed misgivings about a parliamentary tier (NAI, TSCH/2004/21/625, Dermot Nally and Seán Donlan, report on meeting with Brian Faulkner, October 1973). The Alliance Party adopted a similar position, moving away from its earlier support for a British–Irish Council. For its part, the British government accepted that it would not be represented in the inter-ministerial council (though mechanisms would be established to protect its financial interests), and that there would be a parliamentary tier and a dedicated secretariat; and it agreed that the council should have some executive functions, as well as consultative and advisory ones (PRONI, Department of Finance (FIN) 30/R/2/A/3, annex A: Inter-Party Consultations: Council of Ireland, 21 November 1973). At a meeting with their Irish counterparts on 28–9 November 1973, British officials indicated their broad acceptance of the Irish plan, though with some reservations (NAI, TSCH/2004/21/627, Council of Ireland: structures, 28 November 1973).

The success of the Sunningdale talks was facilitated by this convergence among the various parties, though the actual negotiations were tough and intense.[8] Pressure was reduced by a decision to hold a second-stage formal ratification conference once the Northern Ireland Executive was up and running, giving extra time for negotiation of matters of detail. The agreement provided for a Council of Ireland that closely resembled the Irish government's blueprint. The biggest structural differences were that the Consultative Assembly would be elected in equal numbers by the Dáil and the Assembly (rather than reflecting the one-to-two North–South population ratio), and no provision was made for the proposed Economic and Social Committee. Long-term funding arrangements and the list of functions for executive action by the Council were to be finalised later following further discussion, but the broad fields for co-operation were outlined. The Council would also have an important role in EEC-related matters, and a potentially significant one in the area of security and policing. Crucially, though, these institutional provisions were linked to two other issues: recognition of the status of Northern Ireland and security co-operation.

Implementing the Council of Ireland

As is well known, the Northern Ireland Executive took office on 1 January 1974 and functioned for five-and-a-half months along the lines originally envisaged, if against a backdrop of a continuing IRA campaign and growing Loyalist protest. The Council of Ireland, however, not alone failed to come into existence; its very character was undermined in the early months of 1974, and the ambitious scope planned for it was used to blame it for the collapse of the Executive. Failure to deliver on the quid-pro-quo implicit in the Sunningdale Agreement offered a powerful weapon to opponents of the Council: in return for accepting a Council of Ireland, Unionists expected formal recognition of Northern Ireland's status within the United Kingdom and enhanced security co-operation, but it was perceived that the Southern government delivered on neither of these.

Following the Sunningdale talks, the Irish government proceeded with determination to press for conclusion of the formal agreement. By the end of January 1974 it had produced a draft statute for the Council for transmission to the British side, and by the end of February it had completed a draft of the formal agreement within which this would be embedded (NAI, TSCH/2005/7/625, Draft statute of the Council of Ireland, 28 January 1973; NAI, TSCH/2005/7/626, Draft agreement between the Government of Ireland and the Government of the United Kingdom, 28 February 1974). Most of its energy, however, went into the detailed planning of the functions of the Council of Ireland. Responsibility for drafting this was given to the newly created Department of the Public Service, which was to work in consultation with the Departments of Finance and Foreign Affairs (NAI, TSCH/2004/21/627, Memorandum for the Government: Anglo-Irish conference at Sunningdale, 10 December 1973). Inter-departmental tensions quickly manifested themselves, though. The deputy secretary of the new department planned a meeting with Northern Ireland civil servants for 18 December to 'test out what might be on and what might not be on', a formulation that invited reconsideration of what had already been agreed (NAI, TSCH/2004/21/628, Note from Charles Whelan, 14 December 1973). The Northern civil servants indeed stressed the 'administrative complexities' to which the transfer of functions would give rise, and listed five financial constraints that would impede any kind of significant executive role for the Council (NAI, TSCH/2005/7/624, Administrative aspects of transferring functions to a Council of Ireland [record of meeting], 18 December 1973). The Minister for Foreign Affairs, not implausibly, saw this as an 'attempt by the Department of Finance to secure in collaboration with "minimalist" Northern Ireland civil servants what they had attempted but failed to achieve in conjunction with other departments during the discussions in the Interdepartmental Unit before Sunningdale, namely a narrowing down of the potential role of the Council of Ireland' (FitzGerald, 1991: 225).

A meeting on financial matters with British officials in London two days later threw further cold water on Irish ambitions, with the British expressing reservations about giving the Council independent financial resources, preferring to confine funding to the running of the secretariat itself (NAI, TSCH/2005/7/624, Council of Ireland – financing: preliminary discussions by officials, 20 December 1973). Perhaps not surprisingly, an official in the Taoiseach's department warned at the beginning of the new year that if a political meeting were not held soon to clarify what was meant by 'executive action', 'it may not be possible to get much further than to have the Council act in a general advisory or consultative role' (NAI, TSCH/2005/7/624, Dermot Nally to Taoiseach, 3 January 1974).

Political difficulties gave rise to further impediments. A *Sunday Press* report of an interview with the Taoiseach on 16 December, and the defence adopted by the government after Kevin Boland challenged the constitutionality of the agreement in the High Court on 17 December, were seen as undermining the solemn declaration on the status of Northern Ireland made by the Irish government at Sunningdale; this, in Faulkner's view, 'robbed him of all credibility' (PRONI, Office of the Executive (OE) 1/29, Note of the meeting at Baldonnel Airport on Wednesday, 16 January 1974, between the Chief Executive Member of the Northern Ireland Executive and the Taoiseach of the Irish Republic). There were also perceived serious failures in security co-operation. Faulkner's position was further weakened when the Ulster Unionist Council, the highest organ of his party, narrowly rejected the notion of the Council of Ireland on 4 January 1974, precipitating his resignation as party leader three days later (though he continued to lead his supporters in the Assembly). This pushed Faulkner to the view that there was 'no hope' of completing the Sunningdale Agreement until the status and security issues had been resolved (NAI, TSCH/2005/7/625 Note of meeting at Baldonnel (PRONI); and Note of meeting between the Taoiseach, Mr Cosgrave, and the Chief Executive, Mr Brian Faulkner, at Baldonnel, Co. Dublin, on 16 January 1974).

At a meeting of Northern and Southern ministers in Hillsborough, Co. Down, on 1 February 1974, the Southern side pushed forward provisions for the Council of Ireland. Faulkner, whose officials feared that 'too much haste, too grandiose a scheme at the start could ruin not only the Council but the Executive', suggested that the council be established first, and that a decision as to which functions it should have could be made later.[9] The two sides agreed on a list of possible areas for transfer, and appointed a group of officials to examine which functions should be transferred, and when (PRONI, OE/1/29, Record of Hillsborough meeting, 1 February 1974; NAI, TSCH/2005/7/626, Report on intergovernmental meeting, Hillsborough, 1 February 1974).

The group reported within three weeks, but the impressive volume it produced showed agreement on the transfer of only a few innocuous areas. It identified ten 'areas for executive action', but half of these were modest cross-border activities or projects: management of Carlingford Lough and of Lough Foyle, restoration of the Ballinamore–Ballyconnell canal, management of cross-border drainage, and policy on cross-border railways. Three more were vague: cross-border industry studies, physical strategy/regional planning, and 'aspects of human rights'. Two more concrete all-Ireland forms of co-operation were identified: management of horse racing and blood-stock, and joint tourism marketing. A second list covered 11 areas 'for executive decision and implementation by existing agencies at the council's direction', and there was a third list of seven areas for 'studies and consultation'. The most impressive list was the fourth (further areas for far-reaching executive authority), but these were proposed only by the Southern officials. The report noted drily that 'the steering group from Northern Ireland did not agree with this identification' (NAI, TSCH/2005/7/665, Transfer of functions to the Council of Ireland: joint report of officials from Government of the Republic of Ireland / Northern Ireland Executive, February 1974). As a covering memorandum from the Department of the Public Service put it, the 'executive' functions in the first list were 'minimal', and it would be desirable that some, at least, of those in the fourth list should also be transferred to the Council of Ireland (NAI, TSCH/2005/7/637, Proposed transfer of executive functions to the Council of Ireland, 22 February 1974).

At this stage, a more serious obstacle intervened. A UK General Election on 28 February 1974 resulted in the replacement of Ted Heath's Conservative government by a Labour government headed by Harold Wilson who, though a public supporter of Irish unity, was less wedded to the Sunningdale Agreement than his predecessor. In Northern Ireland, the election was fought in effect as a referendum on the agreement. Unionist opponents of Sunningdale won a majority of votes cast, and 11 out of Northern Ireland's 12 seats in the House of Commons. The following day the Irish Supreme Court ruled that the Sunningdale Communiqué (issued at the conclusion of the talks on 9 December 1973) did not amount to recognition of the right of the people of Northern Ireland to determine their own future, and was not incompatible with the Irish constitution.[10] Following a meeting of his Assembly party, Brian Faulkner issued a statement on 4 March stating that 'no discussion or cooperation between North and South could be contemplated' until the issue of Northern Ireland's status was resolved (NAI, TSCH/2005/7/627, Statement by Mr Brian Faulkner on 4 March 1974).

In these circumstances, it proved impossible to settle on a date for the formal agreement. When Cosgrave proposed Friday 5 April as a completion date, Faulkner responded that the Council of Ireland as agreed 'does not at present enjoy sufficient support in Northern Ireland' (NAI, TSCH/2005/7/628, Cosgrave to Faulkner, 21 March 1974; NAI, TSCH/2005/7/607, Faulkner to Cosgrave, 31 March 1974). As his permanent secretary put it at a meeting in Dublin shortly afterwards, the implementation of Sunningdale 'just was not on at present, so far as the Protestant community in the North were concerned' – they were 'at breaking point'. He proposed instead that the council be established, but that implementation of its executive functions be deferred, and that the idea of a consultative assembly be dropped, at least for the present (NAI, DFA/2007/111/1863, Discussions with permanent secretary of Northern Ireland Executive, 8 April 1974).[11] While British officials still accepted the need for speedy completion of the agreement at a meeting with their Irish counterparts in Dublin on 1 May, they were more preoccupied by security issues (NAI, DFA/2007/111/1863, Meeting of British and Irish officials, Iveagh House, 1 May 1974).

By now, the Executive was in deep trouble. On 15 May a subcommittee of the Executive produced a last version of the Council – just a day after the start of the Ulster Workers' Council strike that was to have such devastating consequences for the Executive. In the new version, the Council of Ministers would provide a forum for 'consultation, cooperation and coordination of action' in an impressively long list of areas, but only two of these (horse-racing and bloodstock, and marine resources) provided for anything like executive authority. In most areas, the Council would do no more than conduct studies, promote a joint approach and encourage co-operation (PRONI, OE/2/24, Memorandum by the Secretary to the Executive, 15 May 1974). On 22 May, the Executive itself finally agreed to this truncated package for immediate implementation, with other components (including the Consultative Assembly, and executive powers) to come into operation only after the next Assembly election.

This compromise was insufficient to save the Executive. Its collapse on 28 May 1974 not only brought to an end Northern Ireland's first experiment in power sharing but also buried the idea of a Council of Ireland, at least in the short term. An Irish government discussion paper in June 1974 signalled a policy shift, designed to secure stability rather than to pursue any ideal solution. Given existing realities in respect of power sharing and the Irish dimension, the paper suggested that the government should 'exert pressure, discreetly, directly and indirectly e.g. through EEC partners and others on the British to continue direct rule', and 'conduct here a discreet educational exercise among the public on the (1) security, and (2) economic consequences of a British withdrawal', while also investigating the possibility of United Nations participation (NAI, TSCH/2005/7/606, Policy on Northern Ireland: discussion paper, June 1974). Though the government kept a wide range of options on the table in principle, including a new Irish dimension at some time in the future, in practice the Irish dimension was put on the long finger (NAI, TSCH/2005/7/633, Minister for Foreign Affairs' memorandum to the Government entitled 'Policy options and actions with regard to Northern Ireland', 16 July 1974).

Conclusion

It took a quarter of a century for institutionalised links between Northern Ireland and the Republic of the kind first agreed at Sunningdale to come into existence: the North/South Ministerial Council and its associated implementation bodies. A second, parliamentary, tier appeared finally in 2012, though now transformed into a North/South Parliamentary Association, a designation implying a weaker identity than the Consultative Assembly of 1973. It is also noteworthy that on the occasion of the Good Friday Agreement, as at Sunningdale, pressure for North–South links of this kind came from the Nationalist side, with Unionists hesitant or resistant. This reversal of roles since the first Council of Ireland that of 1921–25, is striking: at that time, it was Nationalist Ireland that was reluctant and suspicious.

The contrast between these early and late twentieth-century experiments is instructive. In the 1920s, and right up to the end of the 1960s, the notion of an intergovernmental or interparliamentary Council of Ireland was objectionable to Nationalists because it implied recognition of Northern Ireland, seen as an illegitimate entity; indeed, it implied recognition of Northern Ireland on a basis of equality with the South. In the 1970s, this view was still held by Sinn Féin and the IRA; but other Nationalists increasingly came to embrace the notion of the Council either as a form of embryonic Irish government and parliament, or as a form of sensible, pragmatic co-operation with Northern Ireland, or as something in between. For Unionists, the acceptability of the Council depended precisely on which of these interpretations seemed most applicable.

This takes us back to the question with which this chapter started out. How might we interpret the North–South relationship from the perspective of theories of political integration? From the onset of partition until at least the end of the 1960s, the form of coercive unity that was associated with the Irish government's position is hard to relate to any of the three models discussed at the beginning of this chapter. To the extent that it was based on a 'top-down' political solution, it resembled the federal model. The actual institutional formula advocated, however, was not the classic federal one; it rested instead on an asymmetric arrangement, with Northern Ireland retaining its autonomous institutions and the whole island being governed under the terms of the 1937 constitution. Two variants of classical federalism were advocated at particular points in time. In 1971 the newly formed 'Provisional' Sinn Féin proposed a federal Ireland based on the four traditional provinces, with Northern Ireland expanding to include all of Ulster but being matched by three units with the same status in the other three provinces. A form of dual federalism linking the two existing jurisdictions under an all-Ireland federal umbrella was also put forward from time to time, notably by the New Ireland Forum in 1984. But Sinn Féin reverted in 1982 to the unitary state model, and the report of the New Ireland Forum also expressed its preference for this model over federation, confederation or joint rule.

The strategy of pragmatic engagement with Northern Ireland that began in the 1960s implied a departure from the solution of imposed unity; it was implicitly based on a long-term policy of construction of everyday contacts between North and South of a kind that would ultimately undermine unionist objections to unity by demonstrating the advantages of co-operation. It thus resembled the neofunctionalist approach to European integration.

Indeed, as argued above, neofunctionalist arguments were explicitly advanced by civil servants and politicians involved in the negotiation of the provisions governing the Council of Ireland, reflected in particular in the debate over the types of functional area that might be transferred to the all-Ireland body. From this perspective, the Council of Ireland was not an end in itself but an instrument for building confidence and trust that might encourage momentum towards a deepening of North–South co-operation, leading ultimately to some form of unity.

Notwithstanding occasional irredentist rhetoric, public and elite opinion in the Republic seems increasingly disposed to accept or even support the current boundaries of the state (Coakley, 2002; 2009). For those indifferent or hostile to Irish unity, an intergovernmental strategy is appealing: institutional links between North and South, to the extent that they exist, may be confined to practical areas where a pragmatic case for joint action can be made, without prejudice to the sovereign right of the two states which share the Irish border to exclusive jurisdiction within their own states. The Sunningdale process illustrated the extent to which more ambitious aims yielded to proposals for modest co-operation along essentially intergovernmental lines and, notwithstanding other provisions of the Good Friday Agreement that define a pathway towards Irish unity, the 'Strand Two' (North–South) institutions that came into existence in 1999 appear to fall into the same category.

The position of the Irish government in relation to that central institution in the Sunningdale Agreement, the Council of Ireland, reflects all three of the classic approaches to political integration that were discussed at the beginning of this chapter. Individual actors are likely to have varied in their preferences for these approaches, and to have shifted perspective. It seems likely that by mid-1974 few committed advocates of federal-type arrangements remained among the political elite, that intergovernmental approaches were now much more attractive, and that neofunctionalist perspectives were more cautiously expressed. This rearrangement of political positions was, however, highly vulnerable to shifts in British policy. Had a British withdrawal from Northern Ireland taken place in late 1974, a realistic possibility whose implications have been little explored in the academic literature, this configuration of perspectives would have been thrown into the air, and a radically new Irish government strategy would have been called for.

The Sunningdale episode and the Council of Ireland negotiations represented, then, a steep learning curve for the Irish political elite. One lesson was an obvious one: Ulster Protestant determination to resist 'rule from Dublin' was as strong in 1974 as it had been in 1912. Indeed, many Unionists were prepared to resist not just Dublin rule but also Dublin influence – an important hardening of attitudes since 1912, when most aspects of everyday life in the Northern counties, as elsewhere in Ireland, were managed by Irish civil servants in Dublin. Ulster resistance in 1974 was, however, less securely grounded than it had been earlier, though this was not obvious to all Unionists: it could no longer rely on the support of the British government, and it was confronted by a Nationalist minority (a noun that still applied in 1974) that was growing in self-confidence and in political weight, a trend reinforced by demographic developments.

The second lesson was less obvious. The exercise in trying to establish which functions Dublin government departments might be prepared to cede to all-Irish institutions had revealed strong support for the status quo among Irish civil servants. This may have been shocking to committed neofunctionalists such as Garrett FitzGerald; but it was also, perhaps, inevitable. This was, after all, the same civil service which had resisted, with some success, its own dismemberment in 1921–22 as part of the partition settlement (Maguire, 2008: 93–169). Like other bureaucracies, it had a strong sense of self-preservation, and was not likely to welcome reform that would reduce its mandate, whether by territorial partition as in the 1920s, or functional differentiation as in the 1970s. Sunningdale, as is well known, defined the limits, at that time, on North–South institutional co-operation; but it also exposed the unpalatable nature of such co-operation to many senior decision-makers in the South.

Notes

1 In addition to discussion of the Sunningdale Agreement in several of the standard book-length studies of the Northern Ireland conflict, a more specialist set of articles focuses precisely on efforts to interpret the agreement; see, for example, Farren, 2007; Farrington, 2007; Gillespie, 1998; Kyle, 1975; McDaid, 2012; McGrattan, 2009; McLoughlin, 2007; O'Donnell, 2007b; O'Duffy, 1999; Power, 1977; Rose, 1999; Wolff, 2001.

2 McLoughlin points out that there is some doubt about what Logue said (his remarks were an off-the-cuff response to a heckler following an address in Trinity College); this exchange was not reported in any of the three Dublin morning newspapers the following day, 17 January 1974.

3 See also the modified position of the Taoiseach Jack Lynch (1972: 615–16), which was drafted by a Foreign Affairs official, Noel Dorr, and later redrafted by another official, Eamon Gallagher; witness seminar on Sunningdale Agreement, Institute for British–Irish Studies, University College Dublin, 7 September 2005. Thanks are due to the Irish Research Council for the Humanities and Social Sciences for its support of this project.

4 Pre-Darlington References to a 'Council of Ireland' by political organisations and spokesmen, NAI, Department of Foreign Affairs (DFA) 2004/7/2599. The idea of

a Council similar to that of the 1920s had already been considered by the British government (Smith, 2011: 172–5) and advocated by the opposition Labour Party (Callaghan, 1973: 154–5).

5 On internal difficulties see NAI, TSCH/2004/21/624, Charles Whelan, Inter-Departmental Unit on Northern Ireland, 3 August 1973.

6 This point is reinforced by Austin Currie's recollection of surprise on the part of Northern civil servants at the reluctance of their Southern counterparts to cede any significant powers to the Council of Ireland; witness seminar, 7 September 2005.

7 NAI, TSCH/2004/21/627, Council of Ireland financing: estimates of the numbers of staff who would be transferred from central government departments and of the costs involved, 28 November 1973. At different points in time, other numbers of staff (sometimes much larger) were given; witness seminar, 7 September 2005.

8 See note 1, and autobiographical writings such as FitzGerald, 1991.

9 Brief for Chief Minister, 30 January 1974, PRONI, OE/1/28.

10 See 'Boland v. an Taoiseach', Irish Reports, 1974, pp. 338–72.

11 Faulkner wrote in similar terms to the SDLP leader Gerry Fitt on 12 April, NAI, TSCH/2005/7/629. At the same time, Irish officials explored ways in which the profile of the formal agreement could be lowered; Sunningdale Agreement: implementation of arrangements, April 1974, NAI, TSCH/2005/7/629.

5

British government policy post 1974: learning slowly between Sunningdales?

Eamonn O'Kane

The collapse of Northern Ireland's power-sharing Executive in May 1974 represented the failure of the policy that the British government had hoped would restore stability to the region. As Dixon noted, Merlyn Rees had told the House of Commons when the consultative Green Paper was launched in 1972 that, if the plan was rejected, 'it would mean needing to face up to a complete reappraisal of policy by any British government, because the basis on which that government had been working would have been shown to be false' (Dixon, 2008: 128). This policy failure was intensified by the fact that there was little agreement within British policy-making circles as to what could be put in its place. As Harold Wilson recorded in his memoirs, after the collapse in 1974, 'while it may have seemed negative, almost defeatist, the Government inevitably had no new proposals for the future of the Province. The initiatives taken at Darlington, and Sunningdale, the policies of the Heath government and of our own had reached a dead end. No solution could be imposed from across the water' (Wilson, 1979: 78).

To an extent this illustrates an underlying problem for the British government when dealing with Northern Ireland in this period and subsequently. The level of violence, constitutional obligations, responsibility for law and order as well as domestic and international expectations, meant that there was a necessity for the government to have a policy on Northern Ireland.

Britain was though hampered by several factors. There was significant British inexperience and a lack of understanding of Northern Ireland in the early 1970s, with an NIO official acknowledging that the 'depth of ignorance' of the problem was 'pretty horrific' (Kerr, 2011: 34). The incompatibility of demands and expectations of the political parties and paramilitary groups within Northern Ireland (which Sunningdale arguably entrenched), and divisions between British policy-makers over what could and should be done, resulted in governments of various hues failing to develop a policy that would enable the restoration of sustained devolved government to Northern Ireland for over thirty years. In the post-Sunningdale period British policy towards Northern Ireland appeared to oscillate between policies that were often contradictory or divergent. At times the British considered: Irish unity; full integration of Northern Ireland into the United Kingdom; devolution without an Irish dimension (or indeed much power to share); repartition; an independent Northern Ireland and increased co-operation with the Irish government without power sharing, before apparently returning successfully to the Sunningdale model in the late 1990s. This chapter examines the reasons for this apparent inconsistency in policy. It argues that whilst the British government was a key player in the Northern Ireland conflict, its ability to shape the agenda and secure the outcome that it desired was seriously curtailed by its inability to force or persuade other actors to accept the policy choices it proposed. Britain's own policy preferences were dictated not by an outcome it sought to achieve but by what the government felt was possible and in line with its own obligations and objectives.

Cillian McGrattan has correctly noted that the British government did not have 'a long term or consistent policy vision' for Northern Ireland (McGrattan, 2010: 89). Academics have debated whether British policy was marked by consistency or inconsistency (see Cunningham, 2001). The problem with some accounts is that they seem to suggest that if British policy had been clearer, more consistent or different the comparative stability that Northern Ireland enjoyed post Belfast/Good Friday Agreement (B/GFA) could have been achieved earlier. Brendan O'Leary, for example, has been highly critical of the contradictions of British government policy and argued these inconsistencies were the result of the 'policy learning, albeit painfully slow learning, [that] has been taking place'. O'Leary claimed that many of the policy-makers in the Thatcher and Major governments 'took two decades to learn what Edward Heath mostly understood in 1973' (O'Leary, 1997: 675). Similarly Etain Tannam has argued that the developments in Northern Ireland and the achievement of the B/GFA, as opposed to Sunningdale (and the 1985 Anglo-Irish Agreement) was the result of 'policy learning' by the British (and Irish) governments (Tannam, 2001). However, when the apparent vagaries or oscillations of British policy are examined in the context of the events of the period, such accounts appear questionable. The problem with 'slow learning' explanations is that they imply that there was an 'answer' to the problem that, once discovered, could be applied with successful results. They suggest too much power is available to the British government and fail to appreciate the (changing) context of the events in Northern Ireland. The reason that the British moved away from what Heath had 'learnt' in 1973 is that the failure of Sunningdale altered the context in Northern Ireland, entrenched the incompatible objectives amongst the parties there and meant that the Sunningdale model was not applicable in the years after 1974 (leaving aside the debate as to whether it was applicable in 1974). In contradiction to what O'Leary suggests, the experience of 1974 illustrated the inability of the government to 'coerce' unionists or nationalists 'to drink at the well of institutional concessions' (O'Leary, 1997: 675–6). Whilst McGrattan is correct in his observation regarding a lack of a coherent British policy for Northern Ireland, it is possible to identify British objectives, and it was these objectives that influenced the policies they developed (or failed to develop) for the region. These objectives remained relatively constant but their saliency ebbed and flowed as the characteristics of the conflict altered, and as a result policies were amended, developed or dropped as the situation appeared to dictate. This is not to argue that the British made no mistakes in relation to Northern Ireland (mistakes were clearly made in all the relevant fields of policy: political, military and economic) but that the policies were logical given the constraints that the British faced over the period. When the objectives and the context are considered it becomes less surprising that there was not a developed, durable and coherent British policy towards Northern Ireland. The narrative then appears to point to policy adaptation and construction (at times considered and imaginative, at others ill-judged and ill-informed) rather than slow learning.

British objectives

At least four objectives can be identified that were instrumental in influencing the policies that British governments developed between Sunningdale and the B/GFA. These were as follows.

End or minimise the violence in Northern Ireland

The re-involvement of the British dovernment in Northern Ireland of the late 1960s to early 1970s was largely a result of the increasing level of violence that was engulfing the region and the increasing perception that the Northern

Ireland government and security forces could not deal with it. As has been well recorded, the decision to send in the troops was not one that was taken lightly or enthusiastically by the British government of the day. There was a fear that once the troops were deployed it would be difficult to extract them again. Similarly the decision to introduce direct rule in 1972 reflected a belief that the Unionist government was unwilling or unable to introduce the necessary reforms that might have created conditions that would have reduced the violence or to accede control of security to Westminster. Yet neither the deployment of troops nor the introduction of direct rule enabled the British to end the violence or, despite the aspirations of the Home Secretary, Reginald Maudling, in December 1971, enable violence to be reduced to an 'acceptable' level. The hopes that Sunningdale and the resultant power-sharing Executive would bring the political stability that would marginalise those who sought to use violence for political ends proved ill-founded. As a result, an objective of the British over the following decades in Northern Ireland was to try to create conditions that would lead to an end to the violent aspects of the conflict. At times they prioritised security measures and at times political measures to seek to achieve this end. But this objective of dealing with the violence in Northern Ireland remained a primary objective for the British government throughout.

Reduce the impact of Northern Ireland on British politics

The British government's reluctance to become more directly involved in the affairs of Northern Ireland in the late 1960s to early 1970s was indicative of a long-standing desire to insulate British politics from the question of Ireland, which had historically been so problematic in British politics. The creation of the Stormont government in the 1920s and the Speaker's Convention, which meant that matters devolved to Stormont could not be raised at Westminster, had largely succeeded in this objective for fifty years. The emerging violence of the late 1960s and the imposition of direct rule meant this was no longer possible. However, the imposition of direct rule did not challenge the widely held belief in British politics that Northern Ireland was a 'place apart'. The question was how could British politics be insulated from the potentially corrosive issue of Northern Ireland whilst meeting its obligations as the sovereign power for the region, with all that entailed? Sunningdale offered an answer to this question. When this failed it left Britain, as noted earlier, bereft of a coherent alternative policy that would meet this objective. As will be examined below, plans were mooted for alternative ways to achieve the end of reducing the impact of Northern Ireland on wider British politics. These plans were scuppered by a variety of factors (though ultimately it was the inability to secure a sufficient consensus amongst the parties in Northern Ireland and the belief that they would actually exacerbate the problem that explains most of the failures). The outcome was that in its quest to achieve its objective of reducing the impact of Northern Ireland on British politics, the British government had to remain deeply involved in the politics of Northern Ireland.

Reduce or manage international criticism of their administration of Northern Ireland

There has been an interesting debate over the role that international criticism has played in the construction of British policy towards Northern Ireland. This has been particularly pronounced in relation to the role of the United States in the peace process in the 1990s and 2000s and in relation to whether the end of the Cold War was a significant factor in its emergence (English, 2003, Snyder, 2013) and as to whether the Bush administration's envoy, Mitchell Reiss, was instrumental in forcing Sinn Féin to alter its approach and the British to change policy in the mid-2000s (Clancy, 2010). The role of the United States was also though a consideration in the debate over the attitude of the British government in signing the Anglo-Irish Agreement (AIA) in 1985 (O'Kane, 2007). Some of these accounts have overstated the importance of the international dimension, in shaping British policy during the period. It is the case that in almost all cases the shifts in British policy and the decisions taken in London and Belfast are explicable by domestic considerations. At times the British were subject to international criticism as a result of their Northern Irish policy (for example during the 1981 hunger strikes) and the available evidence suggests that British governments were keen to ensure that such criticism was muted and, in particular, to avoid criticism from the American government. As a result the avoiding criticism from the international community was a consideration and an objective of the British but not to the extent that they constructed policy, or failed to pursue a favoured policy, primarily in response to international pressure.

Upholding the principle of consent

A fourth objective for the British government was its commitment to upholding the principle of consent. The 1973 White Paper stated that 'Northern Ireland remains part of the United Kingdom, and will not cease to be part of the United Kingdom without the consent of the people of Northern Ireland' (Paragraph 33). This remained the position of the British government throughout the Troubles period. At times it came under strain but making sure that British policy was compatible with this commitment to the principle of consent remained an objective of British policy-makers throughout. It should be noted that the objective of upholding consent should not be inter-preted as a commitment to Northern Ireland remaining part of the United Kingdom. As Quentin Thomas, a senior civil servant at the NIO between 1988 and 1998, argued, 'Consent is absolutely fundamental. It was absolutely a matter of principle that would sustain against any challenge to the right of the people of Northern Ireland, or a majority of the people of Northern Ireland to do what they wanted.' However, Thomas also noted that the British were not proscriptive of what the people of Northern Ireland should consent to. 'We had some interests but basically our position was that if everyone would consent to something, if they had consented to the proposition that the moon is made of blue cheese, fine. What do we care?' This meant that unity by consent was acceptable to the British, 'If they want to go we will hold the door open. We've said it' (O'Kane, 2007: 186–8). A similar point was made in an unguarded moment by the then Secretary of State, Sir Patrick Mayhew, when he told a German newspaper in 1993, 'Most people believe we would not want to release Northern Ireland from the United Kingdom. To be entirely honest, we would with pleasure' (O'Clery, 1999: 215). But this apparent lack of an emotional or ideological commitment to the Union amongst (most if not all) British policy-makers did not lead to an active policy of seeking to create the conditions for an agreement to end the Union. As a result the commitment to policy construction in line with the principle of consent remained an important objective for British governments.

These four objectives can be seen as the considerations that underpinned British policy-making between the failure of Sunningdale and the success of the B/GFA (and subsequent St Andrews Agreement). When we consider the policies adopted by British governments since Sunningdale in relation to these objectives, in the context of the conditions in-play in Northern Ireland at the times the policies were developed, British policy appears less marked by 'slow learning' than by what the former head of the Northern Ireland Office (NIO), Sir John Chilcott, described as 'necessary opportunism'. The British were under pressure to seek 'movement in any forward direction', but the problem they faced was they were unsure how to achieve this (O'Kane, 2007: 195).

Developments in British policy

The 1970s

The Wilson government's policy towards Northern Ireland in the mid- to late 1970s was heavily influenced by the failure of Sunningdale. In the immediate aftermath of the collapse of the Executive there was little prospect of resurrecting devolved government in a similar form. The government created an elected Constitutional Convention in 1975, in line with Wilson's observations that, given the rejection of the Sunningdale model, 'we had to throw the task clearly to the Northern Ireland people themselves. Let Parliament see what they would come up with and we would consider it – a Northern Ireland solution' (Wilson, 1979: 78). The results of the election only underlined the divisions within Northern Ireland and the hardening of attitudes with the anti-power-sharing UUUC winning over 54 per cent of the first-preference votes and 47 of the 78 seats. This effectively meant that there was no chance of the Convention recommending a system of government that would be acceptable to the Social Democratic and Labour Party (SDLP). In November 1975 Convention supported a UUUC report that called for a restoration of majority rule and rejected power sharing and an institutionalised Irish dimension.

Wilson himself had long been sympathetic to the idea of a united Ireland. His policy adviser, Bernard Donoughue, noted that Wilson had 'radical instincts on the Irish question' and in May 1974 had drafted his own 'Doomsday Scenario' to consider the possibility of British withdrawal. At one level this could be seen as in contradiction to the objective noted above of ensuring British policy remained consistent with the consent principle. However, there are two reasons why this is perhaps not the case. Firstly, Wilson was not considering simply withdrawing from Northern Ireland; what he proposed was 'dominion status' for Northern Ireland: 'Ulstermen would remain subjects of the Queen' and sovereignty would be transferred to a new government in Northern Ireland with minority rights protected and financial support being phased out over five years (Donoughue, 1987: 129). The reality was though that such a plan would, as Paul Bew has argued, have 'effectively returned Northern Ireland to Protestant majority rule, would provoke international outcry and could have led to massive bloodshed' (Bew, 2007: 517), thus failing to meet most of British objectives in policy-making. There is little doubt that Wilson himself favoured exploring the options for British withdrawal, a view that was shared by other in the government, including the Home Secretary Roy Jenkins and Bernard Donoughue. However, the second reason that the idea of British withdrawal did not represent a break with the commitment to consent is that it never became British policy. Wilson's belief in the desirability of a united Ireland was also in part related to the objective of reducing the impact of Northern Ireland on British politics. In December 1974 Donoughue recorded in his diary that the prospect was 'an endless period of direct political rule – which is why HW wants to get some movement towards pulling out' (Donoughue, 2004: 253). Although it was favoured by Wilson and the objective of a united Ireland was supported by other key members of the government such as James Callaghan, there was a realisation that it was likely to lead to a deterioration in the situation in Northern Ireland and would have been incompatible with the other British objectives such as reducing the violence in Northern Ireland. In March 1974 the Foreign Office had considered 'the international, legal and other repercussions of a decision to disengage entirely, severing all constitutional links between Northern Ireland and the rest of the United Kingdom'. Stuart Aveyard notes that the document 'was entirely dismissive, arguing that Britain would be viewed 'significantly less attractive as an ally, as a political and economic partner ... as a place to invest in or a country to lend money to, or a country with a claim to international influence' (Aveyard, 2012: 533). The Irish government was highly nervous at the prospect of British withdrawal. The then Irish Minister of Foreign Affairs, Garret FitzGerald, raised his concerns with the US Secretary of State Henry Kissinger, and the British Ambassador in Washington reported that the US government was against withdrawal 'with or without a period of notice' (Bew, 2007: 518). In addition to the concerns of the Irish government, there were those in British policy-making circles who were concerned with the apparent consideration of the withdrawal option. Senior civil servants within Number 10, such as Robert Armstrong, were 'clearly worried' about the option being considered (Donoughue, 2004: 130) and the NIO's Frank Cooper had argued in 1974 that it was not realistic (Aveyard, 2012: 533). Opposition to the idea from within and outside the government and the realisation that it was not practical, or likely to improve the situation, meant that it was eventually dropped, despite being supported by key people, including the Prime Minister. Similarly the idea of integrationism that was periodically considered (and favoured by sections of the Ulster Unionist Party (UUP)) was rejected as it would have resulted in Westminster having to be more involved in Northern Ireland (and the question becoming more of a focus of Westminster politics, rather than less) (Dixon, 2008; 155).

In addition to considering ways to extricate itself from Northern Ireland the Wilson government held talks with the Irish Republican Army (IRA) in the mid-1970s. There was a precedent for this as Whitelaw had met members of the IRA in 1972 (and Wilson had also met them whilst in Opposition). The 1974–75 'truce' saw the IRA declare a ceasefire and seven incident centres were created throughout Northern Ireland to monitor the situation and enable problems to be resolved between Sinn Féin and the British government. There has been a great deal of debate regarding the 1974–75 'truce', over whether it was a serious part of an attempt by the British to withdraw from Northern Ireland (as the IRA believed at the time) or whether it was an attempt by the British to undermine the IRA (as the British subsequently claimed) (English, 2003: 179; Bew, 2007: 518–23; Dixon, 2008, 159–65). The truce though had consequences for British policy and the IRA. The IRA's capacity to carry out its campaign was undermined by the truce, and in the aftermath of the ceasefire the British significantly increased their arrest and prosecution of IRA members, having improved their intelligence during the ceasefire period. The internal debate within the Provisional IRA and the recriminations over the failure of the ceasefire led to the emergence of the new 'Northern' leadership of the republican movement under Gerry Adams and Martin McGuinness and an intra-republican feud resulted between the Provisionals and the Officials (Moloney, 2002: 143–5). The ceasefire period and the linked speculation of British withdrawal also led to a significant increase in the levels of loyalist violence in the mid-1970s. This further high-lighted the fact that movement towards withdrawal was likely to increase violence, not enable the British to reduce the influence of Northern Ireland on British policy, was unlikely to secure the consent of a majority of people in Northern Ireland, and would have led to international criticism of Britain.

By the mid-to-late 1970s then the British government was effectively 'forced' to pursue direct rule as policy. This was not, from London's perspec-tive, ideal, but the alternatives of Irish unity, integration, devolution, reparti-tion or an independent Northern Ireland were likely to worsen the situation rather than improve things. The British government under James Callaghan concentrated on improving the security, and accepted that no new political initiatives were likely to be successful (and indeed no new ones were pro-posed for the rest of the 1970s). The British government had moved away from the Sunningdale approach not as a result of a reformulation of policy but due to the fact that the opposition to the approach had changed the context in Northern Ireland and meant that the approach could not be suc-cessfully implemented, and the British could not find an acceptable alterna-tive to it.

The Thatcher years

The Conservative government elected in 1979 had suggested a move towards an integrationist approach in its manifesto, but this was soon dropped in favour of another attempt at devolution (the author of the approach, Airey Neave, was killed by an Irish National LIberation Army (INLA) car bomb in the House of Commons car park in March 1979). The election of Mrs Thatcher's government might have been thought to lead to a shift in govern-ment policy, given that she was widely taken as being the prime minister with the greatest commitment to the Union. However, the relative continuity in approach is the result of the constraints that Britain faced in formulating policy in Northern Ireland, which were highlighted by the 1970s post-Sunningdale considerations, discussed above, and the fact that the Thatcher government's objectives were the same as those that had been in play under Heath, Wilson and Callaghan. Just as Wilson's instinctive support for Irish unity and British withdrawal had not led to a fundamental shift in approach, nor did the instinctive Unionism of Mrs Thatcher lead to a more Unionist-friendly policy. Indeed it was Mrs Thatcher who signed the 1985 Anglo-Irish Agreement, which institutionalised a consultative role for the Irish government over Northern Ireland, and which was negotiated in secret over the heads of the Ulster Unionists and which did not have an accompanying devolved legislature in Northern Ireland.

The new government explored the possibility of establishing common ground between the parties in Northern Ireland with a view to devolving government back to Northern Ireland. The Secretary of State, Humphrey Atkins, launched a series of talks between the parties in Northern Ireland but the shadow of Sunningdale continued to hang over British policy-making and his White Paper in November 1979 did not make reference to an Irish dimension (though after the SDLP threatened to boycott the talks Atkins agreed that the Irish dimension could be discussed in parallel talks). As the talks wore on, it became clear that there was little common ground between the parties and the initiative was soon dropped. The lack of options available to the British at the time was nicely summed up by the cartoonist Martyn Turner in *The Irish Times* after the Queen's Speech in November 1980. Turner's cartoon depicted the Queen announcing, 'My Government feels that no programme of legislation would be complete without mentioning Northern Ireland ... Hello, Northern Ireland' (*Irish Times* 21 November 1980). A further attempt in 1982 to devolve power back to Northern Ireland under Jim Prior's Rolling Devolution initiative also failed. The Prior plan did succeed in creating an elected Assembly in Northern Ireland but it achieved little due to the refusal of the SDLP to attend on the basis that it did not acknowledge the Irish dimension. Indeed Thatcher had forced Prior to remove a section from the proposals that dealt with relations with the Republic (Prior, 1986: 197).

Shortly after coming to power, Mrs Thatcher held two meetings with the new Irish Taoiseach, Charles Haughey, in 1980. Although she was initially charmed by him, the perception that he had 'oversold' the significance of the December 1980 meeting and the belief that he had misrepresented the significance of the 'joint studies' that had been commissioned by the two governments and the possibility of 'new institutional structures' (which concerned Ulster Unionists) led to a cooling of relations. One British official claimed that Thatcher 'liked being led up the garden path by Haughey but didn't like the garden when she got there' (Moore: 2013, 595). Thatcher believed that the Haughey government was suggesting that constitutional issues were up for discussion and the Prime Minister admonished her Irish counterpart at a European meeting in March 1981, pointing out, 'I said nothing about the constitution, nothing whatsoever was said'. Dermot Nally argued that the episode destroyed the idea that she could reach a deal with Haughey and her faith in him (Moore, 2013: 603). The problem for Mrs Thatcher, however, was that, despite her innate Unionism and her mistrust of Charles Haughey, the security situation was not improving in Northern Ireland and indeed deteriorated significantly as a result of the 1981 hunger strikes. The strikes also led to wider international consideration of British policy in Northern Ireland and forced the topic back towards the centre of British political life, suggesting that current policy was not really achieving its objectives.

For Mrs Thatcher security considerations were paramount and she believed that assistance from Dublin was essential but inadequate (Thatcher, 1993: 385). The question of how helpful Dublin was in co-operating with the British over security issues is a difficult one. Heath, for example, in 1971, reacted to a suggestion from Paisley that the then Taoiseach Jack Lynch should do more to stop 'illegal forces' drilling in the Republic, by claiming, 'He can't stop them, poor man' (Ziegler, 2011: 303). The Irish position was that the IRA posed a greater threat to their state than to the UK's and believed that they were doing everything they practically could in relation to security (O'Kane, 2007: 83–6). Interestingly, recently released British documents seem to suggest that at some levels security and intelligence co-operation between the Irish and British were very good. In a report of May 1985 the British Security Co-ordinator claimed that Britain's Special Branch and MI5 had 'excellent relations' with their Irish counterparts and 'benefit from a degree of co-operation and from a flow of intelligence which we believe to be at a greater level than is suspected by at least some Irish ministers ... A small number of garda officers ... are... prepared to be extremely helpful.' This assistance made 'a major contribution to combating the present terrorist campaign on the mainland' (RTÉ Website, 30 December 2014). However, Henry Patterson has claimed that Irish governments 'failed to take the issue of Provisional exploitation of their territory seriously', which 'objectively facilitated the organisation's ability to carry on its "long war" into the 1990s' (Patterson, 2013: 199). What is not in doubt though is that for Mrs Thatcher the quest to improve security co-operation with the Republic in the hope of achieving the objective of reducing the level of violence in Northern Ireland was a main driver in policy formation. According to Charles Powell, Thatcher's Private Secretary, she was primarily concerned with security considerations and had 'less interest in trying to resolve the political aspects of the problem'. Her preference was for devolved majority rule with safeguards for the minority (LHMCA archive: Powell transcript). Thatcher told FitzGerald during a heated exchange at Chequers in November 1984, that as regards Unionists, 'Power-sharing was just not on for those people. Sunningdale still lives vividly in their memory' (*Irish Independent* 27 December 2014). Yet it was her concern with security co-operation which was instrumental in persuading her to sign the AIA, an agreement that was anathema to Ulster Unionists and seen by them as a betrayal. The strength of the reaction to the Agreement and the anger they directed at her was both disappointing to Mrs Thatcher and confusing. Powell claimed that there was nothing in the AIA that should have 'given the Unionists a moment's loss of sleep'. He claimed that

> Mrs Thatcher's great hurt in her subsequent dealings with the Unionists was that they didn't take her word for it. She would say 'but you know I am a great supporter of the Unionists, surely they would trust me, surely I am the one person they can rely on to make sure that Unionist interests were thoroughly protected', and I think that really rather altered her view of Unionism and the Unionists in an extraordinary way because up until that point she had really thought that she was the safeguard for their interests and that they would accept and acknowledge and honour that. (LHMCA archive: Powell transcript)

The deteriorating security situation after the hunger strikes and the comparatively successful decision by Sinn Féin to contest elections in Northern Ireland (it secured over 10 per cent of the vote in the 1982 Assembly election) had increased instability in Northern Ireland. This led to concern within the British government that the situation might deteriorate further and lead, according to Prior, to Northern Ireland becoming 'a Cuba off our Western coast' (Dixon, 2008: 187). The Irish Cabinet Secretary, Dermot Nally, recorded in a memo that Thatcher told FitzGerald at Chequers, 'There was a real danger that a Marxist society could develop. She did not ever want that to happen. When she looked at the strategic aspects of the problem she understood what the US feels about Nicaragua' (*Irish Independent* 27 Decmeber 2014).

Such considerations explain why Mrs Thatcher went against her own instincts to pursue a policy that appeared inconsistent with her preferences. She later claimed that she had signed the AIA in the hope of gaining the support of the Irish government in the fight against the IRA but it had failed as 'our concessions alienated the Unionists without gaining the level of security co-operation we had a right to expect' (Thatcher, 1993: 415). Mrs Thatcher arguably saw the AIA in too narrow terms and it is questionable whether it was, for the others involved in negotiating it, driven by security considerations to the same extent (Howe, 1994; Hurd, 2003). However, it is again indicative of the restraints that the British government faced in constructing policy and in designing an approach that would meet both their objectives and the policy preferences of the British politicians and officials. The most Unionist of Prime Ministers signed an agreement that was as unacceptable as Sunningdale to Ulster Unionists (but one which, given it did not require their co-operation, they were unable to overturn).

The peace process

By the late 1980s the British government had tried a variety of policies in Northern Ireland but were apparently no nearer to succeeding in developing one that would help them achieve their objectives. The AIA had increased Unionist distrust of the British state and made it less likely that they (Unionists) would agree to a new initiative with a strong Irish dimension. The AIA persisted, albeit with some disappointment over its record amongst some British policy-makers. Yet within a decade the Belfast/Good Friday Agreement would be negotiated, which was underpinned by a devolved power-sharing government and a significant Irish dimension (though it would take almost another decade to achieve these on a sustained basis). Again though, to understand why this was achieved and Britain's role in it, the discussion has to be grounded in the context of events in Northern Ireland and the attitude of the parties to the conflict.

The peace process was largely built upon the decision of the IRA to declare a ceasefire in 1994, but this did not simply 'happen'. The British government of John Major had worked hard to achieve this (in conjunction with the Irish government). An important development in this was their attempt to persuade the IRA to end its violence and to pursue its objectives by peaceful means. To this end there was a movement from the approach of seeking to build agreement between the 'moderates' in Northern Ireland and exclude those who supported the use of violence (as had been the case under all initiatives that sought to achieve devolved government to Northern Ireland since Sunningdale) to one of seeking to persuade those who supported the use of violence to end their campaign and enter the political process (primarily aimed at Sinn Féin and the IRA). The approach of excluding Sinn Féin from the political process was not based primarily on moral considerations: as noted, the British had dealt directly with the IRA in 1972 and 1974–75 as well as indirectly during the hunger strikes of 1981. It rested on the belief that the cost of dealing with the IRA whilst it pursued violence was too great in terms of the impact that it had on other parties, international opinion and levels of violence in Northern Ireland. What changed in the early 1990s was a growing belief within British policy-making circles that there was a con-stituency within the Republican leadership that was considering an alterna-tive to the armed strategy. This was explored via the 'backchannel communications' that were conducted via the Derry link, led by the business-man Brendan Duddy, who acted as intermediary between the British and the Republicans. There remains confusion and misunderstanding over the role and reliability of the backchannel communication (O'Kane, 2015) and a debate over why the IRA was amenable to considering a ceasefire by the early 1990s (Dixon, 2012; Bew and Frampton, 2012) and whether the approach of the British government was sufficiently even-handed or the outcome the best that could be achieved (Neumann, 2003; Bew et al., 2009).

However, what is important for the purposes of this chapter is the fact that the British began to believe that such a debate was taking place and started to examine ways to influence that debate. The prospect of a role in all-party talks, aided by the outline of a possible approach laid out in the intergovernmental Downing Street Declaration in December 1993, was instrumental in the IRA calling its ceasefire in August 1994. This had a transformative impact on politics in Northern Ireland. This was of course simply part of the equation, and the willingness of Unionists to remain engaged in a political process that included Republicans (albeit not directly engaging with them) was another key factor in the success of the negotiations that led to the B/GFA. In part this was a result of an unforeseen impact of the AIA. The leader of the UUP in the 1990s, David Trimble, had been influenced by the failure of the campaign against the AIA and was unwilling to risk Unionists becoming further marginalised during the subsequent negotiations in the 1990s (Godson, 2004). The role of the SDLP, loyalists and, later, the DUP also needs to be considered to understand the develop-ment and outcome of the peace process. The process was a fraught and stut-tering affair and its trajectory and success were far from clear for many years. The election of the Blair government in 1997 gave it a new impetus and the New Labour administration deserves great credit for the effort it put in to the process and the successes it achieved (Powell, 2009; Blair, 2011; Camp-bell, 2014). But again, in terms of policy, the Blair government's was not fundamentally different from that of his Conservative predecessors and in line with British objectives.

The fact that what emerged from the peace process was in outline compa-rable to that which had failed post Sunningdale is explicable by the changed context of the 1990s. These changes were obviously influenced by British government policy, but not the direct and conscious construct of those poli-cies. Seamus Mallon's quip regarding slow learning is perhaps more apposite than it is largely taken to be, given its relative overuse in the literature. The slow learning that occurred took place on all sides: for a variety of reasons all parties to the conflict changed their approaches and ultimately what they were willing to settle for. In this regard there was slow learning, but it was not, as some of the literature suggests, policy learning by the British government that taught it what its predecessors knew a quarter of a century before that enabled the breakthrough that the peace process achieved.

Conclusion

British policy post Sunningdale oscillated widely but this was due to the changing context of the conflict and the inability of the British to impose their preferences on the parties within Northern Ireland. In relation to the questions posed in the introduction to this book, the differing lessons that the protagonists took from Sunningdale significantly coloured their attitudes towards dialogue and policy agendas. The retrenchment of the parties in Northern Ireland and their belief that Sunningdale represented either the minimum acceptable settlement or more than could possibly be tolerated meant that it cast a long shadow over politics in Northern Ireland and British policy specifically. These considerations led parties at times to see behaviour that frustrated the British government as not only necessary but essential. Sunningdale had illustrated to the British their own relative lack of power, a lesson that coloured their own attitude to dialogue and their policy agenda. It also illustrated to governments over the coming years not only the difficulty of dealing with those who felt alienated from mainstream politics and so advocated the use of violence but also the difficulty in dealing with those who *represented* mainstream politics in Northern Ireland. British politicians, even those who were instinctively sympathetic to Unionism or Nationalism and interested in the politics of the region, found Northern Ireland's politics and politicians difficult. That the British failed to find a solution to the conflict for so long should be discussed, but so should whether there was a solution there to 'find'. Much is made of the success that the peace process represents and (international) consideration is given to whether lessons can be learnt. But it is instructive to consider British policy-making in the longer term and necessary to appreciate the constraints and failures that the British government faced in seeking to secure its objective in Northern Ireland. British policy did significantly alter between the failure to achieve sustained devolved power-sharing government with an Irish dimension in 1974 and the success in achieving this objective in 2007. The situation in the 1990s and 2000s was though hugely different from that of the early 1970s, and to suggest that what was achieved then should have been introduced decades earlier is to take too broad a brush to the historical record.

6

British security policy and the Sunningdale Agreement: the consequences of using force to combat terrorism in a liberal democracy[1]

Aaron Edwards

Throughout these difficult years, it has always been said that a solution lay in a two-pronged approach: a vigorous onslaught against the terrorists, coupled with political advance. That political advance will shortly be a reality.
  – Rt Hon Francis Pym MP, Secretary of State for Northern Ireland, speaking after the Sunningdale Conference in December 1973 (*House of Commons Debates* (Hansard), 13 December 1973, Vol. 866, Col. 675)

This chapter considers the impact of the Sunningdale Agreement on security policy in Northern Ireland. It analyses the consequences that the nine specific clauses in the Agreement relating to security had in determining Britain's subsequent response to political violence, especially as the Conservative government in London sought to shift the operational focus away from military-led counter-insurgency and towards law enforcement-led counter-terrorism (see also Newsinger, 1995). Although the policy of 'police primacy' did not emerge as Britain's preferred option for tackling terrorism until 1975–76, this chapter argues that the seeds were sown by the British government's handling of the Agreement and the urgency by which it sought a cross-border arrangement with the Republic of Ireland that would enhance the security forces' powers of pursuit, arrest and extradition of terrorist suspects. Moreover, the chapter asks whether the Conservative Party's return to power in 1979 finally heralded a reinvigoration of 'police primacy' in a more systematic way than that enacted by the Labour government between 1974 and 1979 (see also Aveyard, 2012). The chapter also highlights the theme of democratic control over the military that would remain extant up to the signing of the Good Friday Agreement in 1998 and beyond. Finally, it makes the case that London's use of the military instrument as an option of last resort is fundamental to our understanding of Britain's long war against the IRA. This is relevant today, of course, particularly as Britain faces a residual armed challenge from dissident Irish republicans. In general terms the chapter reflects on how liberal democracies have responded to the challenge posed by terrorism in broader terms.[2]

Many myths have crept into our understanding of the role of the military in Northern Ireland during its long deployment in aid of the civil power between 1969 and 2007. None is more powerful than the widely held view that the British Army oversaw a counter-insurgency strategy that eventually contributed to forcing the Provisional IRA to the negotiating table by the early 1990s. In archival research, as well as in qualitative interviews and consultation of the secondary literature, there appear to be competing narratives that either accept the view that the military instrument played a decisive role in ending terrorism or reject the idea by stressing that force was incidental to the 'peace process' which emerged in the early 1990s (Tonge et al., 2011). As with all good myths, both have some foundation in empirical reality. However, when it comes to testing the hypothesis about the instrumentality of force, both narratives lack precision in their basic understanding of how – in strategic terms – the military-led counter-insurgency phase (between 1971 and 1976) failed to prevent political violence and in some respects may even have prolonged it. The reality is that the military instrument only contributed to the ending of terrorism when it was strategically subordinated to the political lead provided by the Northern Ireland Office and – in operational terms – by the Royal Ulster Constabulary (RUC) from the late 1970s onwards (Edwards, 2014; Evelegh, 1978).

This chapter argues that the seeds of this wresting of control of security policy back from the British military lie in the Sunningdale Agreement of December 1973, when the London government sponsored talks between the constitutional Unionist, Nationalist and Alliance parties in Berkshire. While some commentators make the case that Sunningdale ultimately failed because it did not include the extremes, others argue that it moved the need for dialogue closer to the mainstream of political activity by London (Tonge, 2000). What these accounts tend to overlook, however, is that Sunningdale actually included nine clauses relating specifically to security policy. The British government was concerned with the deteriorating security situation and made consistent efforts to stabilise the political environment in order to take the sting out of the tail of the armed conflict. By recognising that there could be no 'military solution' to the violence, British strategic thinking opted out of trying to persuade unionists and nationalists to accept an externally imposed political settlement (Neumann, 2003: 81). By the closing weeks of 1973, London was instead heavily investing in the search for an internally agreed democratic consensus that would eventually culminate in the signing of the Good Friday Agreement, a shift which would ultimately facilitate the normalisation of the security situation and the ending of emergency legislation.

Why did the military take the lead in security policy?

Before going on to discuss the security implications of the Sunningdale Agreement it is important to provide an evaluation of military activity in the opening years of the Troubles. The deterioration of the security situation in Northern Ireland was the result of the coalescence in a number of factors, which included the onset of civil rights demonstrations, civil disturbances between rival Protestants and Catholics in Belfast and Londonderry, and the emergence of paramilitary groupings across Loyalist and Republican areas in the late 1960s. Although the only deaths attributable to terrorism in the immediate aftermath of the IRA's border campaign of 1956–62 were part of a sinister conspiracy involving members of the fledgling Ulster Volunteer Force (UVF) and a conglomerate of other extremist Protestant organisations and right-wing members of the ruling Ulster Unionist Party, they none the less had a destabilising effect on community relations in the late 1960s. The inability of the RUC and auxiliary Ulster Special Constabulary (USC; also known as the 'B Specials') to contain the violence meant that by the middle of August 1969 a slump in police morale led the RUC Inspector General, Anthony Peacock, to request military assistance. The British Army had historically been garrisoned in Northern Ireland with a brigade-level force (approximately 2,500 troops) like other parts of the United Kingdom. It had been deployed in aid of the civil power before in Internal Security operations during the IRA border campaign. Then the British could call upon the experience of its soldiers who had fought insurgents and terrorists in Kenya and Cyprus to provide expertise in tackling the IRA flying columns that were attacking police stations and military training camps across Northern Ireland. However, this was largely a limited intervention by the military and remained the only instance of support offered to the civil power since the formation of the Northern Ireland state in the early 1920s.

By 1969 the army found itself under increasing pressure to assist a police force unable to cope with the demands of internal security operations

(Hamill, 1986). The inappropriateness of using colonial policing tactics, a lack of proper public order equipment and training, not to mention a widely held belief that their deployment would only be temporary, led the General Officer Commanding (GOC), Sir Ian Freeland, to issue a strongly worded statement to the press:

> The Army therefore came in in August not to impose Law and Order by force, but to 'keep the peace' between two rival factions in the Community and help the people regain their confidence and overcome their fears. The ring would thus be held while the New Deal for Ulster and the reorganisation of the Police forces were being worked out by the Government and the Hunt Commission. The aim of the Army all along was to work towards the re-establishment of the RUC in all areas as soon as possible. (IWM, Freeland, 79/34/3a)

Freeland made it clear that the army was only a short-term fix for a crisis that required a long-term political solution. Interestingly, his comments irked both British ministers at Westminster and many Nationalist politicians who feared that the military would be used in a politically partisan way by their Unionist rivals. One former British government minister, Lord Chalfont, outlined the dilemma now facing London at the time: 'As in all internal security operations winning "hearts and minds" is as vital as winning the tactical battle. In the context of Northern Ireland in what way can the security forces help in fostering community relations and bridging the gap between rival factions?' (Chalfont, 1972: 61).

Army commanders on the ground who were tasked with enforcing a fragile peace between warring factions of Protestant Unionists and Catholic Nationalists were not wholly unaware of the nuances inherent in the security situation. Lieutenant-Colonel Mike Gray, Commanding Officer of the 1st Battalion the Parachute Regiment, told participants attending the GOC's Study Day in Lisburn in December 1969: 'As always in the Hearts and Minds battle the main link in the chain has been the British Soldier, who has again proved what a most capable and popular ambassador he can be' (IWM, Freeland 79/34/3b). As far as these officers were concerned, the average soldier was perfectly capable of adapting to whatever the situation demanded of him. In a prescient observation, Colonel Gray even suggested that

> As a by-product of these relationships, the soldier on the streets has become an intelligence gatherer. By passing on rumours and other information from the conversation he hears it has been possible to collate intelligence. This also now acts as a very useful indirect 'early warning' system for any trouble which is brewing, though sympathetic admirers. (Ibid.)

Beyond acting as an early warning system, soldiers had a duty to behave in a manner akin to local police officers 'on the beat'. In Gray's words:

> Once the main troubles had ceased the problem was to win 'Hearts and Minds', to make contact with the people, regain their confidence and respect in order to ease the tension and allay the fears of old and young alike, many of whom were not directly concerned in the incidents. This was done by each soldier on the streets, adopting an almost fixed friendly smile – whether he felt like it or not – being polite and talking to people, and lending an impartial and sympathetic ear for the many who wanted to let off steam. (IWM, Freeland, 79/34/3c)

In short, argued Gray and other military commanders, British soldiers could play a preventative role in Northern Ireland by deterring terrorists and reassuring the general population. This kind of optimism proved short-lived as the security situation shifted from one of civil unrest between rival communities to a determined terrorist campaign by the fledgling IRA. As a direct response to the upsurge in political violence the British state authorised the introduction of internment in August 1971. However, this failed to arrest the decline in security and by the opening weeks of 1972 the situation had once again deteriorated. By looking to the army to take a harsher line with those in civil disobedience, the Unionist administration in Belfast and the Conservative government in London created the permissive circumstances wherein escalation of violence soon came to pass. The immediate consequences of this escalation included the shooting dead of 13 unarmed civilians by the Parachute Regiment in Londonderry on 30 January 1972, later known as 'Bloody Sunday'. After Bloody Sunday there was little prospect of the IRA losing support amongst the minority population as long as the security forces were perceived to be taking a heavy-handed approach to dealing with civil unrest. As we now know, the Provisional IRA's 'Derry Brigade' grew from a motley band of forty to fifty volunteers in the city to several hundred members. British military intelligence assessments of IRA strategy by the beginning of the summer raised the prospect of burgeoning activity:

> The group is also planning to extend guerrilla warfare to rural areas of south Co Londonderry. Hideouts and arms dumps are being constructed for this purpose. Active Service Units from Eire together with local units are expected to take part in hit and run attacks against Security Forces, and it is hoped that some of the Roman Catholic rural areas will become No-Go areas. There is a suggestion that this rural campaign is being prepared in case the IRA are forced out of the Bogside and Creggan, should their activities become unpopular there. (The National Archives (TNA), DEFE, HQNI INTSUM, No. 19/72)

In response to Bloody Sunday the IRA stepped up its bomb attacks on businesses owned by Protestants in Londonderry in a bid to force them out of the city. Given the increasingly sectarian nature of the armed conflict it would not be long before the IRA sought out other soft targets within the wider Unionist community. In Belfast the Provisionals carried out the

'Bloody Friday' atrocity on 21 July 1972 in which 11 people were killed in the space of an afternoon when 26 car bombs exploded across the city. Despite urging restraint on military operations, the Conservative government sought to rebalance the strategic calculus by capitalising on the revulsion expressed across the two communities for the co-ordinated bomb attacks in Belfast. Downing Street gave the order for the dismantling of 'no-go areas' in both cities and the reimposition of governmental writ. The operation was a success and led to a drop in attacks from 2,595 shooting incidents in the three weeks before the so-called Operation Motorman to only 380 in the three weeks after it had gone in (Neumann, 2003: 80). The predominantly Protestant town of Claudy, just a few miles outside Derry, was the first to be hit by reprisals when a no-warning car bomb exploded in the main square, killing nine people and injuring scores of others on a busy shopping day. Even with the strategic success offered by Operation Motorman, 1972 would still none the less emerge as the worst year of the Troubles. In that year 497 people lost their lives, ten times that number were injured and the IRA had carried out over twelve hundred operations, mainly in rural areas. In strategic terms, the government proved that the military instrument had utility, if used proportionately and only when operating according to clear political objectives.

This interpretation of the role of the military in the early years runs contrary to orthodox interpretations of the army as either incredibly naïve or overly repressive in the conduct of operations in Belfast and Londonderry. It is also at variance with the understanding of how adaptable the army was when it came to adjusting its tactics to meet what was fast becoming a fluid security environment. As Lord Chalfont wrote at the time:

> The first point to be made is that they have been forced, by the obvious and understandable limitations of the RUC, into tactics which are alien to the whole concept of military operations in aid of the civil power. The classic method is to hold military forces in reserve until the police are no longer able to control the situation; then to deploy troops quickly and decisively, using the minimum force, but enough of it to restore order; and then as soon as possible to withdraw the armed forces, handing over again to the civil power. (Chalfont, 1972: 61)

The problem with so many interpretations of the tactics utilised by the army is that they rarely augment discussion with an understanding of the political context within which the military instrument operated, as if force was devoid of strategic purpose or direction. Prior to the collapse of Stormont, security policy was a somewhat convoluted process involving multiple actors; after the imposition of sirect rule, however, it became much more straightforward in theory. As the historian Huw Bennett argues, 'the civilian leadership broadly exercised control over the military'. Consequently, 'it is important to note the activist stance taken by the senior generals in defining the strategy in detail' (Bennett, 2010: 516).

The British search for a political solution

By the beginning of 1973 the British government was running out of options. The violence showed no signs of abating despite the political breathing space created by Operation Motorman. Naturally, the IRA sought to regain lost momentum by moving its operations to the UK mainland, leaving the British eager to find a political solution capable of taking the sting out of the tale of violence. By now London began to present itself as a 'neutral arbiter' in political terms: an umpire refereeing a fight between two warring factions. There were limits to this form of liberal balancing between individual liberty and collective security in a deeply divided society, not least at a time when the British state was acting very much in its own national interests to reduce the levels of violence.

Brendan O'Leary (1989) argues that the British basically adhered to four basic policies to service this self-effacement of 'neutral arbiter'. First, they gave the outward appearance of being an 'honest broker', by denying unionists the political opportunity to return to their pre-1972 form of majoritarian rule. This kind of supremacism was ruled out and the balancing between rival communities became the mainstay of British attempts to impose a solution. Secondly, London enacted legislation that would consign the old ethnonational logic shoring up '50 years of unionist misrule' to the dustbin of history in favour of a vibrant reform agenda. This was so successful that some constitutional nationalists were declaring in 1972 that it had actually begun the process of deconstructing discriminatory practices in employment, housing and the electoral franchise, which disproportionately affected the minority Catholic community. To be sure, the idea of equal citizenship had been a main plank of the third labour tradition in Northern Ireland for much of the fifty years of unionist domination at Stormont. Thirdly, the British sought to criminalise political violence and deny the IRA and Protestant paramilitaries the opportunity to gain support for their activities. Internment, therefore, was cited as an example that became discredited because it was viewed as synonymous with unionist hegemonic control. 'None the less an awesome array of security forces and legal instruments had made Northern Ireland exceptionally repressive amongst liberal democracies by the late 1970s.' Crucially, writes O'Leary, British politicians emphasised Northern Ireland's exceptionality as something alien to those values and norms pertaining on the UK mainland. Essentially, this served to quarantine Great Britain from the Irish 'disease' of ethnic intolerance. It was in this context that a political solution was sought alongside a more effective security response that reinforced the need for the police to work in partnership with the community. Much would now hinge on the tripartite talks at Sunningdale in late 1973.

The main aim of the Sunningdale conference was to reach an accommodation on Northern Ireland's constitutional future. The Nationalist Social Democratic and Labour Party, which had been gradually moving to the right, reaffirmed its commitment to a United Ireland based on 'unity established by consent'. The Unionists, led by the former Prime Minister of Northern Ireland Brian Faulkner, reflected the position of the 'majority of the people of Northern Ireland to remain part of the United Kingdom'. The Irish government accepted that position and this was reaffirmed by the British government, which stated that it would countenance a change in Northern Ireland's position only if the majority of people 'should indicate a wish to become part of a United Ireland'.

Controversially, however, the conference agreed to establish a Council of Ireland, which would 'comprise a Council of Ministers with executive and harmonising functions and a consultative role, and a Consultative Assembly with advisory and review functions'. According to Peter McLoughlin, even though the SDLP 'championed the body as an engine of Irish unification', the 'North–south structure actually agreed at Sunningdale could *not* be a harbinger of Irish unity' (2007: 11), because the principle of consent had been built into its architecture. Notwithstanding McLoughlin's dismissal of Unionist fears, the fact remains that the perception amongst Unionists at the time was that the proposal would give the Irish government a direct say in the internal affairs of the British state. Unsurprisingly the Council of Ireland sparked widespread protest from Unionists, with the fundamentalist right-wing preacher Ian Paisley leading calls to bring down the power-sharing institutions. The clarion call was that 'Dublin is just a Sunningdale away'. What is often overlooked in the haste to critique the constitutional crisis that the establishment of the Northern Ireland Executive triggered is that the Agreement included nine clauses relating to the security situation. It was this that was given equal weighting under Sunningdale, and its implications would have far-reaching consequences for London's security policy.

In short, Sunningdale envisaged the extradition and the arrest of persons committing crimes of violence and the creation of a 'common law enforcement area in which an all-Ireland court would have jurisdiction'. This clause was unprecedented and would effectively mean that both sovereign states would have a greater say in each other's internal affairs. Another clause in the Agreement underscored the Irish government's position on seeking the British to agree to the adoption and ratification of the European Convention on Human Rights.[3] Other clauses dealt specifically with policing and the need to 'ensure public support for and identification with the police service throughout the whole community', as well as, most radical of all, the devolution of 'responsibility for normal policing'. The point was to build confidence in the police amongst all sections of the community and saw the British government give an undertaking to 'bring detention to an end in Northern Ireland for all sections of the community as soon as the security situation permits'.

McLoughlin makes an important observation in relation to security by questioning whether both governments were serious about linking policing to the Agreement more formally. As he perceptively argues:

> Whether or not Whitehall ever genuinely considered the possibility of such a quid pro quo in order to obtain better policing of the southern side of the Irish border is a moot point: when the cards were on the table at Sunningdale, it was clear that London, still mindful of such disasters as the introduction of internment and Bloody Sunday, was not prepared to relinquish any control over security in Northern Ireland, nor even to give Dublin the kind of consultative role that it would concede a decade later in the 1985 Anglo-Irish Agreement. (2007: 16)

Nevertheless, the fact remains that Britain did intend to commit itself to the terms of this international treaty by agreeing to pass legislation in Parliament as quickly possible in the wake of the tripartite talks at Sunningdale.

The then Shadow Secretary of State for Northern Ireland, Merlyn Rees, articulated the view that even though he found it desirable 'to hand over to those in Northern Ireland as quickly as possible [and] as much as possible of the running of their own country', the process by which they arrived at this situation should not be forgotten. As Rees continued, 'we went through a traumatic experience during the years of the last Government and this Government before we got security into the hands of Westminster'. In his opinion, for '[a]s long as there are substantial numbers of British troops in Northern Ireland, it is vital that their control should be vested in Westminster and nowhere else' (*House of Commons Debates* (Hansard), 13 December 1973, Vol. 866, Col. 683). This position would continue to be exercised by the London government and would later be accepted as a point of principle when Labour came to power within weeks of the parliamentary debate on the Sunningdale Agreement.

Exercising the 20:20 vision offered by the benefit of hindsight, the SDLP's deputy leader, John Hume, blamed both the new British Labour government for demonstrating 'one of the most squalid examples of government irresponsibility in our times' and the Unionists for resisting and jettisoning 'any British policy for Northern Ireland which involved conceding power to the minority'. Ironically he praised the Conservative government for showing 'the political courage and imagination' to establish power sharing. Hume never believed in the efficacy of political violence on either side (saving special disdain for the Provisional IRA in whom he saw 'a ruthless terrorist force which can compensate in terms of experience and technique for what it has lost in political support' making their activities both 'savage' and 'immoral') (Hume, 1979: 308) but grossly misinterpreted the British government's own self-interests in seeking to maximise its national security over and above forcing unionists into an agreement they did not want. He continued, 'A hard headed people [the unionists] should logically draw the conclusion that an arrangement with the south is in its best interest. I have no doubt that they would do so now were the problem of Northern Ireland purely economic. Of course, it is not' (Ibid.: 303).

Even though it ultimately failed in the face of large-scale Unionist opposition protests, Sunningdale none the less set the tone for British preoccupation with dealing with the security situation more robustly. It permitted the army some much-needed top-cover in carrying out its aggressive counter-insurgency operations that began with the disasters of internment and the highly controversial tactics practised by the Military Reaction Force in recruiting informers, not to mention the liberal fire control orders its operators seemed to be following in their reckless game of cat and mouse with the IRA. Some of the techniques adhered to by the security forces at this time would later implicate Britain in the inhumane and degrading treatment of terrorist suspects. Moreover, the litany of failed colonial-era tactics only served to alienate the minority Catholic community and would, arguably, set back community relations by a generation. With the return of a Labour government in February 1974, a policy of bipartisanship now appeared to be operating in relation to security policy in Northern Ireland. Merlyn Rees, who had become Secretary of State for Northern Ireland, informed the House:

> Let me say again quite clearly and categorically that sufficient numbers of the Army will remain in Northern Ireland to assist in maintaining law and order. But we believe that in the long term it must be the community itself and normal police activities, not military operations alone, which will finally defeat the terrorist. (*House of Commons Debates* (Hansard), 4 April 1974, Vol. 871, Col. 1469)

The return of a Conservative government under Margaret Thatcher saw the final strategic outmanoeuvring of the military and the enshrinement of the primacy of policing, despite the IRA twin bomb attack at Warrenpoint, Co. Down (in which 18 soldiers were killed), and the assassination of Lord Mountbatten in Co. Donegal, just over the Irish border, in August 1979. By the early 1980s the RUC was firmly in the driving seat of security policy, building up its covert counter-terrorist capability in a more meaningful way (Edwards, 2014).

Constitutional politics and the British Army

Strategic theorists generally agree that 'the idea of force as an agent of political purpose is generally persuasive' (Gray, 1999: 29). However, this is somewhat disputed in the literature on Northern Ireland, for there remains a reluctance to see the clear strategic lines that connected policy to the military tactics used by the Security Forces. During the 1970s this included deterrent activities such as public order drills employed by the army to contain serious street disorder, vehicle check points to disrupt terrorists from carrying out attacks, through to more coercive measures like internment without trial and the exchange of fire with terrorist gunmen. Colonel Robin Evelegh put this best when he wrote in his influential book *Peacekeeping in a Democratic Society* about how 'Political factors interweave with everything that the military do in a counter-insurgency campaign, right down to the tone of voice used by the most junior soldier in talking to civilians on the street' (Evelegh, 1978: 110). The need to ensure the pendulum in security policy swung back in favour of the police would later be more effectively pushed by Harold Wilson's Labour government after 1974.

In his celebrated book *Governing Without Consensus* (1971), an account of Northern Irish politics before the fall of the old Stormont regime, the renowned political scientist Richard Rose wondered whether the crises of authority in divided societies could ever be overcome. In a particularly telling observation, he declared that even an absence of violence could not be a guarantee of political consensus. In his view, the challenge remained simply a question of how one managed conflict in a peaceful manner. As he put it, 'In so far as political discord arises from substantive issues, then the crucial question is the extent to which the chief issues are bargainable. Peaceful bargaining is possible, if the matter in dispute permits negotiations that can lead to an outcome acceptable to all' (Rose, 1971: 371). The key, in Rose's view, was to find a formula that satisfied all belligerents in conflict without them needing to pursue a more decisive end goal wedded to violence. Rose concluded how 'Whether or not an issue is bargainable is reflected by three characteristics: whether it involves a zero-sum conflict; whether it involves private or collective goods, and whether competing claims are stated as absolute values or advanced as demands for more or less of something'. By the 1980s it seemed clear that both the British and Irish governments had moved towards the institutionalisation of their policy-making process, with the key motivation behind co-operation being the need to effectively tackle violence and security (see O'Kane above).

How should a liberal democratic state respond to terrorism? Should it rely on its law enforcement agencies to inflict attrition on violent non-state groupings through systematic evidence-gathering, arrest and imprisonment, or should it deploy the military in a policing role? And, moreover, if it does this and manages to inflict serious damage on the terrorist grouping, when should it seek to end the violence and by what means? If the state has entered into a bargaining process with a terrorist organisation how much ground should it cede and what are the consequences?

In Britain the constitutional effects of the English revolution of the mid-seventeenth century, where the New Model Army interfered directly in the politics of the time, were still being felt three hundred years later. Few would countenance the British Army being deployed as readily on the streets of British soil as quickly as they had been deployed to quell rebellious uprisings across the empire. For the moment the army was the only organisation that could respond effectively to the terrorist situation. By the late 1970s the pendulum had swung back in favour of the police, and the Conservative government under Mrs Thatcher began the long process of dismantling the security apparatus that had outstayed its welcome in security policy terms.

Throughout the remainder of the Troubles the army would play a supporting role to the RUC (renamed the Police Service of Northern Ireland after 2000) and would work within a law enforcement framework that emphasised good old-fashioned evidential-based crime-busting methods to combat the terrorist threat. By the 1990s the nascent 'peace process' had locked Republicans in and gave them a stake in its success. After the signing of the Good Friday Agreement it became clear that further 'normalisation' of the security situation was required in order to bring violence to an 'acceptable level'. By 2007 the army would finally draw down its presence and thereafter return to pre-1969 force levels. One of the last GOCs to oversee this normalisation described the process as making Northern Ireland like Hampshire or Surrey. The constitutional imperative of reducing military force levels made perfect sense to those who were not used to the sight of vehicle checkpoints, army patrols on land, on sea and in the air, or the fortification of residential areas on the scale that had come to mark out Northern Ireland as atypical of Finchley.

Conclusion

Liberal democracies risk much when they tackle the scourge of terrorism. Essentially, by engaging in the threat or actuality of violence, terrorists are issuing a challenge to the state that it cannot hope to protect its citizens in a meaningful way. As it was made clear by the Provisional IRA in the wake of the bomb attack on the Grand Central Hotel in Brighton in 1984, they only had to be lucky once – the implication being that the state had to be lucky all of the time if it was to stand any chance of stopping terrorist violence. For the architects of the Sunningdale Agreement the optimism they imbibed over what the Communiqué represented became a salutary lesson on how politicians could act independently of their electorate and misjudge the mood prevailing at the time. Although the majority of people displayed no support or sympathy for Loyalist paramilitaries, they were less likely to accept the need to relinquish their rights as British citizens. This much was proved in May when the UWC called a stoppage in the main industrial centres of Northern Ireland, putting enormous strain on public services and ensuring that the British government would have to rely disproportionately on the army to step in in an attempt to maintain services while people stayed away from work. Westminster may have thought they correctly understood the need to reassure unionists that they were committed to maintaining the Union (Neumann, 2003); however, in the zero-sum game of Northern Irish politics, the British concern to balance this commitment to the Union with the so-called Irish dimension in favour of Nationalists saw them underesti mate the power by which Unionists would resist any return of devolution with Dublin interference.

Notes

1 The views expressed in this chapter are the author's and do not necessarily represent the views of the Royal Military Academy Sandhurst, the Ministry of Defence or any other UK government agency.

2 Terrorism is taken to mean the threat or use of force by a non-state actor for the purposes of influencing a government by placing the public, or a section of the public, in fear of their lives, liberty and property. It is inherently a rational political activity and can be seen in contradistinction to crime, despite its pejorative connotations.

3 Ironically, only a few years later, the Dublin government would take the British government to the European Court of Human Rights in Strasbourg in response to the army's 'inhumane and degrading treatment' of terrorist suspects.

7

Sunningdale and the limits of 'rejectionist' Unionism

Stuart Aveyard and Shaun McDaid

To understand Sunningdale and its legacy it is necessary to grapple with divisions within Unionism, many of which preceded the Sunningdale Agreement. Divisions on power sharing crystallised between the publication of the Northern Ireland Constitutional Proposals in March 1973 and the collapse of the power-sharing Executive at the hands of the Ulster Workers' Council (UWC) in May 1974. Opposition to Sunningdale created short-lived unity among rival strands of rejectionist Unionism, which subsequently disintegrated after the executive collapsed. After May 1974, Unionists experienced a prolonged limitation of their capacity to influence policy. The absence of a local administration that Unionists could focus their protests against and the consistency of the British government's stance on nationalist involvement in any devolved settlement ensured that the demise of power sharing in 1974 was the zenith of rejectionist Unionism. There remained a cleavage within Unionism between a diminishing minority prepared to countenance some form of compromise with constitutional Nationalism and a majority who continued to demand a return to the old Stormont system. The failure of Unionism to compromise only served to reinforce Westminster's reluctant acceptance of direct rule. While elements within the UUP showed some flexibility in contemplating new forms for this system, it became increasingly clear over the course of the following decade that it would not fulfil Unionists' hopes for a closer relationship with Great Britain.

The loss of Stormont

The collapse of Stormont brought the ideological divisions within Unionism into stark relief, divisions which had begun to manifest before the introduction of direct rule. Whilst, at the time of the prorogation of Stormont, the Ulster Unionist Party (UUP) was still the dominant party in Northern Ireland, it faced an increasing number of challenges from hard-line Unionists, opposed to any hint of compromise with Nationalists. Attempts by the former Prime Minister, Terence O'Neill, to make overtures to Catholic opinion, though cosmetic, caused consternation among hard-line Loyalists (Mulholland, 2000). In particular, Ian Paisley's Democratic Unionist Party (DUP), formed in 1971, began challenging the UUP in certain areas. Paisley drew upon his extensive network of evangelical fundamentalist supporters, highly attuned to the prospect of treachery, for the core support-base of his new party (Bruce, 2007; Tonge et al., 2014). Likewise, the UUP (and its leader Brian Faulkner) faced challenges from an internal pressure group, Ulster Vanguard. Vanguard, formed in February 1972, cautioned against compromise with Nationalists and sought tougher action against the Provisional Irish Republican Army (PIRA). It was led by the Stormont minister William (Bill) Craig. The group's mass meetings, and Craig's fiery rhetoric, made it reminiscent of a far-right organisation. Addressing a rally of fifty thousand Loyalists, Craig referred to 'liquidating' the Republican enemy, and warned that his supporters would 'do or die' before accepting direct rule (*Sunday Independent* 19 March 1972).

Direct rule was duly introduced in March 1972 amid a deteriorating security situation and an acceptance within the British government that internal reform could do little to reduce violence (Bew, 2007: 508). Anti-British sentiment swept Northern Ireland. The Union Flag was replaced by the Ulster banner at Belfast City Hall, and loyalists jeered British troops on the streets (*Irish Independent* 28 March 1972). A hundred thousand Unionists gathered at Stormont for a Vanguard rally. Faulkner joined Craig, leading his Cabinet members on to the balcony of the former parliament in solidarity against what they regarded as the undemocratic actions of the British government. The last Prime Minister of Northern Ireland felt discomfort standing beside one of his leading critics but it was the British government's insistence that power sharing must accompany any return of devolution that ensured this show of Unionist solidarity was short-lived (Hennessey, 2007: 339; Patterson and Kaufmann, 2007: 151).

Government policy was elucidated in an October 1972 Green Paper, and a subsequent March 1973 White Paper, entitled *The Northern Ireland Constitutional Proposals* (Northern Ireland Office (NIO), 1973). The White Paper proposed a new devolved Assembly, elected by proportional representation. However, the proposals specifically ruled out the formation of any executive that drew 'its support and its elected representation virtually entirely from only one section of a divided community'. This categorically excluded the possibility of a return to Unionist-only government, as pertained under Stormont. That same month, the governing body of the UUP defeated a Vanguard motion to reject the British proposals. This precipitated a formal split within the UUP, with Craig and his followers forming the Vanguard Unionist Progressive Party (VUPP). Concerns about the nature of Northern Ireland's democratic system were central to the VUPP's opposition to reform.

For Vanguard, anything less than a majoritarian system underpinned by British parliamentary norms failed the democratic test. For the first time, Vanguard's *Community of the British Isles* contended, 'civil government in Ulster no longer has the consent of the majority and can thus no longer be termed democratic' (Ulster Vanguard, 1973a). The party subsequently threatened to disrupt the proposed Assembly, and accused the Secretary of State, William Whitelaw, of usurping constitutional authority in Northern Ireland, by attempting to impose a power-sharing settlement (Ulster Vanguard, 1973b).

The DUP was also firmly opposed to any form of power sharing, even with constitutional nationalists such as the Social Democratic and Labour Party (SDLP). It conflated sharing power with the non-violent SDLP with rewarding the violent extremists in PIRA. The DUP also opposed the involvement of any political party from the Republic of Ireland in any future talks, accusing Fianna Fáil of giving 'support to the IRA'. However, the DUP accurately suggested that a working power-sharing executive would not 'of itself bring about an improvement in the security situation' (The National Archives (TNA) (1973), note of a meeting between the Prime Minister and leaders of the DUP, 29 August, Foreign and Commonwealth Office (FCO) (87/283)). At this time, the DUP favoured the complete integration of Northern Ireland with the rest of the UK. If the DUP was largely united behind Ian Paisley, the opposite was true of Brian Faulkner's UUP.

The departure of Vanguard from the party's ranks foreshadowed a more serious split within the UUP, manifest in the summer of 1973. The British White Paper made provision for Assembly elections, duly held in July of that year. Ten of the UUP's 39 candidates declined to support Faulkner's policy on power sharing. Faulkner had earlier stated he would not enter government with those whose 'primary objective' was breaking the link with Great Britain. However, if the SDLP was prepared to accept devolution in a UK framework, then breaking the link with Britain could no longer be its primary aim (Faulkner, 1978: 194). This left open the possibility of power sharing with Nationalists, which the ten UUP dissenters, led by the former Stormont minister Harry West, refused to countenance. West led a breakaway faction of 'unpledged' Unionists opposed to the Faulknerite wing of the party (McDaid, 2013: 19).

The Assembly elections saw Faulkner's UUP return as largest party, with 24 seats. The SDLP came second, with 19, and the non-sectarian Alliance Party took eight. However, anti-power-sharing Unionists fared well, with eight seats each for the DUP and West's 'unpledged' UUP and seven for the VUPP. Overall, a majority of Unionist voters supported anti-power-sharing candidates (McDaid, 2013: 21). These three factions issued a joint statement calling on all Unionists to unite in opposition to power sharing (*Irish Times* 20 September 1973). Whilst the democratic legitimacy of the institutions was frequently critiqued, some Unionists attempted to mobilise opposition to the Assembly by appealing to the more atavistic fears of Unionists.

Vanguard's Kennedy Lindsay, for example, claimed that those Unionists who participated in any power-sharing executive faced possible expulsion from the Orange Order, the Royal Black Institution or the Apprentice Boys (*Irish Times* 17 September 1973). Rejectionist Unionism, then, comprised an uneasy alliance of parties that were at once in competition for votes, divided on the question of devolution, integration, or an independent Ulster, and encompassed individuals and groups who combined both constitutional and sectarian motives for opposing power sharing. The formation of a power-sharing executive, and the subsequent Sunningdale talks in England, however, enabled this fractious coalition to unite in opposition to the new arrangements.

Sunningdale and the UWC strike

In November 1973, following lengthy negotiations, a power-sharing executive was formed. Its membership was drawn from Faulkner's UUP, the SDLP and the Alliance Party. It was scheduled to take office on 1 January 1974. Prior to this, in December 1973, talks between the Executive designate and the British and Irish governments took place at Sunningdale, Berkshire. Anti-agreement Unionists were invited to attend and air their views, but declined since they were to be excluded from substantive discussions. The subsequent 'Sunningdale Agreement' cemented the power-sharing executive, but also made provision for a Council of Ireland to oversee co-operation between Northern Ireland and the Republic of Ireland on matters of shared concern (McDaid, 2013: 25). The Council of Ireland provisions enraged Unionist opinion, and inspired further resistance from them. Anti-power-sharing Unionists, from Vanguard to the Orange Order, criticised the agreement, with Craig promising to make it unworkable (*Daily Mail* 10 December 1973).

The omens were thus not good for the power-sharing Executive, which took office on 1 January 1974. The Executive parties initially worked well together, but recognised the difficulties they faced in terms of Loyalist opposition. However, it was felt that if concerted, all-Ireland action against Republican paramilitaries was forthcoming this might broaden support for both power sharing and Sunningdale (PRONI, OE 1/2/1A Executive minutes, 8 January 1974). It was not long, however, before anti-agreement Unionist factions had an opportunity to seriously undermine the Executive.

In February 1974, Edward Heath called a UK General Election, prompted by the miners' strike in Great Britain. In Northern Ireland, the election was fought on the issue of support (or otherwise) for Sunningdale and the Executive. Anti-agreement Unionists, styling themselves the United Ulster Unionist Coalition (UUUC), fought the election under the slogan 'Dublin is just a Sunningdale away'. At this time, most UUUC members favoured the return of majority-rule devolution. UUUC candidates won 11 of Northern Ireland's 12 Westminster seats, with only one seat (the SDLP's Gerry Fitt in West Belfast) going to a pro-power-sharing candidate.

The election results met with mixed responses from the executive. Nationalists tended to argue that what was needed was a rapid implementation of the Sunningdale Agreement, whereas Unionists cautioned against ignoring a mass protest on this scale. One Unionist minister felt that fears of the Council of Ireland were inflated, but that this message did not get through to 'the people in the high flats' in Loyalist areas of Belfast (PRONI, OE/10/10, Executive minutes, 5 March 1974, note of a discussion on the political situation following the results of the general election 28 February 1974). However, the scale of the UUUC victory demonstrated that opposition to Sunningdale, and to power sharing, was not confined to the Loyalist working classes. A majority of Unionists, across classes, opposed Sunningdale, and many Unionists considered that the February election further undermined the Executive's claims to democratic legitimacy.

The UUUC led the Loyalist clamour for fresh Assembly elections, which, it claimed, would show that the wider community rejected power sharing and Sunningdale. Parallel to the UUUC's political campaign hard-line loyalists with links to paramilitary groups were becoming more politically engaged. In late 1973, the UWC held its first meeting at the VUPP headquarters in

East Belfast. The UWC comprised Protestant trades-unionists and members of groups such as the Ulster Defence Association (UDA), Ulster Volunteer Force (UVF) and Red Hand Commando (Wood, 2006: 33; McAuley, 2010: 40–1). Even within the Executive, which generally remained united, there were suggestions that some of Faulkner's allies (notably Roy Bradford) were identifying more closely with the opponents of Sunningdale. The British government's ministerial committee on Northern Ireland was aware of these developments, noting that Faulkner was being intrigued against by some of his 'erstwhile closest collaborators who felt he was out of touch with events' (TNA, FCO 87/350 Brief: Cabinet, Ministerial Committee on Northern Ireland by ROI Department, 29 March 1974). This further illustrates how uncomfortable even moderate Unionists were with the Sunningdale package, and the susceptibility of the Faulknerites to paramilitary-inspired pressure. That pressure came to a head in May 1974, with the onset of the UWC strike, which led to the Executive's collapse.

On 14 May, the Assembly voted on a loyalist motion calling for the renegotiation of the Sunningdale Agreement, tabled by the independent West Belfast Loyalist Coalition (WBLC). The previous day, the Executive had agreed to implement the controversial Council of Ireland in phases, with the proposed all-Ireland institutions established only subject to a satisfactory test of public opinion. However, this was not announced at the time; thus the general public was unaware the Executive had decided on a more cautious approach (PRONI, OE/2/21 Executive minutes, 13 May 1974). The WBLC motion was easily defeated in the Assembly, but had serious consequences for the Executive. The following day, the UWC began a general strike, ostensibly linked to its demand for fresh Assembly elections. The UWC claimed that the strike was motivated by the Executive's undemocratic nature. However, its view of democracy was not only majoritarian but sectarian and exclusory. It claimed, for example, that the strike was about maintaining Ulster as the last bastion of the Protestant faith in Europe, and escaping the 'shackles of Rome' (*News Sheet* May 1974).

The strike was quick to tap into latent reservoirs of support among the wider Unionist community, who held serious fears about Sunningdale; fears that were inflated by the SDLP's inaccurate portrayal of the Council of Ireland as an embryonic all-Ireland government (McDaid, 2012). It has also been argued that not enough was done by the government to reassure Unionists that their place in the UK was secure (Dixon, 1997: 6). It is unlikely, however, that any such reassurances would have dissuaded loyalists from supporting the UWC's objectives (Gillespie, 1998). The UWC controlled the electricity generating stations, and this proved crucial to the eventual success of the strike (Fisk, 1975; Aveyard, 2014). The strikers were also boosted by an unfortunate intervention by the Prime Minister, Harold Wilson, who accused the UWC of 'sponging on Westminster' and assaulting democratic methods (Aveyard, 2012: 533–4). By 28 May, with the prospect of Belfast's drainage system succumbing to power-shortages, the Executive collapsed. Loyalists, and not only the working-class variety, celebrated its demise 'as if it was VE day' (Kerr, 2011: 246).

The strike was the zenith of anti-reformist Unionist unity, and the cross-class anti-Sunningdale alliance did not outlive the Executive. The uneasy alliance between gunmen and 'law-and-order' Protestants was fleeting. The strike also demonstrated the limits to what Unionists could achieve in the face of a British government determined that power sharing must accompany devolution. Unionists, with the help of industrial and paramilitary muscle, could topple a local executive but could not bring back Stormont. In their drive for a return to majority-rule devolution, anti-agreement Unionists were pursuing policies that actually ensured the continuance of direct rule as the decade progressed.

The failure to compromise

The proceedings of the Northern Ireland Constitutional Convention underline the inability of the Unionist coalition to find a form of government which could serve as an acceptable alternative to Sunningdale. After the UWC strike, the Labour government felt that the next political initiative should press Northern Ireland politicians to engage in discussions without direction from either Great Britain or the Irish Republic. The Northern Ireland Secretary, Merlyn Rees, insisted that a political settlement could not be imposed from outside. In July 1974 a White Paper outlined a plan for the Convention, stressing that 'the people of Northern Ireland must play a crucial part in determining their own future'. The Convention members would be asked to consider what form of government would 'command the most widespread acceptance' (HMSO, 1974). Little was expected from the Convention; Rees conceived of it as a process that had to be gone through and which, from the British perspective, would serve the useful purpose of emphasising that it was Northern Irish politicians who were failing to produce a workable settlement. It was also likely that more restricted terms of reference would have prevented any serious dialogue between Unionism and Nationalism occurring at all. The UUUC sought an assurance that Westminster would not impose its will on the issue of power sharing while the SDLP insisted that only power sharing was acceptable. The legislation was worded to avoid an early confrontation and restrict the Convention without explicitly imposing conditions: any proposal had to be acceptable to Westminster and

Northern Irish politicians were left to harbour their own illusions as to what acceptable might mean (Aveyard, 2012).

Election results gave little incentive for the UUUC to modify its stance. It maintained overwhelming control of Northern Ireland's Westminster seats at the October 1974 general election, suffering the loss of Harry West's Fermanagh/South Tyrone seat to an independent republican but increasing its share of the vote from 51 per cent to 58 per cent. Brian Faulkner's new Unionist Party of Northern Ireland failed to win any seats, demonstrating the lack of support within the Unionist community for a compromise with constitutional Nationalism (Patterson and Kaufmann, 2007: 174–5). The UUUC's campaign for the Convention elections in May 1975 was thus based on a complete rejection of power sharing and all-Ireland institutions. The coalition's manifesto insisted on the superiority of 'the traditional British democratic parliamentary system'. A system of all-party backbench committees was suggested to allow 'special opportunities for any minority group' but, it was argued, nothing should be offered that would 'exceed or distort the mandate given by an electoral majority'. The UUUC won 46 of the 78 seats, the Unionist Party of Northern Ireland (UPNI) secured a dismal five and the Alliance Party eight (HMSO, 1975). The UUUC could thus claim to have a clear mandate for the rejection of the principles behind Sunningdale.

The Convention began with plenary sessions which ran from 8 May until 3 July, adjourning for informal inter-party talks during the summer. Having secured a majority, the UUUC was in a comfortable position and primarily sought to avoid appearing intransigent in the debates. There were, however, tensions within the coalition and within its component parties that are revealing of the character of Unionism after Sunningdale. The loss of his Westminster seat undermined Harry West's leadership of the UUP, with James Molyneaux succeeding him as head of the UUUC group in the Commons. This group, joined by Enoch Powell, led to a greater sympathy for integration. Both men understood far better than West that devolution without power sharing was unlikely to be granted and Powell's distaste for the parochialism within his new party marked a very different approach (Walker, 2004: 222; Corthorn, 2012). The committed devolutionists within the UUP were more in line with the attitude of the party membership but the doubters did more to grapple with the lack of realism about hankering after a return to majority rule. Indeed, Powell recognised that devolution would likely only be bought at the expense of some kind of involvement of the SDLP, which, as Patterson and Kaufmann describe, would for him 'represent the start of the process of the "greening" of Ulster' (Patterson and Kaufmann, 2007: 175). Such voices became steadily more important within the UUP during the Convention and afterwards.

The most important event during the Convention was a surprise initiative from Craig during the private inter-party meetings held over the summer. The Vanguard leader proposed a temporary voluntary coalition with the SDLP. The difficulties with this idea are clear from the terms 'temporary' and 'voluntary'. Craig argued that power sharing could be allowed for the duration of the emergency in Northern Ireland. The clerk to the Chairman observed that 'this was a tactical move rather than a change in strategic objective. Craig still wanted [majority rule], but was prepared to accept a voluntary coalition with the SDLP for a few years in order to get it' (PRONI, CONV/1/9, Hayes to Burns, 5 December 1975). It is doubtful whether this would have led to majority rule. It also seems unrealistic given the level of violence in Northern Ireland and the unlikelihood of a temporary coalition doing much to reduce it. Within the British government, Merlyn Rees described Craig as no 'knight in shining armour' (TNA, CAB 134/3921, IRN(75) memo 20, 19 September 1975). If the SDLP and UUUC agreed on it, however, the British government would have found it difficult to reject any scenario advocated by both Nationalists and Unionists. The UUUC negotiating document left room for a temporary agreement for parties to join together in 'the national interest for the duration of the crisis'. On 8 September, however, a UUUC meeting rejected Craig's initiative by 37 votes to one. Thus, the first significant figure within the UUUC to advocate a compromise with the SDLP found his political influence severely damaged, and was forced to resign as leader of the Vanguard Convention group. This split the party, with Ernest Baird forming the United Ulster Unionist Movement (UUUM). Ian Paisley and the DUP were instinctively hostile to the proposal and within the UUP both Powell and Molyneaux weighed in heavily against Craig, arguing that the British government might enlarge on a deal with the SDLP, that co-operation between Unionists would unravel and that the UUP would be most vulnerable in the election that would have to follow. Harry West's cautious support for continuing negotiations was pushed aside (Patterson and Kaufmann, 2007: 177–81). The coalition formed to oppose Sunningdale restricted the manoeuvrability of its component parties and made it highly unlikely that Unionists would accept a compromise which offered little prospect of peace so soon after Faulkner's humiliation and defeat. Votes were to be had in rejecting any settlement with the SDLP, as was clear in the final eclipse of Craig at the 1979 General Election when he lost to the DUP's Peter Robinson.

After the inter-party meetings failed to obtain agreement, each party tabled proposals. The dominance of the UUUC meant that the final report sent to Rees was based on its manifesto. It stated that the system of government should be the same as in Westminster. The UUUC argued that

Sunningdale was a rejection of the principles of democracy. The exclusion of Nationalists was made explicit in an argument that went further than the UUUC Convention manifesto: 'no country ought to be forced to have in its Cabinet any person whose political philosophy and attitudes have revealed his opposition to the very existence of the State' (HMSO, 1975). As before, the SDLP was rejected by the UUUC not because of a purist notion of democratic principles but because of its nationalism.

This was unacceptable to the British government. In mid-November Rees began talks with the Convention parties. Afterwards he reported that the UUUC claimed to accept Westminster sovereignty but wanted it limited so that devolution could not be abolished, as in 1972 (TNA, CJ4/1440, Burns to Janes, 8 October 1976). A devolved government in which Unionists would be effectively guaranteed control, supported financially and morally by the British government and with little capacity for the latter to influence how it governed, was clearly unrealistic. The Labour government responded by recalling the Convention, with the promise of restoring devolution if there was genuine agreement between both sides. It went some way to accept Unionist fears of all-Ireland institutions by acknowledging that arrangements like the Council of Ireland should not be imposed but develop naturally. Most importantly, the government said the UUUC's proposals did not have the broad support required (HMSO, 1976). The reconvened Convention made no progress. At the UUUC–SDLP meeting on 12 February Harry West gave three 'overriding conditions' for the talks: no negotiation on all-Ireland institutions, no negotiation on power sharing, and a refusal to serve in government with the SDLP. The two groups continued to clash and the SDLP walked out, telling the UUUC it would be willing to talk again when the latter accepted Rees's instructions (PRONI, CONV/1/3, UUUC–SDLP meeting, 12 February 1976). When the Convention returned to plenary debate the UUUC passed a set of motions restating its position. In response Rees abruptly announced the end of the Convention on 4 March (PRONI, CONV/1/3, Chairman's phone conversation with Cooper, 4 March 1976).

The breakup of the UUUC: resisting direct rule

The rejection of the UUUC's proposals marked the Labour government's public commitment to continuing direct rule until Unionism was willing to compromise with the SDLP. Devolution would not be restored except under conditions acceptable to a portion of the Nationalist community. Following a period of unity in opposing power sharing, tensions emerged within the UUUC on how to respond to the British government's rejection of majority rule. After the Convention the UUUC formed a new organisation to resist direct rule, the United Unionist Action Council (UUAC). In addition to the political parties it also included the UWC and all major loyalist paramilitary groups. Uncomfortable with Ernest Baird's violent rhetoric, however, the UUP decided to dissociate itself from the UUAC, seeking instead to pursue the same objectives by methods that Westminster would deem more responsible (Patterson and Kaufmann, 2007: 185–6). Secret talks took place between the UUP and SDLP. Initially, the UUUC approved but in June Ian Paisley leaked news of the talks and accused the Ulster Unionists of double-dealing. The talks were broken off in June, resumed later in the summer, and then came to an end in September with neither side having deviated from its stance on power sharing (TNA, CJ4/1440, Burns to Janes, 8 October 1976). When Roy Mason succeeded Rees as Northern Ireland Secretary in September 1976 the Unionists hoped he would be more sympathetic than his predecessor. Harry West wrote an open letter to the Prime Minister James Callaghan asking him to implement the Convention proposals. Northern Ireland Office officials rejected his claim that 'politicians who dismissed our proposals out of hand in the heat of Convention debate have been able to consider all the implications more calmly' (TNA, PREM 16/1342, West to Callaghan, 15 September 1976; TNA PREM 16/1342, Stewart to Meadway, 17 September 1976). Mason stuck to the principle that both Unionists and nationalists would have to come to an agreement and recognised that there was 'no sign of a meaningful consensus' (TNA, PREM 16/1342, Mason to Callaghan, 1 October 1976).

The other parties within the UUUC returned to the hope of coercing the British government into carrying out their wishes through unconstitutional methods. In April 1977 the UUAC organised a demonstration in support of five members of the Ulster Service Corps, a small paramilitary organisation, charged with mounting an illegal roadblock. The DUP, Ernest Baird's UUUM, the UWC and all major loyalist paramilitary groups sought to use the UUAC as a vehicle for another general strike. Ian Paisley 'called for the expenditure of "blood, sweat and tears" in a campaign which would restore Stormont, return control of security policy to local hands, and lead to the extermination of the IRA' (*Irish Times* 25 April 1977; TNA, CJ4/1566, Elliott to Neilson, 25 April 1977). The declared objective of the strike was to force the British government into implementing majority rule. Having already distanced themselves from the UUAC, the Ulster Unionists refused to support a strike. Harry West was joined by Bill Craig in a statement which condemned 'any loyalist action which might embarrass the security forces' (TNA, CJ4/1566, Elliott to Neilson, 25 April 1977).

The gulf between Ian Paisley's conception of Britishness and that of politicians from Great Britain is illustrated well in his angry public exchanges with

Roy Mason at the start of the strike. Mason warned Paisley that he was 'playing the IRA game' and had no support in Parliament (TNA, CJ4/1567 Mason to Paisley, 3 May 1977). He received an abusive reply: 'when I think of the blood of fellow Ulstermen and women, for which you and successive British governments and parliaments are responsible, I care very little about the opinion of "all parties" in the House'. Paisley attacked 'the drunkenness, lewdness, immorality and filthy language' of British politicians, declaring that 'Ulster Protestants are not interested in gaining the goodwill of such reprobates'. Mason wanted 'to crush the Protestant majority, destroy Protestant liberty, foist republicans into the government of Northern Ireland, and eventually bring Ulster into a united Ireland'. The Labour government 'had supported the IRA "war" for years' (TNA, CJ4/1567, Paisley to Mason, 3 May 1977). Such arguments served only to further enhance the mutual alienation between Great Britain and Northern Ireland. While embracing coercion in order to remove a devolved institution had been successful three years earlier, the 1977 strike proved the difficulties of using it to construct one. The UUAC strike was a close-run affair, with the British unable to overcome many of the logistical difficulties as before, but it did not have the support of Unionist opinion and did nothing to convince Labour ministers that a return to majority rule might be in the British government's interest. Paisley sought to portray a small number of concessions on security policy as a victory when the strike was called off, but it instead marked the failure of unconstitutional action and the end of the UUUC (Aveyard, 2014).

The integrationist argument

After the breakup of the coalition Unionist politics can be characterised as a two-horse race between the UUP and the DUP. The elements of Vanguard which sided with Craig during the Convention drifted back into the UUP while Baird and his supporters suffered after the failure of the 1977 strike. The politics of the DUP remained static, rejectionist and entirely at odds with Westminster politics. Roy Mason considered the party 'as dogmatic and sectarian as ever and unwilling to contribute in any constructive sense' (TNA, PREM 16/1344, Mason to Callaghan, 31 May 1977). Within the UUP, however, the idea of administrative devolution developed out of Enoch Powell's integrationism. His insistence that devolution would be restored only with Nationalist involvement was naturally persuasive after the British government's rejection of the Convention proposals. Reforming direct rule might therefore provide an opportunity for Unionists to develop a better relationship with Westminster while securing greater involvement in administering the region. In December 1976 James Molyneaux advocated an increase in Northern Ireland's Westminster MPs and the granting of 'administrative devolution'. He questioned the value of a devolved legislature, arguing that the Northern Ireland government had been 'effectively bound by legislation passed in the United Kingdom'. Molyneaux claimed that the 'intolerable' aspect of direct rule was 'the lack of control over the application and execution of the law', rather than the law itself. Thus, the British government should devolve administrative responsibilities instead (*House of Commons Debates* (Hansard), 13 December 1976, Vol. 922, Col. 1042–5).

The response to Molyneaux's proposals from within his own party illustrates that, while Unionism was not so inflexible as to be incapable of producing new ideas, it continued to hanker after majority rule in spite of Westminster's repeated rejections. Harry West, still leader of the UUP, held out for the implementation of the Convention report, rejecting 'a purely administrative body masquerading as an Ulster government'. Molyneaux was forced to modify his position, claiming that he had been misunderstood and was only advocating a new tier of local government rather than a substitute for devolution (*News Letter* 25 January 1977; *Irish Times* 25 January 1977). He admitted to NIO officials that he avoided a direct confrontation with West in the UUP executive to avoid splitting the party (TNA, CJ4/1866, Ramsay to Mason, 3 February 1977).

Even if the UUP had been united in support of Molyneaux's proposals, the British government would have rejected them. The conditions might have seemed favourable to Molyneaux; Labour's position as a minority government rendered it open to dealings on the increase of NI representation at Westminster, and the Conservative spokesman Airey Neave spoke favourably of upper-tier local government (Bew, 2007: 525). Nevertheless, devolution with Nationalist participation remained the British government's objective. In June 1977 Mason reported to Callaghan that the SDLP saw a new tier of local government as a step towards integration and 'a device to secure the re-establishment of Protestant dominance' (TNA, PREM 16/1344, Mason to Callaghan, 22 June 1977). Meeting Molyneaux and Powell with Callaghan at the end of the year, the Northern Ireland Secretary argued that the Unionists should pursue a system 'acceptable to all parts of the community'. Powell remarked that they 'were not fool enough to accept a position where the majority and the minority were treated as being of equal weight' (TNA, PREM 16/1721, Meeting between Callaghan, Molyneaux and Powell, 21 December 1977). Powell's objections neatly show that even with its internal divisions, Unionism stuck to a simple principle after Sunningdale: Nationalists should not be allowed to participate in government. This principle remained with the passing of the Labour government and the arrival of Margaret Thatcher in Downing Street.

Conclusion

The Unionist response to Sunningdale and its perception of the agreement after the collapse of the Northern Ireland Executive were tied up entirely with a sense of loss and alienation from Westminster after March 1972. The imposition of direct rule and attempts to impose power sharing in Northern Ireland were deeply resented not merely by politicians but by the wider Unionist population as well. Combined with the tremendous violence of the period, this meant that a willingness to compromise marked individuals out for electoral punishment, bringing to an end the political careers of Brian Faulkner and Bill Craig. Most Unionists' conception of democratic legitimacy could not be reconciled with a system that was not majoritarian. Such a conception naturally excluded from power any political grouping with aspirations towards Irish unity. Craig's initiative in the Convention illustrates how this exclusion extended even to temporary, voluntary coalition.

By refusing to share power, Unionists forced the Labour government and its Conservative successor to accept the continuation of direct rule. The limits of unconstitutional action were made clear in 1977, when it was proved that, while Unionists had the power to reject one constitutional settlement, they could not construct another without outside support. Afterwards, the DUP and UUP offered the Unionist electorate a choice between a fiery, worthless rhetoric that only enhanced the contempt for Ulster Unionism in Great Britain and a more respectable but ultimately weak approach which could do little to sway the British government from its commitment to a settlement involving both traditions. The section of the UUP which became comfortable with direct rule as the conflict entered its second decade misunderstood its true character. The impulses behind Sunningdale still found their way into the administration of Northern Ireland. They did so in drastically modified forms but ones which offered little hope of integration. An all-Ireland dimension was at the heart of the next major constitutional development. As Paul Bew has rightly argued, the Anglo-Irish Agreement of 1985 was 'in effect, merely a rather significant "green" appendage to the direct-rule machine' (Bew, 2007: 509). Such modifications of the machinery were made to boost moderate Nationalism. Rejectionist Unionism succeeded in preventing power sharing for over two decades, but ultimately it failed in its attempts to keep Irish Nationalist voices out of the governance of Northern Ireland. Over time it was forced to accept the will of Westminster.

8

Stan Orme and the road to 'Industrial Democracy': British attempts at the politicisation of working-class Protestants in Northern Ireland, 1973–75

Tony Craig

In the months immediately following the collapse of the Sunningdale Agreement it was very much apparent that power sharing as a potential political solution to the problems of Northern Ireland would not work. Whether because of the obvious opposition from its numerous vocal opponents or because of its failure to include those actually conducting the conflict in Northern Ireland, it can be logically stated that consociational democracy in the way it had been foreseen in the Sunningdale Communiqué was not an immediate legacy of that agreement's failure. Arguably the power-sharing Executive, supported by an assembly elected on 28 June 1973, did not represent the people of Northern Ireland deeply enough to lead, and have them follow. There was no consensus for power sharing and deep opposition within the Unionist community towards the Council of Ireland. But power sharing was not the only option available at the time and it was clear that, if consociationalism were to work in future, it would need to operate in an environment where a much broader consensus with regard to how politics was constituted had been achieved. There is no doubt that the strength of feeling aroused by the Ulster Workers' Council (UWC) against Sunningdale came as a surprise, and not simply to the British and Irish governments but to Northern Ireland's mainstream political parties too. But it was also clear that any future political solution would not work unless at least some of those who organised and participated in the UWC strike were brought into mainstream party politics.

As Minister of State in Northern Ireland 1974–76, Stanley Orme MP (1923–2005) worked at the heart of British government policies that attempted to ameliorate and politicise the membership of a number of those loyalist groups that had successfully brought down the power-sharing Executive in 1974. Whilst Orme had first followed, and then extended, the Secretary of State Merlyn Rees's policy of often secret engagement with those outside the mainstream of Northern Ireland politics; a policy that successfully brought about the Provisional Irish Republican Army (PIRA)'s 1975 ceasefire, but which failed to bring the Ulster Volunteer Force (UVF) into electoral politics with the dismal performance of the Volunteer Political Party in the 1974 general elections. Orme's alternative new approach, outlined in the 1975 pamphlet 'Industrial Democracy' (HMSO, 1975) encouraged workers' participation in the newly nationalised Harland and Wolff shipyard and was an indirect – though purposeful – attempt to politicise the Protestant working classes of Belfast.

With industrial democracy Orme was attempting to redirect the support of Belfast's shipyard workers away from both the existing militant groups that at this time included the Ulster Defence Association (UDA), UVF and Ulster Vanguard, as well as the more mainstream Unionist political parties. Orme's view was that skilled industrial workers belonged within the fold of progressive social democracy and that the extension of government-backed syndicalist activity in the shipyard would empower the workers and help shift Northern Ireland as a whole from sectarian models of political activity to a class-based system similar to the rest of the UK. Though Northern Ireland already had a Labour Party, by the early 1970s this group was riven with division with elements supporting power sharing in 1974 and with others supporting the UWC strike. For Orme something radical and new was needed, 'Industrial Democracy' was the 'Last Chance for Northern Ireland' ('The Last Chance for Northern Ireland?' Draft Speech [undated] c. 17–23 November 1972, Orme 1/3, LSE) and a potential solution to the province's ills. Industrial Democracy could widen representation in Northern Ireland to the point that the constitutional problems could be resolved by those that more fairly represented the diversity of opinion in Northern Ireland, creating the potential for the consensus so badly lacking in 1973 and 1974 to be established. Orme believed that 'If the working-class people of Northern Ireland can be convinced that, whatever their religious denominations, they have economic interests in common, they will be able to approach the constitutional problem ... with open minds' (Ibid.). Using a combination of Orme's official and private papers, this chapter seeks to explore and critique Orme's motivation, his policy and its effect.

As a junior minister, Orme worked closely with the Secretary of State Merlyn Rees, the Prime Minister Harold Wilson and the Northern Ireland Office (NIO)'s Permanent Under Secretary Frank Cooper. While his official role encompassed economic development and industrial relations he also made time to convene private talks held at the NIO's offices at Laneside. Orme's background as a Salford engineering works shop steward is important to explaining how his approach and emphasis differed from others in the Cabinet and in the NIO. Whereas Rees and Cooper held views that echoed with what we would now call *consensus democracy*, expanding participation to those who feel they have been left out of private talks and briefings, Orme was in favour of a more radical departure, expanding consensus through Industrial Democracy and through the trade unions.

Orme's approach arguably stemmed from a number of both short- and long-term influences and included his numerous talks with loyalists at Laneside throughout 1974 and the friendship he developed with the UWC chairman Glen Barr at this time. Barr, the chief organiser of the 1974 UWC and local shop steward of Orme's own union (Amalgamated Engineering Union, AEU) held the junior minister in high regard despite their sometimes opposing political views. Barr remembers, 'Stan Orme and me communicated quite a bit ... Stan and I got on very well' (Author interview, 2010). However Orme's burgeoning relationship with Protestant trade Unionists in Northern Ireland was overshadowed by his longer-term understanding of the historic growth of the Labour Party and British democracy as well as his own experience in Salford. These ideas made him more amenable than others to accepting the need for the deepening of Northern Ireland's democracy – by whatever available means – following the collapse of Sunningdale.

Laneside as 'mainstreaming'

Between 1971 and 1976 British government officials based in offices and accommodation on the shores of Belfast Lough known as 'Laneside' discreetly conducted dialogue with the widest possible variety of people in Northern Ireland. While it is clear that Laneside conducted talks with groups ranging from the Catholic Church to the Democratic Unionist Party, it is most infamously known for the various talks organised from there between its officials and the PIRA (Taylor, 1997; Moloney, 2002; Bew et al., 2009). Laneside's work, however, also brought it into very close contact with Loyalist paramilitaries and their representatives in this era, although British involvement in Loyalist politics is entirely ignored by all three of the (otherwise excellent) main academic studies into the nature of loyalism (Nelson 1984; Bruce 1994; Spencer 2008). Papers released by both the Northern Ireland Office and the Foreign and Commonwealth Office clearly demonstrate the importance attached to talking with Loyalists following Labour's re-election in March 1974. Officials met with representatives of the Loyalist Ulster Defence Association (UDA) eleven times (The National Archives of the United Kingdom (TNA), FCO 87/342, FCO 87/343 and FCO 87/344) and Ken Gibson of the UVF on seven occasions from April to December 1974 (TNA, FCO 87/341 and FCO 87/342). Stan Orme as junior minister often led these NIO talks with Loyalists, as well as other groups linked with Loyalist paramilitaries and thus became personally familiar with many of those who led the UWC strike that year. These talks at Laneside after Labour returned to power in 1974, took on a quite different air from previous initiatives undertaken by the Conservative government when it had opened up backchannels with Republicans in 1972. Sinn Féin's Seamus Loughran noted at meeting in July 1974 how the attitudes of the British officials he met had changed from two years before when they had 'looked down on me as if I was something that had crawled out of a bog' (TNA, FCO 87/342).

Dean Pruitt's work on negotiation and the use of backchannel talks in conflict situations helps theoretically categorise what occurred at Laneside from Orme's perspective. For Pruitt (2006: 371–94) there are five general and overlapping strategies available for dealing with terrorist groups and they are:

- capitulation
- combat
- isolation/marginalisation
- mainstreaming
- negotiation.

Whilst Pruitt himself never talks of victory or defeat in his work (indeed such situations rarely arise in the types of ethno-national conflicts he concerns himself with), the normative aim of his research is obviously towards the sustainable and peaceful resolution of all conflicts. Indeed Pruitt criticises the self-defeating tactics used in combating terrorist groups. He illustrates this well by citing Bruce Hoffman's (1998: 52) analysis of the Irgun's fight to end British rule of Palestine:

> [Menachem Begin] banked on the fact that the massive disruptions caused to daily life and commerce by the harsh and repressive countermeasures that the British were forced to take would further alienate the community from the government, thwart its efforts to obtain the community's cooperation against the terrorists, and create in the minds of the Jews an image of the army and the police as oppressors rather than protectors.

For Pruitt, state actors like Orme are better off marginalising, mainstreaming and negotiating; to end conflict by granting concessions to supporters in an effort to undermine extremist terrorist groups, to lure those groups into normal politics, and eventually to negotiate a settlement (through the use of backchannels at first, if necessary).

Though what Pruitt demonstrates would have sounded familiar to Stan Orme, he would not have expressed the sentiment in quite the same way. Orme's view was far more closely linked to contemporary historical axioms within the British left about how Britain had avoided violent revolutions in the eighteenth and nineteenth centuries. This narrative was essential to the Labour Party's origin myth and, though typified in E.P. Thompson's *The Making of the English Working Class,* it was perhaps exampled best in Hugh Gaitskell's pamphlet on Chartism, in the works of G.D.H. Cole (a tutor of both Gaitskell and Harold Wilson at Oxford) and by Max Beer. Asa Briggs noted that the postwar labour movement considered itself 'part of this "great march" across time' (1998: 5). And, although this debate continues, it remains widely asserted today that it was the gradual expansion of representative politics that derailed revolutionary fervour in Britain (Irish migrants held key roles among the Chartists of course, as they did in the emergent Labour Party). From this origin, we can see the generation of Labour MPs then in power as proponents of an aspirational form of Guild Socialism, where democracy was not limited to the political sphere alone and where 'workers in the guilds, should have substantive decision making authority and power over collectively owned wealth' (Lamb, 2010: 586–7). Through this method, democracy could be deepened so as to transcend national politics and create new opportunities for social self-expression. In Britain, these ideas were promoted by the likes of Ken Coates, Tony Benn and the Institute for Workers Control. But in Northern Ireland, no one was able to challenge the zero-sum sectarian divide that had created monolithic Unionism (with its unelectable Loyalist fringe) and monolithic Nationalism (with the IRA lurking in the wings). Under these conditions power sharing had no hope of being successful, but if the groundwork could be done by deepening democracy, through encouraging more accurate representation of, among others, the Protestant working class, then perhaps a new political consensus could be one day reached.

It was hoped this historical process of 'mainstreaming' would identify those willing to offer compromise and ideas that did not include violent revolution. It rewarded those who could lead their constituencies with other benefits in the form of status, patronage and political power. In this sense, this system of post-feudal patronage was the foundation stone of British democracy, the carrot waved to lead the revolutionists away from violence whether they were the Anti-Corn-Law League, the TUC, the Labour Party, the Suffragettes or the Communist Party of Great Britain. Each of these radical groups was subject to a process of 'mainstreaming' whereby their original aims were cut back, room made for their leaders at the top table of British politics, their victory declared and their radical fringes cast into obscurity without clamour.

Reading the papers relating to Laneside's loyalist talks through this lens one can see that with the election of Labour's minority government Stan Orme joined the Permanent Under Secretary, Sir Frank Cooper, and set about engaging Loyalist paramilitary groups in this manner. Within weeks of taking office for example, Merlyn Rees de-proscribed the UVF along with Sinn Féin and opened channels of communication with both these groups through Laneside. Contacts with the UDA were established through broader umbrella organisations from which the paramilitaries were soon siphoned off (TNA, CJ 4/404). Merlyn Rees later noted that he had also been aware that there were elements of the UVF and he wanted to encourage these, if possible (1985: 49).

By May 1974, of course, it was clear the Unionists who had rejected power sharing had won out. The UWC strike successfully brought down the Northern Ireland Executive, those whom Wilson had described as 'spongers on British democracy' (25 May 1974) had demonstrated their pivotal power and authority on the streets of Belfast and elsewhere. But Loyalist paramilitary groups like the UVF remained unelectable, demonstrated in the October 1974 General Election when the UVF ran Ken Gibson on a Volunteer Political Party ticket but polled just 2,690 votes in West Belfast.

Industrial Democracy/Guild Socialism: widening political representation

The failure of power sharing and the collapse of the Sunningdale Agreement did not result in a change of personnel, or even strategy, at the Northern Ireland Office. Laneside remained open long after the UWC strike had succeeded and the goal of mainstreaming Northern Ireland's unrepresented fringes was maintained. In response to the strike the NIO instituted two initiatives designed to get the larger political parties back on track. The Gardiner Report, published early in 1975, recommended the ending of internment without trial and the 'criminalisation' of terrorism offences which would eventually lead to the ending of Special Category Status for paramilitaries, and provided a foundation for the later policy of 'Ulsterisation' or Police Primacy and the expansion of juryless 'Diplock' courts for terrorism offences. The second important initiative was the very public 'back-to-the-drawing-board' exercise that was the Constitutional Convention: a series of talks between the main political parties that was of course destined to collapse like its predecessor unless something could be done to secure stability on the streets and in the countryside. The Convention rather predictably talked itself in circles until its acrimonious collapse in March 1976.

Discussed elsewhere is a third, secret initiative from Laneside officials that helped bring about the IRA's 1975 'truce' (Craig, 2014: 307–19). This initiative included direct talks with Sinn Féin at the home of the intermediary businessman Brendan Duddy as well as indirect contacts between Sinn Féin and the Security Forces through government incident centres staffed by the Northern Ireland Civil Service (Ibid.: 312–13).

Industrial Democracy was a small but significant part of this broader strategy of mainstreaming being practised at Laneside. With Harland and Wolff, Orme and his civil servants could take advantage of the collapsing profits of the shipyard, and the works' high rate of trade union membership to radically alter the way that working-class Protestants in East Belfast were represented in democratic politics. Harland and Wolff had been struggling for a decade and in 1973 was hit by a series of unpredicted problems. By 1975, the oil crisis had damaged its order books, industrial unrest in Britain affected its supply of raw materials and the UWC strike had damaged production. Thus, the work of the shipyard had fallen behind schedule and as a result its ships were being produced at significant losses. Rampant inflation, fixed-price contracts used to gain orders from fierce global competitors and fines imposed for late delivery compounded these losses further (Department of Commerce Northern Ireland, 'Harland and Wolff Ltd' [Information document made available to Members of both Houses of Parliament], 15 September 1975; 6–7, in Orme 1/2).

The government was warned in June 1974 by Harland and Wolff's management of its insolvency crisis and responded with a promise of significant new investment tied to a restructure of the company's board in which the NIO would take an executive position and the existing chairman would be forced to resign (McCluskie, 2013: 98).

Though nationalisation may have left the chairman 'stunned' (Ibid.), the figures put to Parliament by the Northern Ireland Department of Commerce, made Harland and Wolff's woeful financial position plainly clear. The yard had not posted a profit or paid a dividend since 1964 (Orme, *House of Commons Debates* (Hansard), 1 August 1975, Vol. 896, Col. 2475). And this despite government subsidies, of one form or another, amounting to £79.3 million between 1966 and 1973 (Department of Commerce Northern Ireland, 'Harland and Wolff Ltd', 15 September 1975: 13). The government's auditors began their work in July 1974 and reported that despite healthy order books of £270 million the yard would continue to run at a loss of a further £41 million between 1975 and 1978 (Orme, *House of Commons Debates* (Hansard), 1 August 1975, Vol. 896, Col. 2475).

Although Harland and Wolff directly employed over ten thousand people in 1974, as Northern Ireland's largest company, its prospects were long considered by successive governments as a barometer for the province's economic confidence, and its demise would have an unfathomable impact on the economic performance of the region (Ó Murchú, 2005: 860). What is rarely stated is that, while Harland and Wolff was making a loss, overall manufacturing in Northern Ireland (some of which was itself reliant on Harland and Wolff contracts) was actually performing quite well in the early 1970s despite the shock of the initial years of the Troubles. Manufacturing output for instance continued to grow from 1968 until 1973 before it stalled and began to fall in line with the wider recession in the Western world.

In March 1975, with the reports from the auditors and the prospects of private-sector investment in the yard looking gloomy for the foreseeable future, the NIO announced a package that would save the yard but at the same time transform the way it was run. The plan, proposed and fronted by Stan Orme and backed by a further £60 million investment, would effectively nationalise Harland and Wolff and introduce worker participation in its management. This scheme would create the first large-scale example of Industrial Democracy in the UK. The £60 million was fêted as a last chance for the yard to return to profitability, and for this to occur, it was thought, greater participation of the workforce in strategic decisions would be needed. Along with the announcement a pamphlet was published, written largely by Orme, making Harland and Wolff a test bed for this policy in the rest of the UK (and thereby also getting around the thorny issue of the yard *not* being included in the wider nationalisation of the rest of the UK's shipbuilding industry). Orme was free to sell his idea that the yard would belong to the 'people of Northern Ireland' despite opposition from the recently elected South Down MP Enoch Powell about who it really belonged to (*House of Commons Debates* (Hansard), 1 August 1975, Vol. 896, Col. 2483).

The idea of nationalisation was broadly welcomed by the press in Northern Ireland and made the front pages of all the local newspapers. The prospect of workers' participation was initially met with enthusiasm too by the editors even if *some* of the workers held firmly to a 'couldn't care less attitude' (*News Letter* 27 March 1975). So, too, the vast majority of local politicians welcomed the news though the Northern Ireland Labour Party (NILP) candidate and Harland and Wolff shop steward Sandy Scott described how some of the workers felt that the takeover 'might be another move to pave the way for British withdrawal' (*Irish News* 27 March 1975).

'Bigots': lacklustre reception in Britain

In Britain, though not front-page news, the announcement was covered in a number of national newspapers (Orme 1/2, LSE) though the emphasis here was on the proposed experiment in Industrial Democracy, rather than on the fortunes of the yard itself. But only one of these stories, carefully archived by Orme himself and appearing in the *Salford City Reporter*, noted the Junior Minister's personal interest in the issue and his background in a Trafford Park engineering works. The headline said it all, 'It's a Dream Come True for a Former Shop Steward' (*Salford City Reporter* 11 April 1975).

The plan itself was for a negotiated restructure and began almost immediately with the appointment of a new managing director at the yard, Ronald Punt, whose interview was chaired by Orme and included two trade unionists (one of whom was the aforementioned Sandy Scott). The scheme would be implemented gradually and by agreement with the recognised trade unions as Orme's pamphlet stipulated no overriding structure of management as such but left this up to the workers and management to decide.

Other than the fact that this was being implemented in Northern Ireland's working-class Protestant community (whose members Tony Benn had described privately as 'bigots' in 1966) (Ramsay, 2009: 18), the proposals looked on the surface to have been inspired by the Benn–Foot strategy being promoted at the time as part of the 'Alternative Economic Strategy' proposals of June 1975. Industrial Democracy as a programme had been approved without the need for a card vote at the Labour's 1973 annual conference and trade union leaders like Hugh Scanlon of the AEU and Jack Jones of the TGWU meant that the policy 'was firmly on the Left's agenda' at this time (Callaghan, 1990: 215). In Britain, industrial democracy had other supporters too, the Institute for Workers Control run by Ken Fleet and the Industrial Participation Association run by D. Wallace Bell. Both had an interest in promoting workers' control and had been on the lookout for some time for failing British companies that the government could nationalise and implement these reforms on. The IWC's 1975 conference, hosted at Sheffield University, included Benn – recently demoted from Secretary of State for

Industry – and two other Labour MPs, Joan Maynard and Audrey Wise, among its speakers. Also on the schedule was a talk from a Portuguese trade union delegation (the textile workers' union Mercellino Abrantes) though when Orme proffered a talk about his grand Northern Ireland example, the Institute could not find space 'for other platform speakers over and above those already invited' (Orme 1/2, LSE).

The fact that Northern Ireland was not on the agenda of Labour's radical left in the later 1970s was only one of a number of reasons why Industrial Democracy failed to establish itself as a permanent feature in the shipyard. Soon Britain's liberal left would have more comfortable visions of the policy's implementation at Triumph in Meriden, the Scottish Daily News in Glasgow, and KME in Kirkby. Orme's plan for Harland and Wolff, and the yard's reputation as a bastion of working-class Loyalism, made it an unwelcome addition to the experiment in Britain. But the plan was doubly doomed: the facts that moves had already been made to move the Labour Party back to the centre and Benn had been demoted from the Department of Industry to the Department of Energy ostensibly because of his opposition to EEC membership meant that 'the government was allowing workers' co-operatives to sink' (Callaghan, 1990: 220). The promised Bullock Report of 1977 killed the project in the Commons when it was published along with a 25-page minority report written by all three members of the inquiry team who represented business, management and commercial interests. The rather one-sided report published by the other members of the inquiry (academics and trade unionists) was widely considered a non-starter and thus 'no legislation on industrial democracy ever appeared' (Ibid.).

Harland and Wolff's emptying order books, of course, did not help either and the stipulations by the government – that, as the main shareholder, it would not approve orders unless buyers satisfied its requirements with regard to shipbuilding mortgages (McCluskie, 2013: 98) so as to ensure the projects taken on were profitable (Orme, *House of Commons Debates* (Hansard), 1 August 1975, Vol. 896, Col. 2479) – undermined the newly forming *régiment* in Harland and Wolff before it even got started. 'If the company can't do this it will be time for the government to call a halt and to permit the run down and even closure of the business' (Ibid.: Col. 2480), Orme informed the Commons. The uncertainty such statements caused in the minds of those inquiring about the construction of new vessels, along with the vetting process now required simply to place an order, meant that 'positive inquiries failed to develop into firm orders' (McCluskie, 2013: 98) or, in other words, 'No ships were ordered at all in 1975 and 1976' (Bardon, 2005: 722).

If there was a window of opportunity, it was closing fast. The long and convoluted collapse of the IRA's supposed 1975 ceasefire led to a renewed emphasis on security by the late autumn of 1975. The deployment of the SAS to South Armagh in an attempt to stem the sectarian cycle of killing there arguably marked the end of this period of engagement that a truce – in public at least – had allowed scope for. In March 1976 Harold Wilson was replaced as Prime Minister by Jim Callaghan, a change in focus meant that by June Stan Orme was back in Britain, promoted to Secretary of State for Social Security, and Laneside was closed. Merlyn Rees was rotated out in September 1976, and promoted for his efforts to Home Secretary. Rees was replaced by Roy Mason, a no-nonsense former coalminer, who would actively pursue the security agenda of the Gardiner Report, whilst closing off the other routes that had been pursued by Rees and Orme, as well as Whitelaw and others before them (Craig, 2012: 97–117). Mason told the Labour Party conference in 1976 that 'Ulster had had enough of initiatives, White Papers and legislation for the time being and needed to be governed firmly and fairly' (*Daily Telegraph* 18 April 2004).

Thus the short experiment in Industrial Democracy can be said to have ended by the winter of 1976–77. A Northern Ireland government report distributed on 9 December stated that, while an agreement had been reached on the establishment of a Trade Union Resource Centre and participatory structures, 'difficulties' had emerged regarding the procedures for the election of worker directors. Although it is unclear whether these difficulties stemmed from disagreement among the twelve recognised trade unions or within management, without Orme no one would intervene to save the idea. Similarly with the Bullock Report: when its minority report categorically stated that 'those who work in industry are not ready for the radical changes' and that 'In the trade union movement itself there is abundant evidence of conflicting thinking on this subject' (Bullock Report, 1977: 170), no one was left in any senior position of the Labour government prepared to take on and win a debate on this issue.

Demise of mainstreaming

Despite the clear failure of Industrial Democracy's implementation both in Harland and Wolff and more generally, Orme's policy was not without its successes. In the case of the 1977 UWC strike, Harland and Wolff workers were evident by their absence from the protests. Crucial to this was the tireless work of Sandy Scott.

Alex (Sandy) Scott had been politically active in East Belfast as a Harland and Wolff shop steward for some years. In August 1969 he led a token stoppage at the yard in opposition to sectarianism. Scott was an active member of the NILP and was part of the delegation to first suggest Laneside contacts with the paramilitary UVF (TNA, FCO 87/341). But by 1975 Scott was prepared to go further and actually attended talks with Merlyn Rees at Stormont Castle as part of the Ulster Loyalist Central Co-ordinating Committee that included the UDA's Andy Tyrie, the founder of the Red Hand Commando John McKeague, and the UVF's Ken Gibson (TNA, FCO 87/341). Elected by a 78 per cent 'ballot of all the workers' (Orme, *House of Commons Debates* (Hansard), 1 August 1975, Vol. 896, Col. 2477), Scott played a crucial role as one of the two trade unionists involved in the appointment of Harland and Wolff's new managing director (an interview chaired by Orme that spring). By May, Scott was running for the Constitutional Convention on an NILP ticket (though as he was included on the same ballot as the leader David Bleakley in East Belfast he achieved only 530 votes). By 1977 Scott was openly siding with the government and against the UWC at the shipyard, explaining to an Associated Press journalist that 'the economy is in bad shape, the men realised a strike could finish it and cost them their jobs' (*The Evening News* 9 May 1977; *The Gadsden Times* 10 May 1977). Years later, recollecting his early months as Junior Minister, Orme stated that 'People like Sandy Scott in the shipyard ... had been great crusaders for peace' (Orme quoted in *British Policy in Northern Ireland 1970–1974, Kings College London, 11 February 1993*: 38). Scott's effective opposition to the UWC call to arms in 1977, where he had failed in 1974, demonstrated that the Harland and Wolff workers could be convinced to back their jobs over the demands of the UWC. He demonstrated that Loyalist paramilitarism in East Belfast could be broken by the promise of responsibility and the widening of participation in decision-making, even if Orme's hopes of Industrial Democracy had not been fully achieved there.

Conclusion

Power sharing between the mainstream Unionist and Nationalist parties failed to deliver stability in Northern Ireland in 1974 because the extremists on both sides who were left outside the conference room opposed it. Working-class Protestants in Belfast and elsewhere were not embedded deeply enough into the political system of Northern Ireland to have taken part in the Sunningdale talks and acted instead as spoilers of the agreement. Industrial Democracy – like consociationalism – sought compromise and consensus and was one of a number of attempts made by Merlyn Rees, his Junior Minister Stan Orme and their staff comprising diplomats and intelligence officers at Laneside to widen democratic engagement to as many viewpoints as possible. Industrial Democracy was chosen for Harland and Wolff partly because the workers represented those who had so keenly brought down Sunningdale.

The aim of the initiative was to give those workers' representatives the tools and experience not only to negotiate with their management but to represent their own views on wider issues and to partake fully in the democratic process for themselves. The initiative at Harland and Wolff ran in parallel with a separately managed initiative established between the Provisional Republican Movement that resulted in that group's 1975 ceasefire (Craig, 2014: 307–19). Whilst the effects of both these initiatives are difficult to see, they offer not only a glimpse of a perhaps more inclusive road-not-travelled in Northern Ireland's prolonged Troubles but also evidence of a more committed and holistic approach to British security policy in Northern Ireland after Wilson's 1974 'spongers' speech than was previously assumed. The experiment in Industrial Democracy was therefore a genuine attempt to deepen Northern Ireland's democracy by encouraging a process that would enhance the ability of Harland and Wolff's workers to represent themselves. This, it was hoped, would then spill over and energise a section of Northern Ireland's Protestant working class to participate more fully and directly in the local political system than they had done before. If Sunningdale and power sharing had been rejected by the Protestant working class because their consent had not been sought, then any future agreement that included deeper consultation had the potential to win wider support and reduce the number of those intent on spoiling any deal.

9

Power sharing and the Irish dimension: the conundrum for the SDLP in Northern Ireland

Sarah Campbell

Seamus Mallon, then deputy leader of the Social Democratic and Labour Party (SDLP) famously remarked in 1998 that the Good Friday Agreement was 'Sunningdale for slow learners'. With this comment, Mallon was reinforcing a teleological narrative of the SDLP's history and contribution to nationalism in Northern Ireland: that the central tenets of the SDLP's founding philosophy – power sharing with the provision of an Irish dimension – had been vindicated. Writing in 1998, shortly after the agreement had been reached, Gerard Murray (1998: 261) also commented that

> The Good Friday Agreement reflects the SDLP impact on contemporary Northern Ireland politics and is a major vindication of Party policy. On close scrutiny it is clear that the SDLP has achieved more of its objectives from this agreement than any other Northern Ireland party. If the Good Friday Agreement becomes operational it will be an endorsement of SDLP commitments to cross-community Government and a significant Irish dimension, reflecting the existence of the Nationalist community in Northern Ireland.

Seán Farren (2010: 343) argues that 'It was an agreement for which a great price had been paid, a price that the party believed had been totally unnecessary. Indeed, in many respects, the agreement bore striking similarities to that achieved in 1973.' The failure of the Sunningdale Agreement and power sharing in 1974 has been attributed to many things, and a popular narrative in nationalist circles emphasises that it was an agreement too soon or a lost opportunity. However, this explanation does not account for the level of intra-party conflict within the SDLP on the ideas of both power sharing and the Irish dimension in the 1970s and 1980s (Campbell, 2015: 179–87). This chapter explores how both these concepts evolved within the SDLP. This evolution was directly influenced by British and Irish policy and the legacies the failure of Sunningdale had on both.

Sunningdale and the SDLP

The Sunningdale Communiqué was a key stage in the evolution of the SDLP from a party of repudiation to a party willing to participate in the Northern Ireland state. The Agreement and experience in government were a 'coming of age' moment of the party. Although the Executive lasted a mere five months, it highlighted that the party was the main voice of the minority in Northern Ireland and transformed the SDLP into a serious political party, with democratic trappings. The failure of power sharing in Northern Ireland in 1974 also had a profound and lasting legacy on the party for a number of reasons. As Ian McAllister (1977: 41–2) argues, the Sunningdale Agreement challenged democracy in Northern Ireland by questioning whether or not the SDLP had the right to be regarded as a 'legitimate opposition'. Brian Faulkner, Chief Executive in the 1974 power-sharing Executive, retrospectively questioned the legitimacy of the SDLP sharing power in Northern Ireland: 'Given the history of the SDLP over the previous years, and particularly their attitude that Northern Ireland had no right to exist, it was natural that unionists should feel strongly against SDLP participation in government' (1978: 189). The emphasis the SDLP attached to the Irish dimension as an integral part of power-sharing eroded the democratic complexion of power-sharing. McAllister (*Irish Times* 18 January 1977) suggests that the making of consent through power sharing conditional on an 'Irish dimension' was necessitated by the SDLP's politically heterogeneous support and an essential guard against Republican accusations that the party was 'Unionist'. But in Protestant eyes it had the consequence of devaluing the party's right to be regarded as a legitimate governmental partner. The legacy of Sunningdale and its failure challenged the uneasy unity of the party and there was a shift from notions of power sharing to a stronger Irish dimension by the late 1970s. This shift represented a 'greening' of the SDLP and would have implications for future party policy (see Campbell, 2015).

The central tenets of the Sunningdale Agreement were embodied within the ideology and policy of the SDLP. The party's first published document, *Towards a New Ireland*, which was submitted to the Darlington conference in September 1972 in its absence, outlined the party's thinking on various aspects of the Northern problem. The document revived the idea of a Council of Ireland, leading to stronger co-operation between Dublin and Belfast: 'The basic function of the Senate should be to plan the integration of the whole island by preparing the harmonisation of the structures, laws and services of both parts of Ireland and to agree on an acceptable constitution for a New Ireland and its relationships with Britain' (SDLP, 1972). At the same time, the party sought an immediate declaration from Britain that 'she believes it would be in the best interests of all sections of the Communities in both islands, if Ireland were to be united on terms which could be acceptable to all the people of Ireland' (1973–74, Assembly Party Report). By demanding that the British government should 'positively encourage' Irish unity, the SDLP was beginning to blur the lines between consent and, if not coercion, then at least compulsion (McLoughlin, 2010: 101–2). This was a line of argument that would reoccur in SDLP thinking throughout the 1970s and early 1980s.

The Darlington conference resulted in the Green Paper, which was a discussion document on the future of Northern Ireland. The document highlighted the slow reworking of Whitehall's attitude to the North. It now accepted the possibility of a united Ireland: 'No UK government for many years has had any wish to impede the realisation of Irish unity, if it were to come about by genuine and freely given mutual agreement and on conditions acceptable to the distinctive communities' (Green Paper, 1972: Para. 77). What London was proposing was power sharing with an Irish dimension, the first time the concepts were formally adopted and what would become the debating points of constitutional talks about the North for the next three decades. In a *Fortnight* poll conducted after the publication of the White Paper in March 1973, there was general agreement in favour of power sharing, with 58 per cent in favour or strongly in favour, and only 12 per cent against or strongly against it. The item that showed most difference between the two communities was the question of a conference with the Republic. On this issue, 70 per cent of Catholics were in favour, or strongly in favour, compared with only 16 per cent of Protestants. More than half the Protestant community (56 per cent) were opposed or strongly opposed (*Fortnight* 16 February 1973). These diametrically opposed concepts, and Unionist opposition to them, would be a recurring feature of conflict resolution in Northern Ireland, particularly throughout the 1970s and early 1980s.

The Unionist understanding of the Irish dimension, as part of the Sunningdale Agreement, was much different from how the SDLP envisaged it. The SDLP envisaged a Council of Ireland with executive and harmonising functions that would be given the freedom to evolve if members of the

Council agreed (Cmnd. 5259, Paras 110 and 112). Unionists saw the Council as a limited institution, its functions bound to the non-contentious areas of economic and social affairs. Far from being an institution with an in-built potential for development and evolution, leading *inter alia* to a politically expressible reconciliation of both Irish traditions, the Council of Ireland would have 'a clearly defined role which cannot pose any threat to the Union' (National Archives of Treland (NAI), DFA/2004/7/2599, 24 October 1973). Brian Faulkner stated in February 1973 that 'There will be no question of any Council of Ireland being open-ended. There will be no question of it dealing with constitutional matters. Its only functions will be economic and social' (Ibid.).

The Irish Fine Gael–Labour coalition government, while agreeing that the Council should contain within itself the seeds of evolution, did not have a shared understanding with the SDLP on what functions should be devolved to the Council. An inter-departmental unit on Northern Ireland recognised that the consequence of too forceful or too rigid an attempt to establish a council in the face of Northern opposition could 'spread ... violence to this part of the country. It is vital, therefore, to encourage Northern consent to participation by stressing explicitly the benefits which could flow, particularly to the North, from a Council' (NAI, Taois/2004/21/441, June 1973). Liam Cosgrave, Irish Taoiseach at the time, agreed that the 'SDLP might well be trying to do too many things at once' (TNA, CJ4/468, 17 September 1973). Garret FitzGerald, as Minister for Foreign Affairs, noted his difficulty in getting departments to agree on what functions should be devolved to the Council of Ireland. Many departments in the South at the time did not envisage a united Ireland. FitzGerald wrote in *All in a Life* (1991: 203) that

> [O]ther departments were notably reluctant to concede parts of their responsibilities to a North–South body, which they seemed to see as some kind of external threat to the institutions of the state. As I had always suspected, partition had struck very deep roots in the South!

The Irish government had yet to come to an ideological decision on the Council. The SDLP was reliant on Dublin to support their vision for a strong Council of Ireland with executive functions, but that support was not as forthcoming, or present, as Unionists tended to believe.

While the Sunningdale Agreement outlined what format the Council would take – a Council of Ministers and a consultative assembly – the executive functions of the Council were not defined or agreed. Yet, as Faulkner argued (1978: 237, 253), the constitutional integrity of Northern Ireland was secure; the executive arm of the Council – the Council of Ministers – had to operate on the basis of unanimity. None the less, it was the Council of Ireland that caused the most problems for the Executive. Immediately after the Sunningdale Agreement was finalised and signed, Faulkner remarked to the SDLP leader, Gerry Fitt, that he thought he could sell power sharing to his supporters, but not the Council of Ireland (Ryder, 2006: 258). The unease the Council caused within the unionist community was given expression in the February 1974 Westminster election, when anti-Sunningdale unionists manipulated the fear and won 11 of the 12 Northern Ireland seats.

The Sunningdale negotiations and experience of government highlighted the divisions that existed within the SDLP. The experience also transformed Fitt's vision of Irish nationalism. It highlighted for him that the power-sharing element of the Sunningdale Agreement was a major advance for consensus politics in Northern Ireland, and he moved to a position where a solution would be found *within* a Northern Ireland context (Campbell, 2015). Commenting in 1980, he stated that a power-sharing arrangement which would lead to the running of Northern Ireland would lead, in time, to a greater recognition of an Irish dimension. But to demand that there must be both an Irish dimension and power sharing together, he suggested, was to defeat the whole arrangement (*Irish Times* 26 March 1980). A public opinion poll conducted in Northern Ireland for the BBC in April 1974 – during the power-sharing Executive and after the disastrous Westminster election – showed that there was a 75 per cent approval for power sharing. However, only 41 per cent thought the Sunningdale proposals for a Council of Ireland were a good idea in principle and 37 per cent thought they were a bad idea (NAI, 2005/7/606, October 1974). So it appeared that Gerry Fitt's proposal to secure power sharing before introducing the Irish dimension would have found at least some approval amongst the more moderate Unionists. Indeed, Loyalists outlined that the main problem with the Sunningdale Agreement was not power sharing but the Irish dimension:

> Power-sharing has been shown to work. The Council of Ireland is not necessary to power-sharing, and is in fact the main danger to power-sharing. If the Council were shelved support for power-sharing would increase rapidly in the Protestant community. (Workers Association, 1974)

After Sunningdale

The remainder of the 1970s in Northern Ireland was overshadowed by the failure of Sunningdale. It established a negative and long-lasting dialectic within the SDLP between power sharing as an internal solution to the Northern Ireland problem and the need for an Irish dimension as part of any arrangement in order to externalise it. The evolution of what both meant to the party was undoubtedly shaped by London and Dublin's changed position in the aftermath of the failure of Sunningdale.

The collapse of power sharing marked a 'point of departure' in the affairs of Northern Ireland for London (TNA, CJ4/492, Northern Ireland – The Next Steps, June 1974). London noted that the power-sharing experiment collapsed because the Unionists could not carry their supporters on both power sharing and the Council of Ireland and they 'must therefore alternate the pressures' (TNA, CJ4/3783, 19 February 1982). In the months after the fall of the Executive, the Labour administration in the UK (which had succeeded the Conservatives at the start of the year) was reluctant to impose a system of devolved government on Northern Ireland. Recognising the lack of obvious support for power sharing with an Irish dimension among working-class Protestants, Britain proposed looking for a solution that would 'lead to power sharing in a new form, but a solution that Ulster works out for itself rather than simply shares in devising' (TNA, CJ4/492, June 1974), in the form of a constitutional convention.

Initially, both the Dublin and London governments agreed that power sharing in government in Northern Ireland would have to be an integral part of any solution. Wilson confirmed that no Westminster parliament would legislate for any solution which did not have power sharing in government (NAI, Taois/2005/7/607, 11 September 1974). By October 1974, however, the British were re-evaluating what power sharing could mean in a Northern Ireland context. After the experiences of 1974, they were reluctant to pursue the same conception of it as outlined in the Sunningdale Agreement. In a secret discussion paper, Frank Armstrong in the Northern Ireland Office (NIO) asked if there was 'any informed individual who really believes that power-sharing in any sense approximating to that of the 1973 Act, is a feasible solution in Northern Ireland?' and questioned whether efforts should, therefore, be directed towards 'the situation which will emerge when the Loyalist two-third majority rejects power-sharing'. He suggested that the government should be trying to define the means whereby majority rule in Northern Ireland could be made, if not acceptable, then as inoffensive as possible to the minority (PRONI, CENT/1/3/24, Secret Discussion Paper: Participation in Government, 22 October 1974).

The SDLP had a profound distrust of Britain's policies in the aftermath of Sunningdale, especially its reluctance to refer to 'power sharing'. The Irish government had also noted that there was a tendency in Whitehall to 'substitute the vague term "participation" for "power-sharing" in official discussions on the subject' (PRONI, CENT/1/3/24, Letter from Cosgrave to Wilson, 9 January 1975). Gerry Fitt believed that the British government wished to refrain from initiating any developments in Northern Ireland until the devolution question within the United Kingdom – namely, the first (short-lived) attempt to provide self-government in Scotland and Wales in the 1970s – was settled. The added problem of a slim majority ensured that the Labour government had an interest in placating the ten unionists at Westminster so they would not vote against the government (*Irish Times* 1 May 1976). They also believed that the British government was drifting towards *de facto* integration, and that they had a pact, if only tacit, with the Unionists at Westminster. In such circumstances, the SDLP turned to the Dublin government for support for their efforts to get Britain to reaffirm its policy and take action. The SDLP was also suspicious that the interim devolution talks were no more than shadow boxing to keep the party, Dublin and the House of Commons quiet (TNA, CJ4/2765: Teleletter from P.M. Maxey, Dublin, 3 January 1978). At the same time, Dermot Nally (Assistant Secretary, Department of the Taoiseach) informed British officials that it was the view of the Irish government that the Irish dimension should neither be emphasised nor pushed aside. It was recognised that there were grave dangers in making an issue of the Irish dimension in the aftermath of the fall of the Executive (TNA, CJ4/806, 11 February 1975). Seán Donlon (NAI, Taois/2005/151/696) suggested that 'We should contribute to the success of the Convention, and particularly of the moderates, by soft-pedalling on the Irish dimension now'.

The elevation of the Irish dimension

The Constitutional Convention failed to produce any agreement or compromise among the parties and it was dissolved on 9 March 1976. The complete rejection of power sharing and an Irish dimension by Loyalists after Sunningdale proved to be a major dilemma for the SDLP. The party had nailed its identity on power sharing with an Irish dimension and found it difficult to compromise on any aspect of this strategy during the constitutional convention. The SDLP came out of the experiences of Sunningdale, the UWC strike and the constitutional convention a greatly disillusioned party (McKittrick and McVea, 2001: 125). An NIO report from December 1976 noted that:

> Rarely, if ever, since the SDLP's foundation as an alliance of anti-Unionist independents, nationalists and socialists, has ideological disharmony within the party been so apparent. Between mid-1972 and mid-1975 the SDLP made its appeal to the Catholic minority as the party that could deliver a place in government for Catholics. Since the fall of the Executive, however, the SDLP has been unable to deliver, and when the breaking-off of talks with the Official Unionists brought the latest active phase of the current policy to a lingering end, the voices of those who were growing impatient

with its lack of success began to be heard. It gradually became apparent that the Fitt/ Hume/Currie/Devlin leadership were out of touch with the various strands of party thinking at grass-roots. (TNA, CJ4/3340, 17 December 1976)

With no prospect of negotiating a new power-sharing agreement with Unionists, potentially divisive debates ensued within the SDLP over the future policies of the party. In the same NIO report above, it was noted that the downgrading of an institutionalised framework for co-operation with the South, such as a Council of Ireland, in the White Paper of January 1976, meant that the importance of the Irish dimension in SDLP party policy had, consequently, been elevated (Ibid.).

The drift of both the Irish and British governments from the central tenets of SDLP policy put considerable strain on the party. The 1976 annual conference highlighted publicly for the first time the divisions that existed within the SDLP. The party's central tenet – advocating partnership government in Northern Ireland – was under serious challenge from some sections of the party. There were 157 motions down for discussion, and included among them was one for independence and one for a British declaration of intent to withdraw (PRONI, D3072/5/6/1–5, SDLP Sixth Annual Conference, 3–5 December 1976). It was the first time either of these ideas had been debated at party level. Seamus Mallon questioned party policy in an internal paper, suggesting that SDLP policy, which was adequate for the Sunningdale Agreement and as the basis of the *Constitutional Convention Report*, was impracticable in the current political vacuum. He advocated a 'radical reappraisal of policy' (Murray, 1998: 53).

The special status that was given to the Irish dimension in the aftermath of the fall of the Executive was certainly brought about by pressure within the SDLP, as opposed to its constituency base, and would have repercussions for the party. The making of consent through power sharing conditional on an Irish dimension had the consequence of devaluing the party's right to be regarded as a legitimate governmental partner in Protestant eyes (*Irish Times* 18 January 1977). In a memorandum by Bernard Crick, a political adviser in the constitutional convention that followed Sunningdale, Crick noted that power sharing 'does stick in the Unionist gullet, "coalition", not: the SDLP are getting wise to this, Devlin and Fitt certainly, but Hume still a bit mystical about power-sharing'. The main problem for the SDLP, Crick pointed out, was that it had committed itself utterly to 'power-sharing' as the prize (PRONI, CONV/1/2, 30 September 1975). The British government suggested that the SDLP should 'seek to make themselves more acceptable by playing down those aspects which most offend Unionist susceptibilities. They are, in a word, "seeking a marriage and must be prepared to woo."' One way they suggested the party could do this was to 'avoid parading their links with the South and appearing to be under the domination of the Republic' (TNA, FCO 87/651, January 1977).

Political parties cannot survive without foreseeable success, and that success must be visible and meaningful (*Irish Times* 18 January 1977). This was lacking for the SDLP in the latter half of the 1970s, when the constitutional convention talks collapsed. Against a backdrop of increasing sectarian violence and little political progress, the party was forced to reappraise its policies. The Irish dimension was a fluid concept for the SDLP – there was no one fixed idea of what it meant, either before or after Sunningdale. Austin Currie concurred that, while the party insisted on recognition of the Irish dimension, Sunningdale had been too much (TNA, CJ4/2765, 9 January 1978). John Hume outlined to Roy Mason in January 1977 the revisions the party had made to its ideas of an Irish dimension:

> They [the SDLP] had already made it clear that they were no longer demanding that the aim of a united Ireland should be recognised. They had already accepted the need to support the institutions of government and of the state of Northern Ireland and the absence of this particular point had been a key feature of the minority's attitude through the years. The SDLP had made it clear that they were prepared to offer the Unionists the guarantee that the state of Northern Ireland would remain until the majority signified they wished the situation to be changed. (TNA, CJ4/3340, 19 January 1977)

Yet, with no noticeable moves from the Unionists, the party was in a complete fix. The party's policy statement, *Facing Reality*, which was adopted by the 1977 party conference, highlighted the SDLP's apparent disillusionment with power sharing and renewed emphasis on the idea of an 'Irish dimension'. Similarly to the British government, the Irish recognised that the SDLP policy had always rested on two legs – recognition of the Irish dimension and power sharing within Northern Ireland. The party's 1977 policy document, they argued, 'would merely reaffirm the existence of the first leg, which had not been emphasised while there was a prospect of an internal settlement in the North' (TNA, FCO 87/651, 30 August 1977). The British government believed that Roy Mason's Five Point Proposals offered a real opportunity to establish the principle of partnership in the exercise of real power, but, without a meaningful Irish dimension, the SDLP refused to consider them.

The British government observed that the party had been in a disheartened and disenchanted mood for some time by 1978. They noted that the political vacuum created by the failure of the Convention, and unionist intransigence meant that

> Although the SDLP continue to accept that there can be no change in Northern Ireland's constitutional position without the agreement of the majority of the people

living there, there has been much less emphasis recently on their desire to have a responsible decision-taking role in a new elected Assembly. Instead they talk more about the need to secure an 'agreed Ireland' and they look to Dublin and, to a lesser extent, to the United States and Europe, to encourage HMG to give this concept serious consideration. (TNA, CJ4/2765, 18 September 1978)

The British government was also concerned that the SDLP would further commit itself to the all-Ireland approach to the Northern Ireland problem and play down its commitment to participation in a devolved government in the region (Ibid.). They were correct in thinking so. By late 1978, the SDLP was no longer seeking a solution to the overall problem in the six-county set-up. John Hume confirmed to the Tánaiste in a meeting in November 1978 that the party was not seeking power sharing in a British context, but was not 'abandoning it publicly'. The granting of the extra seats in Westminster had gone against the whole thrust of its policies. It was now resolutely in favour of British withdrawal, and power sharing was very much pushed into the background (NAI, Taois/2008/148/716, 15 December 1978). The party's annual conference in 1979 highlighted the extent to which the party had abandoned its consent principle and moved away from power sharing in favour of an all-Ireland solution. Delegates at the conference overwhelmingly backed the party's *Towards a New Ireland* policy document which committed the party to press for joint Anglo-Irish moves leading to Irish unity by consent, with or without the initial involvement of the Unionists (NAI, Taois/2009/120/1932; SDLP 1–30 November 1979).

From a Council of Ireland to a three-strand approach: lessons from Sunningdale

The SDLP talked of 'lessons of Sunningdale' throughout the 1970s and early 1980s. It was noted that the party had a 'phobia about having the rug pulled from under them', and therefore, were reluctant in the years immediately following Sunningdale to acquiesce too readily on any policies emanating from the British government at this time (TNA, CJ4/2765, Teleletter from P.M. Maxey, Dublin, 3 January 1978). Emphasis of policy oscillated between ideas of what power sharing could encompass and how robust an Irish dimension needed to be. The years immediately after the failure of Sunningdale were some of the bleakest in the party's history, and this undoubtedly had an impact on shaping party policy and ideology.

Yet, the SDLP had been willing to compromise on its proposals for power sharing. In a meeting with the Secretary of State, John Hume stated that the SDLP had 'accepted that power-sharing would not and should not be permanent and had offered a constitutional review to take place after two Parliamentary Sessions' (TNA, CJ4/3340, 19 January 1977). In a statement to the Secretary of State's conference in January 1980, Hume essentially outlined that the SDLP definition of power sharing was synonymous with 'partnership', highlighting a change of emphasis:

> The alternative role to conflict is partnership. Partnership between the two Irish traditions is a necessary means whereby we can reduce prejudice and misunderstandings between us and replace them with trust and confidence. Partnership is not an end in itself; it is an artificial form of government but we have a totally artificial situation which requires, in the short term, artificial means. Partnership is not, as I say, an end in itself. It is a means whereby the people can grow together and can replace distrust and hatred with confidence and trust. (TNA, CJ4/3273/1, 8 January 1980)

James Prior, as Secretary of State, stated in 1982 that, while there had to be moves towards minority participation, he could not deliver power sharing in the form it had been established in 1974 (TNA, CJ4/3783, 11 January 1982). Hume emphasised that the minimum position for the SDLP was a share of responsibility in the administration of the province, but did not offer a definition of what this might mean. Hume still pushed for the British government to 'withdraw the guarantee' and, by the early 1980s, sought to promote a federal Ireland in which the Protestants would retain a majority voice in the North. However, the British noted that there were some indications that privately Hume might have been willing to contemplate an 'internal settlement', provided that the system incorporated acceptable power-sharing provisions. His main difficulty was getting his party to agree with him. The party conference in November 1981 overwhelmingly passed a resolution calling for 'the removal of the constitutional guarantee to Unionists' and affirming that a lasting settlement in the North was possible only 'in the context of a new basis to Anglo-Irish relations which accepts Irish unity' (Ibid.). The British government saw an opportunity to redefine what an 'Irish dimension' might constitute, pointing out that it had made considerable progress in developing relations with the Republic, and had set up the Anglo-Irish Intergovernmental Conference (AIIC). It was this policy – the Anglo-Irish rapprochement – which would provide an Irish dimension, not proposals for a new Assembly. They also claimed that the 'real Irish Dimension is the minority community having its say in the government of the North' (Ibid.). The Irish government's hostile position on the Falklands dispute, however, 'put the lid on the coffin' on this rapprochement (Ibid., Blatherwick, 14 May 1982) (a 'lid' that was lifted following the 1982 change of power to Fine Gael). The SDLP, once again, had failed to deliver on a key component of the party's policy.

This created a conundrum for the SDLP. The survival of the party, particularly in the political vacuum that had existed since 1974, meant persuading successive British administrations not only of the validity of power sharing and a meaningful Irish dimension but of a need for their implementation as well. James Prior's proposals for 'rolling devolution' in 1982 reflected the British government's retreat from ideas of power sharing set out at Sunningdale. SDLP participation in government was at best implied in Prior's proposals, whereas in 1973 seats in government for the SDLP were guaranteed.

The SDLP's failure to achieve progress in both power sharing and the Irish dimension, combined with communal polarisation inside Northern Ireland, pushed the party away from emphasis on social and economic policies, which had characterised it as a new political force in the first instance. Eddie McGrady noted that the party could not fight an election for the Assembly in 1982 without an Irish dimension, especially when the British government had also abandoned previous Westminster insistence on power sharing (Ibid., 13 May 1982). It was noted that, under this tension, differences within the party had become more acute. The party's 1982 election manifesto, *Stand Firm*, showed evidence of the cracks in the SDLP. It divided the party into 'moderate' and 'green' camps. While the 'moderates' may have believed in the need for participation in northern politics, and thought power sharing far more important than the Irish dimension, they knew that the party could not afford to get involved in the Assembly (Ibid., SDLP Manifesto, 1 October 1982).

At a party meeting at Dungannon on 26 August 1982, the party agreed to contest the election but on an abstentionist ticket. It was a compromise decision that avoided an open split in the party (PRONI, CENT/1/11/43, 'Assembly Elections 1982: SDLP'). The election, which took place on 20 October, was the first since the outbreak of the conflict which Sinn Féin had contested. It won 10.1 per cent of the first-preference votes and secured five of the seats. The British noted that 'The existence of so considerable a Republican vote is disturbing' (Ibid.). While the SDLP achieved 18.8 per cent of the first-preference vote, which was marginally higher than in either the 1981 council elections or the 1979 General Election, the distribution of seats inside the Assembly showed a number of striking similarities to the party strengths in the Constitutional Convention of 1975. As in 1975, the various Unionist parties opposed to power sharing won 49 seats with about 55 per cent of first preferences. The SDLP won 5 per cent fewer first preferences than in 1975 and took three fewer seats (PRONI, CENT/1/11/51A, 25 October 1982). It was a disappointing outcome. At the party's annual conference in January 1983, party members felt deeply pessimistic and frustrated. They stridently reaffirmed their rejection of the Assembly and their determination to explore all-Ireland solutions through the Council for a New Ireland. Though differences of emphasis remained inside the party, all were committed to this line (PRONI, CENT/1/12/2A, 31 January 1983). The Council, however, presented difficulties for both Fine Gael and Fianna Fáil in the South, and Garret FitzGerald could only agree to an all-Ireland forum which became known as the New Ireland Forum.

There was a fear in Irish and British government circles that, unless something was done to bolster constitutional Nationalism in the North, Sinn Féin could become the main spokespeople for Northern Catholics (Ibid., 19 January 1983). All the constitutional Nationalist parties in Ireland, with the exception of Sinn Féin, were invited to attend the Forum. Its express purpose was to seek a way in which 'lasting peace and stability could be achieved in a New Ireland through the democratic process and to report on possible new structures and processes through which this objective might be achieved' (*New Ireland Forum Report*, Dublin: The Stationery Office, 1984: Para. 1.1). The first meeting of the Forum took place on 30 May 1983 and the final report was published on 2 May 1984. The report highlighted trends in SDLP thinking. The British government had noted that the hunger strike, the establishment of an Assembly without prescribed power sharing, the electoral success of Sinn Féin and the deterioration in Anglo-Irish relations due to the Falklands war made it difficult to convince Catholics that a constitutional context could advance their aims. The SDLP, therefore, was driven to emphasising its differences with the British government and its Nationalist beliefs, in an attempt to hold support within their community and fend off Sinn Féin (PRONI, CENT/1/12/2A, 1983) and this was reflected in the Forum report. It criticised Britain's policy of 'crisis management' since 1968 and set out three possible options for the future of Northern Ireland: join with the Republic in a united Ireland; joint authority over the region by the Republic of Ireland and Britain; a federal or confederal arrangement (*New Ireland Forum Report*). These prescriptions were unrealistic and could be pursued, if at all, only in ways which were inconsistent with the principles it asserted.

Gerard Murray (1998: 146) argues that the Forum Report played a pivotal role in engineering movement within the Anglo-Irish sphere. As 1985 unfolded, it became apparent that the Report achieved its objective from the SDLP viewpoint, in that it provided a negotiating document between the two governments which the British largely accepted as the nature of the Northern Ireland problem. Peter McLoughlin (2011: 89) also notes that the New Ireland Forum created the opportunity for the SDLP to imbue the Southern state with its political philosophy, and both Dublin and London governments adopted a distinctively SDLP phraseology. The Irish dimension was formally recognised in the 1985 Anglo-Irish Agreement, and the Three Strand approach further built upon in the Downing Street

Declaration (1993), the Framework Documents (1995) and the Good Friday Agreement (1998).

Conclusion

The 1998 Good Friday Agreement was a euphoric moment for the SDLP. It appeared to vindicate the approach the party took to resolving the Northern Ireland problem since it was founded in 1970. In the aftermath of the failure of the Sunningdale Agreement in 1974, however, the party's policies on both power sharing and the Irish dimension – the cornerstones of party policy – underwent a major re-evaluation. The rejection of both policies by Unionists in the years immediately after Sunningdale created a dilemma for the party. It led to the Irish dimension taking prominence in party policy and philosophy and diminished the likelihood of Unionists seeing them as legitimate opposition in Northern Ireland politics. The threat of the rise of Sinn Féin led to both the Irish and British governments seeking to reach a compromise of this aspect of SDLP policy. While many of the elements of the Good Friday Agreement looked like those agreed at Sunningdale, the concepts of both power sharing and the Irish dimension were of very different complexions in 1998 than in 1974. This does not mean that a more palatable or better form of democracy emerged because of these changes. The SDLP's ideas on both were fluid and adaptable to suit what was politically viable at any time, and the re-evaluation happened more at a semantic level than any deep change. The experiences of Sunningdale and its failure also changed the complexion of the party – less than a decade after it was founded, the party's moderate wing, and most of its founding members, were completely sidelined or had left the party. This allowed a 'greener' agenda to emerge. Despite the party's achievements in ensuring that their approach was adopted in 1998, the internal divisions that existed over both policies have meant that the party has been unable to deal effectively with post-constitutional issues. As Jonathan Tonge (2003: 47–53) convincingly argues, the party has become a victim of its own success.

10

'1974 – Year of Liberty'? The Provisional IRA and Sunningdale

Henry Patterson

Were Republicans, as the Taoiseach, Liam Cosgrave, claimed, responsible for the collapse of the Executive? Cosgrave's charge was that the campaign of the IRA 'has sparked a massive sectarian backlash' (White, 2006: 215). In response the President of Provisional Sinn Féin, Ruairí Ó Brádaigh, claimed that Cosgrave was looking for a scapegoat for his government's failure to address the 'real cause' of the violence in Northern Ireland: partition and the British presence (Ibid.). In fact Cosgrave's blaming of Republicans was at odds with the negotiating position which his government had adopted both during and after the Sunningdale conference. The Irish position was that Irish Republican Army (IRA) violence, while aimed directly at undermining the attempt to construct a new political dispensation in the North, was fundamentally a symptom of the underlying problem of the Northern state's lack of legitimacy in the eyes of its Catholic minority together with the effects of British security policies in alienating working-class Catholic communities (Patterson, 2013: 49–77).

There was another obvious problem with Cosgrave's charge. In the period from the inauguration to the power-sharing Executive on 1 January 1974 to the collapse of the Executive in May, Loyalists had been responsible for more deaths than Republicans. During 1973, of a total death toll of 263, Republicans had killed 124 while Loyalists killed 78. In the whole of 1974 the overall death toll rose to 304, of whom Republicans killed 148 and Loyalists 131 (McKittrick et al., 2004: 412–44). Thirty-three of those killed by Loyalists had died as a result of three car bombs planted by the Ulster Volunteer Force (UVF) in Dublin and Monaghan on 17 May during the Ulster Workers' Council (UWC) strike. These were not the first Loyalist attacks in the Republic as both the UVF and the Ulster Defence Association (UDA) along with many Unionist politicians claimed the IRA was able to use the South as a safe haven and was allegedly in league with an irredentist state. Whilst it was true that Loyalist violence was to a significant extent aimed at combating the Provisionals by terrifying the broader Catholic community, Loyalist violence was also linked to a broader narrative of the crisis of the Northern Irish state which depicted demands for reform as a Trojan horse for anti-partitionism and saw, first, the civil rights movement and, later, the Social Democratic and Labour Party (SDLP) as part of a broader anti-Unionist alliance to destroy the state. Bitter Loyalist opposition to change was clearly evident, for example in rise of Paisleyism, before the Provisionals were even founded (see Nelson, 1984).

To single out Republicans for destroying the Executive serves to distract from more fundamental problems with the Sunningdale project. These emerge very clearly from the official records of the Executive itself and are registered from its earliest days. On 16 January 1974 the Chief Minister, Brian Faulkner, had been flown to Baldonnel airport for a meeting with the Taoiseach to attempt to get the Irish state to make some high-profile arrests of leading Provisionals to shore up support for the Executive in the Unionist community. By this time Faulkner had lost the support of the Ulster Unionist Council and been badly embarrassed by the Irish government's defence against the legal challenge by Kevin Boland. Already Cosgrave had been pressured by an SDLP delegation to 'lift' leading IRA members and in response the Gardaí had arrested 15 Provisionals. Cosgrave noted that the Gardaí had advised in advance that they had no very firm information which would allow them to charge the people concerned and to the embarrassment of the government 14 of those arrested were quickly released for lack of evidence. Despite this Faulkner pressed Cosgrave for action, mentioning his Minister of Community Relations, Ivan Cooper, who he claimed was being approached by people from his town, Strabane, who expected, now that he was a Minister, for action to be taken against the Provisional unit in Lifford which had practically destroyed the centre of the town (PRONI, OE/1/29, 'Note of Meeting at Baldonnel Airport, 16th January 1974').

Such pressure had limited effects. By the time Harold Wilson came to Stormont to meet the Executive in April, the Deputy Chief Minister, the SDLP leader, Gerry Fitt, could report 'some improvement south of the

Border … he was impressed by the fact that the IRA pocket in Lifford had been virtually flushed out' although he admitted that there were still 'pockets of terrorists' on the Cavan and Monaghan borders (PRONI, OE/1/24, 'Note of a meeting between the Northern Ireland Administration and the Prime Minister, Stormont Castle, 18 April 1974'). But as Fitt admitted, the SDLP faced a major problem with trying to get the Catholic population to support the Royal Ulster Constabulary (RUC) and even more problematic was the continuation of internment and detention without trial: 'the recent signing of some 30 Interim Custody Orders had not helped, it had allowed people to point to the fact that there were more people in detention under the new Labour government than there had been at the end of the former Conservative administration's period of office' (Ibid.).

The SDLP had fought the Assembly elections on a manifesto, 'A New North – A New Ireland', and the Nationalist electorate had largely ignored Provisional Sinn Féin calls for a boycott and voted in large numbers for the SDLP, which had gained 22.1 per cent of the poll, establishing itself in the words of Michael A. Murphy as the 'official representative of the northern minority' (Murphy, 2007: 189). However, the SDLP's policies had situated its political aspirations firmly within a prospectus of radical, if peaceful, constitutional change and also had demanded radical reform of the RUC and declared it would not involve itself in any British initiative until internment was ended (Ibid., 192). In the February 1974 Westminster election, while Fitt had been returned for West Belfast, his vote of 19,554 had fallen significantly compared with his 1966 and 1970 election totals. Provisional Sinn Féin had set out three conditions which would allow it to contest the election: the return to prison in Northern Ireland of IRA volunteers recently sentenced to long terms of imprisonment for bombing London, a revoking of the ban on Sinn Féin and an end to British Army harassment of Catholic areas. Observers at the time thought the demands, which had little chance of being met, were issued to enable the Provisionals to justify a boycott (*Irish Times* 12 February 1974). Albert Price, a veteran Republican whose daughters, Dolours and Marian, were serving time for the London bombs, stood in West Belfast on the issue of repatriation of 'Irish political prisoners' and along with Jack Brady of the Republican Clubs and two Republican candidates amassed a vote of over eight thousand (Murphy, 2007: 204). At a time when the Official and Provisional IRAs were both involved in active armed struggle, this was a not inconsiderable vote. Outside Belfast Bernadette McAliskey and Frank McManus stood as 'Unity' candidates against Sunningdale in Mid-Ulster and Fermanagh/South Tyrone. In the two constituencies the total SDLP vote of 37,782 was only slightly higher than the 'Unity' vote of 32,401 (Staunton, 2001: 276). Enda Staunton has argued convincingly for the existence of two Catholic Norths – a stronger, anti-partitionist tradition west of the Bann and a more moderate 'reformist' Nationalism in the east (Ibid.). The SDLP's initial success was in integrating both traditions but Sunningdale had brought potential conflicts between them to the fore.

Both the Provisionals and the Officials rejected the Sunningdale strategy, although their reasons for doing so were sharply distinguished. In July 1973 at a press conference in Dublin to launch a publication, 'Freedom Struggle', their account of the history of the North since 1969, leading Provisionals predicted that the new Assembly would fail, with the prominent Republican Dáithí Ó Conaill declaring: 'We see it as potentially no more useful than the many television confrontations that have taken place in the last few years'. The IRA would fight on until Britain agreed to their demand for a complete 'withdrawal of her forces' (*Irish Times* 14 July 1973). It was a year since IRA leaders had been flown in secret to London for a meeting with William Whitelaw, the Secretary of State for Northern Ireland and senior officials. Though nothing had come from the talks, the Provisionals interpreted them as one important indication of the leverage their campaign was capable of exerting on the British state, and despite reversals their leaders continued to believe in the imminence of British withdrawal.

Claiming that it was they who had brought down Stormont, the Provisionals incautiously predicted that 1972 would be 'Year of Victory' (Bew and Patterson, 1984: 49). In fact the imposition of direct rule, and the clear intention of Whitelaw to provide both the SDLP and the Irish government with a role in any future Northern Irish settlement, opened up the space for a reformist exit from the crisis. On the military front the reoccupation of the 'no-go' areas of Belfast and Derry by the army in July 1972, after the disastrous Bloody Friday bomb blitz, represented a major strategic loss for the Provisionals who were forced to concentrate their attacks increasingly in rural and border areas. The army was able to build up more intelligence on both IRAs while the Provisionals' capacity to inflict losses on the military, while remaining substantial, was significantly reduced (Hamill, 1986: 118). The Quarter Master of the Belfast Brigade had been recruited as an agent and revealed a large number of arms dumps in 1973 and 1974. In July 1973 the Belfast Brigade Staff including Gerry Adams and Brendan Hughes were all arrested while at a meeting and on the same day most of the staff of the Third Battalion was arrested. Thus in one day the army had put 17 leading IRA members out of action (Moloney, 2010: 151). The effects on the IRA's capacity to kill British soldiers were clear. In 1972, 108 regular soldiers had been killed but in 1973 the figure had been almost halved to 59.

However, some of the means by which Provisional capacities had been eroded did little to lessen hostility to the security forces, particularly in

Catholic working-class areas. The gathering of intelligence through house searches, person stop and searches and arrests ensured a substantial reservoir of disaffection and at least passive sympathy for the IRA (Boyle et al., 1975: 37–53). There was thus danger for the SDLP members in being portrayed as puppets of a British state happy to provide them with the perquisites of office whilst their constituents endured the hard end of state power.

As talks between the Unionists, SDLP and Alliance got under way at Stormont Castle in October 1973, IRA volunteers had been assured by Ruairí Ó Brádaigh that they were in sight of a British declaration of intent to withdraw: 'Mr Heath fully realises it [inevitability of withdrawal] and knew he is slipping deeper into the Irish bog. It was becoming more and more recognised abroad that the North was Britain's Vietnam' (*Irish Times* 24 September 1973). This was more than simple whistling in the dark. As Paul Dixon has pointed out, the heavy losses suffered by the army in 1972 produced a recruitment crisis in 1973 and there was a fear of a populist 'bring our boys home' campaign developing (Dixon, 2001: 126).

It was also the case that although the IRA had suffered reverses in Belfast and Derry it remained a substantial force organised on a 32-county basis whilst the British security forces faced formidable problems in co-ordinating a counter-insurgency strategy with their counterparts across the border. The Provisionals were able to exploit the territory of the Republic as a relatively safe haven from which to plan and launch attacks, import weapons and use for training and fund-raising. After the Sunningdale talks the British prepared a detailed analysis of the border security problem. The document noted that between 1 May 1973 and 30 April 1974 there were 548 recorded border incidents. They included such things as concerted attacks on isolated police stations using rockets, mortars and small arms fire; opening fire on security forces from across the border; placing culvert mines and elaborate ambush bombs in the North, controlled by wires enabling them to be detonated from south of the border, as well as murders and other such activities when those responsible were clearly known to have escaped across the border, sometimes while being pursued by security forces in the North (TNA, FCO 87/371). In South Armagh the Provisionals had imposed a heavy toll on the security forces. In October 1973, when Michael McVerry was the first IRA volunteer to be killed in the area, the IRA had already killed 22 British soldiers (White, 2006: 219).

The Provisionals had also returned to the traditional Republican tactic of bombs in England. The Old Bailey bomb in March 1973 was one of four that the team from Belfast had planted, although only two exploded. In August and September Harrods was bombed along with two railway stations, and a soldier was killed trying to defuse a bomb in Birmingham. Letter bombs were sent to the Stock Exchange, the Bank of England and the House of Commons. Though most failed to explode, one sent to the British Embassy in Washington did detonate, seriously injuring an Irish-born secretary (Ibid., 205).

Thus, although the Provisionals were under severe pressure in the North and faced a new and more hostile administration in the Republic with the arrival of the Fine Gael–Labour coalition in power, their capacity to maintain a campaign in the North was still substantial. For many of the volunteers victory would be achieved simply by maintaining the armed struggle and ensuring that the North remained ungovernable except by exceptional means. They were buoyed up by occasional 'spectaculars' like the landing of a hijacked helicopter in the exercise yard of Mountjoy prison and the escape of Seamus Twomey and two other leading Provisionals in October 1973 (Ibid., 204). This was the sentiment behind the statement in November from the Belfast Comhairle Ceantair of Provisional Sinn Féin expressing solidarity with their comrades, eight of whom had just been sentenced to long terms of imprisonment for their involvement in bombings in London on the day of the Border poll in March 1973. The statement declared grandiloquently if hardly realistically that 'In the "Year of Liberty" 1974, the revolutionary soldiers of the Provisional IRA will be together to celebrate the final destruction of British imperialism' (*Irish Times* 17 November 1973).

As John Bew and his co-authors have noted, the Sunningdale strategy simply ignored the Provisionals' intransigence and refusal to give up armed struggle, hoping that a new dispensation in the North would drain the swamp of Catholic disaffection which it was believed fed the Provisionals. As they note, this underestimated 'the ferocity, ideology and confidence of violent republicanism at the time' (Bew et al., 2009: 48). However, the continuing military triumphalism of the Provisionals also brought tensions when it clashed with those in the leadership of the movement who emphasised that force was an insufficient basis for the realisation of the movement's political objectives. These objectives were embodied in the *Éire Nua* programme which was written by Ó Brádaigh and Ó Conaill and first published in January 1971. It initially sought to define the economic and social programme of Sinn Féin as a form of democratic socialism distinct from Western capitalism and Soviet-style socialism. Like the Irish socialist martyr James Connolly, it looked back to the Brehon laws for Gaelic Ireland for an indigenous tradition of communal property which was not to be updated into worker co-operatives in manufacturing, agriculture and fishing (White, 2006: 165). Having established their economic and social differences with the allegedly 'Marxist' Officials, the Provisionals advocated a form of federal government for Ireland with four provincial parliaments including a Dáil

Uladh based on the historic province of Ulster. The Ulster Assembly was to be designed to demonstrate the Provisionals' fealty to Tone's notion of an Irish republic based on the 'unity of Protestant, Catholic and Dissenter' in that it would demonstrate that republicans had no desire to replace Protestant hegemony in the North with a 32-county Catholic version. Dáil Uladh would place former Unionists in a working majority but there would be a strong Nationalist opposition which would prevent it repeating the excesses of Stormont rule. To Official denunciations of the Provisionals' carbombing of Belfast and other northern towns as sectarian, Ó Brádaigh claimed that the Provisionals' enemy was the British state not the Protestants of Ulster and that they did not want to dominate Protestants in a Catholic state: 'The Northern Protestants must have a share in creating a new Ireland' (*Irish Times* 29 May 1974).

When, in the aftermath of Sunningdale, the prominent lawyer, former Unionist MP and former Paisley ally Desmond Boal proposed that Unionists would be better to rely on themselves to negotiate a settlement with Dublin based on federalism with a six-county parliament, Ó Brádaigh welcomed it as a possible major breakthrough (White, 2006: 213). As some Loyalists in the UVF and UDA had expressed an interest in the proposals, Ó Brádaigh and his supporters claimed to see signs of a possible common front against Sunningdale. Asked at a press conference if Republicans would consider a ceasefire to allow the proposal to be considered, Ó Brádaigh responded that such a move was worth considering (*Irish Times* 9 January 1974). At the time some Provisionals were attempting to work out an agreement with the UVF to end sectarian killings in Belfast and it was hoped that signs of working-class Protestant disillusion with mainstream Unionism would create the possibility of common ground against 'the growing oppression of English forces against all sections of our people' (Patterson, 2010: 57). To facilitate possible engagement with the Loyalists the IRA confirmed that it had instructed its volunteers to cease operations against off-duty members of the Ulster Defence Regiment (UDR) – these killings, which often took place at the homes or places of work of UDR members, were seen as deeply sectarian by most Protestants (*Irish Times* 1 February 1974).

The tensions within the Provisionals over this campaign reflected a North–South divide well summarised by Ed Moloney:

> The Northern Provisionals came in large measure from the Defenderist and, it must be said, sectarian tradition of Irish Republicanism, while Ó Brádaigh and his supporters took their politics from Pearse, Mellows, O'Malley and Liam Lynch. It was fear and loathing of Unionism less than the wish to break the link with Britain that inspired hundreds and thousands of northern Catholics to join the Provisional IRA. (Moloney: foreword in White, 2006: xvi)

The Provisionals had been born out of the sectarian conflagration of August 1969 and their campaign both reflected and exacerbated that sectarianism. In his sympathetic study of Ó Brádaigh, White noted the effects of the mass influx of young Northerners into the Provisionals: by mid-1972 there were more than a thousand volunteers in Belfast alone:

> The bulk of the fighting was being done by young northerners, some of whom were beginning to resent ... control from Dublin. IRA policy only allowed defensive action in the case of sectarian attacks ... But some IRA personnel were willing and able to retaliate. (Ibid.: 180)

He instances the Provisionals' response to a Loyalist attack on a bar in West Belfast by bombing the Bluebell Bar in Sandy Row and firing on Protestant workers (Ibid.). White, like Ó Brádaigh, does not regard attacks on the RUC and UDR as sectarian as targets were selected for membership of the Crown Forces not religion (Ibid.). However, the decision not to target off-duty UDR personnel demonstrated some recognition that whatever Republican rationale such killings were perceived as sectarian by most Protestants. In a sense Ó Brádaigh's Republican purism had made a Faustian bargain with a rampant Northern Republicanism deeply inlayed with sectarianism. Particularly embarrassing was the IRA's murder of the Irish Senator Billy Fox in County Monaghan in March 1974. Fox, a Protestant, was shot dead when he came upon an IRA gang raiding the farm owned by the family of his fiancée. The Coulsons were a Protestant family and their attackers' sectarian motivation was clear when they threw a family Bible on the fire (Patterson, 2013: 667). At first Ó Brádaigh blamed the action on 'pro-British agents' attempting to frighten Dublin into more coercion of Republicans and 'collaboration with the British forces of occupation'. He pointed out that Fox had been prominent in protests against the British Army's cratering of border roads and knew Ó Conaill, with whom he had discussed the Provisionals' federalist proposals (*Irish Times* 13 March 1974). However, it soon emerged that the murder was carried out by local Provisionals, five of whom were given life sentences (Patterson, 2013: 67). The Fox murder was a graphic example of the impossibility of insulating Provisionalism from the visceral sectarianism that pervaded the North.

The clear desire of both Ó Brádaigh and Ó Conaill to get back into negotiations with the British may in part have reflected a recognition that a prolonged armed struggle could not be insulated from barbarous sectarianism. Later in the decade and in the early 1980s the rise to dominance of Gerry Adams and his supporters would be associated with attacks on *Éire Nua* as a sop to Loyalists. At the time while there were no public displays of disunity there were some manifestations of tension. The removal of off-duty UDR personnel from the list of targets did not last long. On 10 April 1974 the headmaster of a primary school in Derrylin was shot dead while having a coffee break. He had retired from the UDR a year previously (McKittrick et al., 2004: 437). Questioned about the killing during an RTÉ interview, Ó Brádaigh broke off the interview when his own membership of the IRA was raised (*Irish Times* 18 April 1974).

The British had not ended all contacts with the Provisionals after the failure of the 1972 ceasefire. There were indirect contacts through intermediaries including the Derry priest Dennis Bradley, and more direct communications through successive MI6 officers stationed in Northern Ireland. These allowed the government to have some idea of the internal dynamics of the Provisionals and of the tensions that existed within the IRA. Thus after meeting two Catholic priests the MI6 officer Michael Oatley identified Ó Conaill as 'anxious for peace and a move to politics' while the Belfast Chief of Staff, Seamus Twomey, was described as the 'most intransigent'. Gerry Adams, already clearly identified as being 'much more intelligent', was seen as someone capable of being persuaded to O'Conaill's point of view (Bew et al., 2009: 50–1). It is in fact doubtful whether Adams would have been amenable to either Ó Conaill's or Ó Brádaigh's point of view. It was certainly the case that his view of the situation, and the respective roles of politics and violence, would have been a more nuanced and subtle one than Twomey's. The latter was nicknamed 'Thumper' for his habit of banging the table to get people's attention (White, 2006: 205). However, it is doubtful that Adams and other younger Provisionals in Belfast had much time for the policies and politics associated with the two architects of *Éire Nua*. According to Brendan Hughes there was from the early 1970s 'a confrontation between the Dublin leadership and the Belfast leadership ... we believed that we knew how to run the war, not those people sitting in Dublin in their safe houses, people like Dáithí Ó Conaill and Ruairí Ó Brádaigh' (Moloney, 2010: 150).

There was certainly an air of almost academic abstraction in Ó Brádaigh's musings on the proposed workings of the new Ireland. In June 1973 Sinn Féin had published a policy document on 'The Quality of Life in Ireland' dealing with amongst other things the environment, pollution and control of technology. At the press conference to launch the report Ó Brádaigh declared himself 'anxious that the public should not see Sinn Féin solely as a support group for the struggle in the North ... There was always more than the gun in the republican movement and what we are now doing is correcting the wrong image which has gone out amongst ordinary people through the media' (*Irish Times* 20 June 1973). Ó Brádaigh's concerns with developing the political side of the movement had provoked the first Chief of Staff, Sean

Mac Stiofain, to try to have him court-martialled for not accounting for the movement's funds and, although an internal inquiry led to the dropping of the charges, there remained many in the IRA who saw Sinn Féin as having little more role than that of a support organisation and had little time for attempts to develop it as a serious political organisation (White, 2006: 192). At the 1973 Sinn Féin Ard Fheis a resolution from Andersonstown in Belfast called for Sinn Féin as a 32-county organisation to play a more positive role in the 'struggle for freedom'. In response a Belfast delegate was dismissive: 'Now that victory is staring us in the face there should be no waste of time with political obstructions'. Another delegate declared that there was no point in Sinn Féin discussing land and housing policy 'when we are not masters of our own land. To secure that is the first objective' (*Irish Times* 22 October 1973).

But if the more militaristic volunteers decried the very idea of serious political involvement this side of British withdrawal, this would not have been the position of those Northerners around Adams. For from the earliest manifestations of a distinct Adams line in the mid- to late 1970s there would be clear echoes of Ó Brádaigh's call for a movement that was more than a military machine (Patterson, 1997: 184–5). More substantial differences lay over the analysis of Loyalism and the increasing evidence that some of the IRA leadership were in contact with the British. Ó Brádaigh's confidence that a British declaration of intent would be forthcoming relatively quickly made him anxious to ensure that the withdrawal was a phased and orderly one – to avoid a 'Congo-style' bloodbath (Moloney, 2010: 166). Talks with Loyalists about the virtues of Dáil Uladh in safeguarding them in future united Ireland were aimed at reducing the chances of a sectarian conflagration. For those like Adams the lessons of the civil rights movement and subsequent sectarian violence was that nothing progressive would emerge amongst the Protestants of Ulster until the British link was broken. Some of the leading younger Provisionals had mixed in the civil rights movement with the left-wing Queens University student radicals of People's Democracy (PD). The chief ideologist of PD, Michael Farrell, produced an early analysis of the Northern state, Unionism and Loyalism which would be very influential on Provisionals like Adams and Tom Hartley. In *The Struggle in the North*, a pamphlet first published in 1969 and reissued in 1972, and in *The Battle of Algeria*, published in 1973,[1] Farrell depicted the mass basis of Unionism amongst the Protestant working class as a product of the British colonisation of Ulster which had created a settler garrison, like the French *colons* in Algeria, with a materially privileged position. Those like the Officials who sought to win the Protestant working class to progressive politics were doomed to failure because Protestant workers had a material interest in the status quo. Only when the state which guaranteed that status quo was destroyed could any section of that working class be won over.[2]

However, if some of the younger Northern Provisionals had little time for overtures to Protestants, it is necessary to quality Moloney's notion of a North–South divide in the Provisionals at this time. As the Billy Fox incident showed, sectarian attacks were not restricted to Northern Ireland. Although the cutting edge of Provisional violence was in the North, the capacity to carry it out was reliant on an infrastructure which transcended the North. Membership of the Army Council in this period was largely composed of Northerners including figures like Joe Cahill, Billy McKee, Kevin Mallon and J.B. O'Hagan (White, 2006: 203). It is important not to read back into this period the divisions over strategic direction of the Provisionals that emerged in the late 1970s and early 1980s as Adams and his supporters mobilised the leadership of Ó Brádaigh.

A key issue in this conflict was the claim by the Adams camp, repeated in Ed Moloney's analysis, that the leadership of the IRA at the time was bamboozled by the British into agreeing to the ceasefire of 1975. During the 1986 Ard Fheis when Ó Brádaigh was waging a rearguard action against the proposal that Sinn Féin should drop its policy of abstentionism for elections to the Dáil, Martin McGuinness attacked 'the former leadership of the Movement' for 'the disgraceful attitude adopted by them during the disastrous 18-month ceasefire in the 1970s' (Ibid.: 306). In fact the ceasefire lasted only from February to September 1975 but the core of the criticism of Ó Brádaigh and Ó Conaill was that they had allowed themselves to be fooled by the British into believing that a British withdrawal was imminent. The current Provisional historiography was expressed in an analysis of newly released British and Irish files on Sunningdale in 2005. It accepted that 'elements within the British establishment' including the then Prime Minister, Harold Wilson, had considered the option of withdrawal but claimed that 'it was not to be a full withdrawal by the British state in any real sense' and that the real British aim was 'to divide Irish republicanism and drag the IRA into a prolonged ceasefire by offering the prospect of withdrawal' (*An Phoblacht* 6 January 2005).

Much of the running on the issue of withdrawal was made by the Secret Intelligence Service (SIS) man in Belfast, Michael Oatley. His later direct contacts with the Republican movement arose out of a meeting with the Derry priest Dennis Bradley towards the end of 1973. Bradley's description of Oatley is telling: 'an incredibly sophisticated man who was very comfortable in church circles with the clergy, but hadn't a clue' (Clarke and Johnston, 2001: 86). Although full-blooded negotiations did not start until after the collapse of Sunningdale, the motivation on the British side was to encourage

THE LESSONS OF SUNNINGDALE

those identified as the more politically orientated Provisional leaders. The Westminster election results and the potentially fatal blow they dealt to Faulkner's legitimacy in the Unionist population began the process of engagement. The return to Downing Street of Harold Wilson, who had made clear his inclination to think in terms of an all-Ireland solution to the conflict, would have encouraged the optimism of the Provisionals (see Bew, 2007: 516–23). Although the security forces had made serious inroads into the Provisionals in Belfast, they still managed to reassert themselves. Thus within days of the arrest of Ivor Bell, the IRA's Belfast commander, in February, the Provisionals were able to set off a series of bombs in the city centre, devastating the Army's HQ at the former Grand Central Hotel, and in March another bomb seriously damaged the Europa Hotel, favourite meeting place for visiting journalists (Moloney, 2010: 166). Such violence did little to encourage Unionist support for Faulkner whilst at the same time exacerbating Anglo-Irish differences. At an Anglo-Irish summit in London on 5 April, the new Secretary of State, Merlyn Rees, emphasised to the Irish the damage the Provisionals were doing to the Executive:

> The recent series of bombings in Belfast, Bangor and other centres had caused great anger. If sufficient numbers of Faulkner's supporters defect power-sharing will come down ... outside the Assembly he is losing support as a result of the recent bombing campaign. He has been publicly and vulgarly abused on the streets of Belfast about his republican friends and what they have brought about. (Patterson, 2013: 73–4)

But although both Wilson and Rees pressed the Irish ministers for more action on border security it was very doubtful if any new measures would have had significant effects soon enough to arrest the tide of anti-Sunningdale feeling amongst the Unionist population.

In an address to an Easter commemoration in Cork, Ó Brádaigh had maintained his optimism about engagement with Loyalists about constitutional future of the North:

> There are those who would mock the feeble attempts of Loyalists in the North to work their way forward to joining hands with us ... Such people should be given every encouragement to discuss and get around the table so we work out a future for our country. (*Irish Times* 15 April 1974)

He predicted the imminent collapse of Executive given that 'it was founded on deceit having two contradictory and opposed concepts which people were told could be achieved at the same time'. This was a not unreasonable criticism and his hopes for the Loyalists were apparently shared by Merlyn Rees who when he lifted the ban on Sinn Féin also legalised the UVF. He also announced the phasing out of internment. The decision infuriated Brian Faulkner, who claimed that Sinn Féin 'was no different from the organisation that had just bombed Royal Avenue in Belfast'. The contradictions of British policy were apparent in the continuing arrests of prominent Provisionals by the army and the RUC. Thus the veteran Provisional and former Sinn Féin TD John Joe McGirl was arrested by troops in Andersonstown on his way to address an Easter Commemoration and Rees signed an Interim Custody Order allowing him to be detained in Long Kesh jail (*Irish Times* 18 April 1974). Austen Currie, SDLP Housing Minister in the Executive, complained about the arrest and expressed concern over a recent increase in the number of detentions although he added that he appreciated the position the British government was in due to escalating Republican violence (Ibid.).

By this time, as Faulkner's Unionists and the SDLP continued to argue over the role and powers of the Council of Ireland, and Wilson's government was already contemplating options in the event of power sharing collapsing, Ó Brádaigh's prediction looked likely to be fulfilled. However, that it was the UWC strike that brought the collapse raised the crucial issue of the realism or otherwise of previous overtures to Loyalism. The strike foregrounded the inadequacies of both Provisional and Official views of the likely political trajectory of the Protestant working class. When the UVF had attacked the proposal for a Council of Ireland and proposed instead a Council of Ulster, this was welcomed by the leadership of Official Sinn Féin, who praised 'its obvious class orientation' (*Irish Times* 4 February 1974). During the Republican Clubs' Westminster election campaign they had declared they were committed to destroying Sunningdale, which was aimed at 'the permanent control of the middle classes' and supported all anti-Sunningdale candidates including Paisley, 'although he was opposing Sunningdale for the wrong reasons' (*Irish Times* 27 February 1974).

Similarly some within the Provisionals took heart from the success of the UWC strike:

> There is evidence that the working class Protestants who comprise the paramilitary groups are strongly socialist in their thinking. This bodes ill for traditional Unionist politicians who have exploited the loyalist working class on the basis of sectarianism. This development could have far-reaching effects if they realise, as they must surely do in time, their community of interest with the depressed Catholic working class. (Cited in Bew and Patterson, 1984: 79)

A more realistic if primordialist sentiment was expressed by the *Republican News* commentator 'Vindicator', who warned of any 'détente' with the Loyalists. The UWC strike should not be seen as indicating 'a significant change in the mentality of the Orange colonists who have for 180 years been the major agents in upholding English imperialism in Ireland' (Irish Republican Information Service, 31 May 1974, quoted in Bew and Patterson, 1984: 79). From this perspective, only British withdrawal would force Loyalists to change: 'Once the British backing was removed the Orange bully-boys would face reality and draw in their horns' (*Irish Times* 29 May 1974).

However, whatever the differences of view on the nature of Loyalism, the Provisionals could only be heartened by the collapse of the Executive. In a traditionalist blast Ó Brádaigh attacked the British for 'caving in in the face of political striking and bombings without warning'. He emphasised the humiliation of the SDLP:

> John Hume used to say that right-wing Unionism would have to be confronted, out faced and beaten. But now the moment of truth has arrived and it is Hume and Currie, their collaborators, who have been outfaced and humbled. The velvet glove is off and the Irish people behold the mailed fist of British imperialism in Ireland. (*Irish Times* 23 May 1974)

British constitutional policy for Northern Ireland was now in the melting-pot and the Provisionals made the easy assumption that, with their having suffered such a defeat at the hands of Unionists and Loyalists, withdrawal was now a much more likely option. Although this was indeed the inclination of the Prime Minister, the very success of the UWC strike, together with the evidence of a relentless Loyalist assassination campaign and Nationalist suspicions of collusion between sections of the security forces and Loyalist paramilitaries, made risks of uncontrollable violence following any withdrawal apparent, not only to a terrified Irish government but to more sensible heads within the British state. The basic fact about the events of 1974 was that the sectarian violence unleashed in 1969–70 had created the conditions for a Provisional campaign with substantial popular support or acquiescence. Capable of destroying Stormont and playing a significant role in the destruction of Sunningdale, it would have the unintended consequence, not of forcing British disengagement, but of a reconstruction of the British connection and a resigned acceptance that the British state was in for a long haul in the province.

Fortuitously for Gerry Adams he was reduced to the role of a spectator for all these developments, incarcerated as he was in Long Kesh. We have no direct evidence of what he thought of the strategy followed by Ó Brádaigh and the army council during this period although Brendan Hughes claimed that from the early months of 1974 he, Adams and Bell were aware of talks between senior Provisionals and the British and were angry and suspicious about their purpose (Moloney, 2010: 168). The problems with the ceasefire were clear from the beginning and are fully recognised in Ó Brádaigh's account of it. A hike in Loyalist killings stoked up internal pressure for retaliation, there was little actual evidence that withdrawal referred to more than the natural reduction of British troops in the event of violence having ended, and, fundamentally, it became clear that 'withdrawal' was meant to mean the British state adopting a 'distancing' role which foregrounded the role of the Northern Irish parties in working out the structures of a future accommodation (McGrattan, 2010: 110–13). In April after the IRA had bombed a business in Belfast to demonstrate lack of progress, the British representative told his Republican interlocutors that a demand for declaration of intend was out of the question but asked for help in 'creating the circumstances out of which the structures of disengagement can naturally grow' (White, 2006: 235). The British also wanted Sinn Féin to stand for the Convention elections to use it as a platform to advocate an all-Ireland convention (Ibid.: 234). But just as they had predicted that Sunningdale would fail, the Provisional leadership could rely on the leadership of Unionism to destroy any faint chance of a convention agreement. Such a failure would, they believed, increase the likelihood of British withdrawal. The core of their failure lay in their overestimation of the willingness of the British state to act in a way that would have risked a massive Protestant backlash and which the Irish government had made clear it strongly opposed. While this led to their replacement by a younger Northern cadre led by Adams, this group, while correctly grasping that the British state was not withdrawing in the short term, incorrectly believed that a 'long war' would succeed where the 'Year of Liberty 1974' mentality had failed.

Notes

1   Copies of both pamphlets can be consulted in the Linen Hall Library's Political Collection.
2   Farrell's analysis was given more substantial historical form in his *Northern Ireland: The Orange State*, first published in 1976. Adams's analysis of Unionism and Loyalism is strongly beholden to this book; see Adams, 1986: 114: 'Colonial powers have long used the plantation of garrisons to keep down rebellious natives. These garrisons were given privileges in return for their loyalty.'

Part III

The legacies of Sunningdale

11

Cultural responses to and the legacies of Sunningdale

Connal Parr

The theatre represents what the director Mick Gordon calls a 'safe thinking space', where the mind intuits 'no danger from the alternative actions, thoughts and feelings being presented'. While this is often cited as a weakness – because what the audience sees does not impact directly upon their lives – 'It is precisely because theatre does not directly affect our normal lives that our minds allow us the thinking space to experience and consider the alternative stories and behaviours in front of us' (2010: 13–14). This may be why drama has often been the preferred form for those culturally approaching the Ulster Workers' Council (UWC) strike of May 1974, at least from within the community who drove it. The strike intrudes on the late Christina Reid's *Belle of the Belfast City* (1989), and it was no coincidence that when the former Progressive Unionist Party leader Dawn Purvis made a recent theatrical foray through the *Flesh and Blood Women* trio of one-act plays – performed at the Belfast Opera House in May 2014 – her story was set during the strike. The time continues to represent a powerful crucible through which to explore identity and intra-communal division, though it was a terrain first mined by Sydenham-born Stewart Parker, whose play *Pentecost* (1989) is arguably the most sophisticated framing of the era of Sunningdale.

Concerned very intimately with 'the state of Protestant political identity as it emerged from the 1974 UWC strike (O'Toole, 1995), Parker's work was not afraid to confront the baser elements in his own background. Echoing old Northern Ireland Labour grandees – who believed that a 'modicum of generosity' from Unionists during the 1960s may have averted the ferocity of the violence from 1969 onwards (Brett, 1978: 153) – one of its characters rails:

> PETER: Can you not see, this whole tribe, so-called Protestants ... all that endless mindless marching, they've been marching away with the lambegs blattering and the banners flying straight up a dead-end one-way blind alley, self-destroying, the head's eating the tail now, it's a lingering tribal suicide going on out there, there was no need for any of it, they held all the cards, they only needed to be marginally generous. (Parker, 1989: 184)

On stage there was, and remains, a probing and self-questioning going on which it is impossible to see taking place through Unionist politicians, whose careers would be curtailed by expressing such sentiments in a zero-sum atmosphere.

In his life and work Parker was obsessed with Northern Protestant identity and devoted to highlighting its multifariousness. As Field Day Theatre Company toured *Pentecost* around Ireland in the late 1980s, the play sought a return 'to the individual, to the "Christ in ourselves", as the source of regeneration and change' (Andrews, 1987: n.p.). Religion was not shunned but, as the ending makes clear, an intrinsic part of the solution. Parker's own proximity to death heightened this conviction,[1] though *Pentecost*'s 'final cure lies not in political action or even social agitation but in a fundamental engagement which alone can give change a moral as well as a sociological dimension' (Andrews, 1987: n.p.). The structure and title of the play were handed to its author by the timescale; the actual dates of the UWC strike gave way to the feast of Pentecost. Its central character of Marian steps 'right across the community divide to investigate someone whose whole history is totally different to her own' (Lynne Parker, interview with the author, 24 March 2012), reaching out to an apparition – a recently deceased lady called Lily Matthews – who is a psychic manifestation of what she believes to be the 'other': the Loyalist community.

Initially Lily is an antagonistic revenant, emerging from the brickwork to deliver, with unapologetic intransigence, the line which seems to define her community's stance: 'I don't want you in my house' (Parker, 1989: 155). Through Marian's engagement, however, flows a plea 'to live now' and move away from the perpetual blaming of the other for all grievance and injustice, reaching 'a reconciliation of sorts: with the collective past' (Johnstone, 1989: 62) as well as an unavoidable present. In the year of the Enniskillen bombing and the residual hostility to the Anglo-Irish Agreement (which to Parker was coterminous with 1974), the essence of *Pentecost* was its imagining of some kind of reconciliation for Northern Ireland when none appeared in sight. This appeared even more pronounced with the mass-mobilisation element of the opposition to Sunningdale, i.e. the democratic majority whose will it flexed. As Stephen Rea, who founded Field Day and acted in the original production, remembers: 'It's only in that small microcosm and room where there are these people that find it impossible to live, end up determining to be reconciled. At the time when *Pentecost* was set you couldn't imagine a future. All you could imagine was people huddling in their houses, hiding from the very frightening violence that was outside' (Interview with the author, 14 August 2014). He affirmed that Field Day's theatrical productions were 'voicing things, heightening the language in which things could be debated, because everything was being fought over rather than discussed.' Plays like Brian Friel's *Translations* (1980) and Parker's *Pentecost* were 'looking for a way out when the ceasefire wasn't even a remote possibility' (quoted in *Irish Times* 11 October 2006: 16). The simple cultural presentation of a possible reconciliation, Rea maintains, 'filters into people's consciousness' and, eventually, their politics' (Interview with the author, 14 August 2014).

Legacy

If Lily haunts Parker's final play, the ghosts of Sunningdale haunt every political arrangement, every set of talks, initiatives, and deliberations undertaken in Northern Ireland ever since. A whole community – or at least the majority of a community – proved in response to a series of perceived political defeats that it could wreck developments as a final veto in the politics of destruction. This became in itself a dominant cultural feature of Ulster Protestant politics. The late John Cole astutely captured how this was reinforced 'by a thwarted sense among many Protestants that they are losing the battle in spite of their superiority in numbers', and for this reason 'the possibility of another strike hangs over every Protestant politician' (*The Guardian* 17 February 1975: 11). Personally comfortable with increasing cross-border co-operation, the Chief Executive, Brian Faulkner, was thought to have underestimated the anxiety the Council of Ireland would foment in the Unionist community and the party he led. Arguing many years later that Faulkner should have 'played harder to get', his own Principal Private Secretary maintained that the Unionist 'veto' was 'never a threat to the overall process in the way it perhaps should have been'. Faulkner's desire 'to get Stormont up and running again' – part of his dynamic persona – was considered, in this reading, a 'weakness' (Ramsay, 2009: 123).[2] Henceforth the position of negotiation in extracting the stoutest settlement for the extremes of Unionism is something every one of its leaders and representatives has had to be mindful of, which is why politicians continue to feel the need to run political agreements past une-lected figureheads.[3]

Alternatively the UWC strike of May 1974 occurred at the end of a longer process taking in the fall of Stormont, the disbandment of the B Specials, the disarming of the Royal Ulster Constabulary and the Sunningdale negotia-tions themselves. During the latter only two members of the process identi-fied that the ensuing settlement constituted Faulkner 'being nailed to a cross' (quoted in Akenson, 1994: 407).[4] Referring to the democratic element which was essential in underpinning Sunningdale, the Northern Ireland Labour Party's David Bleakley – who supported power sharing – concurred that the Agreement's 'Irish Dimension' ensured that the British government 'pressed for more than the Protestant community could be persuaded to accept'. This in turn placed 'an intolerable burden' on the Executive and brought it, ironically, 'into conflict with the basic stipulation of his Constitution Act that government in Northern Ireland should be "widely acceptable through-out the community"' (Bleakley, 1975: 8). Both the Social Democratic and Labour Party (SDLP) and the Irish government would learn lessons for subsequent negotiations, and there is no question that in February 1974 the Westminster election turned into a virtual referendum on Sunningdale, handing the UWC an air of legitimacy (*Irish News* 29 December 2005: 25). The strike's success was a one-off in the sense that future political provisions would always see the electorate of both communities 'adequately consulted and informed *in advance*' (Conor Cruise O'Brien, writing in *The Times* 20 November 1975: 20).

The UWC strike was the most pronounced manifestation of the 'Protes-tant veto' during the early Troubles, temporarily comprising disparate groups which were always liable to fall asunder. The weakness of analysis thus far has consequently been to simplify and homogenise what was in actuality a complex phenomenon, either with facile labels such as 'fascist' or through a nonsensical interpretation of the action as a 'lockout' (see Bell, 1976: 82; Mitchell, 2014: 38). Ironically mirroring the assessment of the then Secretary of State, Merlyn Rees, who insisted that the stoppage was 'not normal indus-trial action' (PRONI, OE/1/16, 'Press Notice'),[5] the failure to realise that the opposition to Sunningdale was built on genuine Ulster Protestant resent-ment, motored by trade unionists from the same background, and secured with the will of a majority, reflects many of the contemporary problems which have arisen through the ongoing politicisation of history. The assess-ment of an Irish labour historian that 'The Ulster Workers' Council had nothing to do with trade unions. It simply deepened divisions' (Devine, 2009: 601) simply defies fact. With the language of the Left claimed – in many ways unconvincingly – by mainstream Republicanism, the strike's more

radical trade unionist character is often neglected and downplayed, frequently by Northern Protestants themselves. Aside from the strike garnering
– with exceptions – the widespread support of working-class Protestants,
'there were a lot of people involved in it who were trade unionists, and who
would remain trade unionists after' (Joe Law, interview with the author, 26
June 2013).[6] Speaking on television days before the strike began, the UWC's
Billy Kelly affirmed that his group was not affiliated to any party and 'only
an organisation for the working-class people' (quoted in PRONI, OE/1/16,
'BBC Scene Around Six').

For many years confined to a few journalistic accounts and the odd article,
the quality of literature on both Sunningdale and the UWC strike has only
been remedied by more nuanced analysis which has emerged in recent years
(McGrattan, 2009; Kerr, 2011; Aveyard, 2014). For far too long events were
not viewed in their continuum. Inherently connected to shifts within Ulster
Protestant politics in the previous decade, Marc Mulholland has established
how until the era of Terence O'Neill (1963–69):

> Unionism had traditionally been led by a social elite distant from the rank and file.
> The leaders had made up for this, however, by paying a populist attention to the opin-
> ions, attitudes and prejudices of their loyalist constituency. By the 1960s, however, the
> middle-class establishment had accepted a liberal consensus, which believed that
> battles over the border had been left in the past. (2000: 199)

O'Neill was supportive of this new consensus and won the leadership of his
party as the figure best suited to steal the Northern Ireland Labour Party
(NILP)'s 'technocratic, economically modernizing clothes' (Mulholland,
2000: 199). His project attracted 'liberal' middle-class Unionists who had
steered clear of his party due to its traditionalist Protestant associations, but
working-class liberals – who supported O'Neill's reforms and many of the
civil rights demands – remained largely steadfast in the NILP. From the start
of O'Neill's tenure, therefore, the 'liberalism' of his brand of Unionism was
'very decidedly identified with the protestant middle class' (Wright, 1973:
272). This is important in the context of Sunningdale because the consensus
was still very much in the air, O'Neill identifying 'remnants of the middle
class moderation he had fostered' in the 1973 Agreement (Mulholland,
2013: 94). While the man himself had left the stage, Sunningdale was looked
on as his achievement by those who sought to demolish it.

Unionism and Loyalism

By 1974 there had been considerable Unionist fissuring with the formation
of the Democratic Unionist Party (DUP) and Alliance, as well as the mild

continuation of the Faulkner Unionists. In keeping with the 'Independent Unionist' tradition, Paisley had always lambasted 'fur coat brigade' Unionists – and the Executive's Minister for Education, Basil McIvor, admitted that affluent 'Liberal Unionists' such as himself were particular 'targets for Loyalist bitterness and anger' (1998: 121). Despite his personal commitment, McIvor was always conscious that Sunningdale's merits might 'not get through to the people in the high flats at Finaghy' (quoted in PRONI, OE/2/10, 'Meeting of the Administration' [5 March 1974]). Thus the strike was directed – as the Ulster Defence Association (UDA)'s former Supreme Commander confirms – against the way

> The Unionist politicians – Captain Terence O'Neill, Brian Faulkner and all the rest – just took it for granted. The fascinating thing was this was the first time that people had said 'Hol' on, we've had enough of this carry-on'. The Council of Ireland was imposed on us. We weren't told, we weren't considered in the argument at all. It wasn't about them (the SDLP) being in government; it was about the attitude of the Unionist politicians. They never were used to making decisions from Partition here. They allowed the civil service to run the place, and it got that bad that we were the lesser-known people within the British government. Our politicians hadn't the sense to realize that they weren't important. They were ambushed. (Andy Tyrie, interview with the author, 9 August 2012)

It is important to remember that effigies of Faulkner, as well as Gerry Fitt, were burned in Newtownabbey's Rathcoole estate on the fall of the Executive (Fisk, 1975: 224).

With this in mind one of the strangest and most ironic of appropriations which has taken place since 1974 has seen Unionist politicians try to take credit for the stoppage's success (see Laird, 2010: 89–90). The *de facto* leader Glen Barr confirmed that such men, aside from precipitating through their absence of 'leadership' his entry into politics, were opportunistically keen to be photographed with the strikers: 'But if you'd have dared mention the fact you were thinking of marrying one of their daughters, they would run a mile.'[7] This apparent class animosity – sometimes wrongly interpreted as 'Ulster Nationalism' – would seem to accord with the estimation of an Executive Minister that the strike was motivated 'as much by a crude class hatred of the landed gentry and local business tycoons who for years had dominated Unionist Party politics as by their fears of a united Ireland via Sunningdale' (Devlin, 1975: 83). It is universally accepted that the only politicians to emerge with any credit from 1974 in the eyes of the Loyalist strikers were Bill Craig and a young Law lecturer at Queen's University by the name of David Trimble.

A window into Unionist thinking on the strike leaders was offered by Sunningdale's Minister for the Environment, Roy Bradford, in the form of his novel *The Last Ditch* (1981), sketching the fall of Sunningdale with fictional characters clearly modelled on real players. Harry Harmonn – an obvious surrogate for Andy Tyrie – is depicted as being secretly elated at rubbing shoulders with high-ranking Unionist politicians during the stoppage: 'It was a step nearer to the Establishment. He affected to despise conventional politicians, but secretly he envied them ... This could be the chance he'd been looking for. If they needed him, if they were prepared even unofficially to bring him in from the cold, he would come' (Bradford, 1981: 50).[8] Aside from conveying the baseless fear that senior Unionists had of being usurped by Loyalists, Bradford's view was that the UWC strike leaders deep down wanted to take their place at the high political table: a fundamental misreading given the sheer lack of Loyalist political success before and since.

At the third meeting of the British/Irish Association two years after the collapse of Sunningdale, the former deputy leader of Vanguard, Ernest Baird, proclaimed: 'There is no middle ground in Northern Ireland, there is no compromise to follow. Sooner or later one side must triumph over the other.' It was Barr of all people who stepped up on the same platform to counter that 'What Ernie Baird has just said is diabolical and does not represent the view of the majority of the loyalist people of Northern Ireland' (quoted in *Irish Times* 10 July 1976: 10). The exchange is revealing in two ways. On the one hand Baird was locating, quite authentically, the space into which Unionism did (and occasionally continues to) situate itself. On the other Barr was correct to qualify that Loyalists did not necessarily tally with Unionist sentiment; that the former were separate and quite often more conciliatory in their political thinking than 'respectable' Unionism. The UDA, for instance, publicly advocated power sharing at a time when both the leadership of the Official Unionist Party and the DUP rejected the idea (*Irish Times* 27 September 1975: 8). Along with Paisley, Baird was strongly identified with a follow-up strike three years later, and, though it was a 'closer-run thing' than many care to recollect (Robert Ramsay, interview with the author, 2 February 2012),[9] to call the 1977 episode a failure in some ways misses the point. What was to leave a lasting cultural mark on Northern Irish politics was the threat, or more precisely the *appearance* of the threat. To give but one instance of this, during the protests accompanying the 1985 Anglo-Irish Agreement the Rev. Ivan Foster and Peter Robinson were among a group who called for a third big Loyalist strike to destroy the latest accord (Hume, 1986: 6). No such action, of course, ever materialised.

The UWC strike accordingly ushered in a new phase in that incredibly ambivalent, often tortuous relationship which has existed between the paramilitaries and Unionist politicians. A prominent journalist on the ground pinpointed the scenario whereby the three traditional pillars of Protestant power – loyalty to the Union, anti-Catholicism and the 'political Toryism which bound the Protestant working class submissively into a single party' (with its betters) – was now 'being quarried away by a section of the garrison', i.e. Ulster Loyalists. For this reason, Neal Ascherson contended that 'the strike has managed to shift the whole centre of gravity in Protestant politics' (1974: 11). When the Rev. Martin Smyth insisted that Northern Protestants had no time for 'thuggery and socialism', Andy Tyrie rounded that men like Smyth 'did politics for a hobby and now they come crawling to us from under their flat stones; they should be ashamed to show their faces' (quoted in Ascherson, 1974: 11). Less than a year after the strike's denouement Loyalists assured Official Unionists at an East Belfast meeting that they would 'wind up in Roselawn' (a cemetery just outside the city) unless they shared political influence with the paramilitaries (*Irish Times* 10 February 1975: 6). At times the DUP did embark on a closer relationship with the UDA, co-operating during the 1977 strike, in the party's habit of running UDA affiliates as candidates (a practice it continues to the present day), and even in the warm ties Peter Robinson reportedly had to the group (Moloney and Pollak, 1986: 292; *Irish News* 2 May 2014: 12). There tended, however, to be much mutual distrust and periodic bouts of invective directed back and forth.

'Spongers'

In a statement on Saturday 25 May 1974 Brian Faulkner observed that the potential damage of the UWC action was 'beyond calculation'. Estimating the loss of 'hundreds of thousands of jobs', he warned that 'If the present deadlock continues much longer we will all be the losers in time to come' (PRONI, OE/1/16, 'Broadcast'). A matter of hours later the British Prime Minister, Harold Wilson, took to the screens to deliver what became infamously known as the 'spongers' broadcast. Many Loyalists were expecting Wilson to announce plans to intern them; instead he railed how

> British taxpayers, have seen their sons vilified and spat upon – and murdered. They have seen the taxes they have poured out almost without regard to cost – over £300 million a year ... going into Northern Ireland. Yet people who benefit from this now viciously defy Westminster, purporting to act as though they were an elected government; people who spend their lives sponging on Westminster and British democracy ... Who do these people think they are? (Harold Wilson, Transcript of Televised Address, 25 May 1974, http://cain.ulst.ac.uk/events/uwc/docs/hw25574.htm (accessed 10 October 2012))

Wilson later explained that 'the idea I was seeking to get across was that Ulster was always ready to come to Auntie for spending money, expressing their thanks by kicking her in the teeth' (1979: 77). Local civil servants remain bemused at the specific phrase, perusing a version of the speech earlier in the day which made no reference to it at all (Maurice Hayes, interview with the author, 26 November 2012). However there was something especially potent in the spectacle of a Labour Prime Minister – a man who helped to establish the Welfare State through his work on the Beveridge Report – addressing this section in such derogatory terms. Its economic tone – reminiscent of successive British governments right up to the present day – was designed for an English audience but also calculated with maximum contempt. A notable piece of high theatre, it invites *all* Northern Irish citizens to consider their status within the UK and its economy.

After listening to the speech in Stewart Parker's *Pentecost*, Ruth dubs Wilson a 'smug wee English shite with a weaselly voice', who fails to respect the sacrifices of Northern Protestants, 'British taxpayers just the same as they are'. When she is challenged by Peter – who fears that 'raw sewage is about to come flooding down those streets out there, and it won't be the English who die of typhoid' – she defies: 'They can't take on an entire community. The strike is theirs' (Parker, 1989: 183–5). Such defiance was not to pass unpunished. Wilson triumphantly withheld a £9 million subsidy from Harland and Wolff, clearly implying that the yard and other industries seen as too close to the strike were to take a hit in the coming years (1979: 75–7). Papers released under the 'thirty-year rule' revealed that during the month of the stoppage the Commerce Minister, John Hume, warned of financial problems at Harland and Wolff and the threat to tens of thousands of jobs. Despite Hume's pleas the company was actually excluded from subsequent plans to nationalise British aircraft and shipbuilding industries (*Irish News* 29 December 2005: 24). Andy Tyrie remains proud that his community 'were the first group that ever took the British government on and won a strike' (Interview with the author, 9 August 2012), but it was in some ways a pyrrhic victory, offering a wounded Labour government the chance to begin eroding its financial contributions to what were frankly Protestant industries. The broader energy crisis and worldwide quadrupling of oil prices further compounded the depressing impact on employment within the Northern Irish economy from then on.

Banditry

One of the other more ominous consequences of the Sunningdale period was the systematising of criminal underworlds. The thin line between vigilantism – which has a long history in Belfast – and criminality was regularly blurred, in a dynamic further exacerbated by the political distress and fragmentation engendered by O'Neill's tenure. This resonates with Eric

Hobsbawm's assessment that banditry fundamentally challenges 'those who hold or lay claim to power, law and control of resources', in a dynamic intrinsically related to 'class divisions' (2000: 7–9). The criminality tar had initially been used in the context of Northern Ireland by the SDLP as 'a useful weapon in its constant battle to distinguish itself unequivocally from the Provos' (Nelson, 1977: 13), but the clash between law and lawlessness was always more pronounced in the Northern Protestant population for the simple reason that it maintained a considerably more loyal relationship with the state than its Nationalist counterpart. As a writer who travelled around Belfast in the 1970s put it, 'for all the endemic lawlessness of the Catholic ghettos their inhabitants have not descended as far into gangsterism as the Loyalists', in part 'because Loyalists have in the past been able to count on certain elements in the RUC "not noticing" their exploits' (Murphy, 1979: 146–7).

A thesis dubiously fostered by contemporary Loyalist leaders proposes that the 'cancer' of criminality basically entered Protestant areas with drug-dealing and the prominence of UDA figureheads in the early 1990s (Jackie McDonald, quoted in Shirlow, 2012: 115). A former leader of the Ulster Unionist Party confirms that problems began decades in advance of this, damaging not just Loyalist politicisation but the societal fabric:

> When they did start up in the 1960s and '70s, their activities in Loyalist areas weren't confined simply to fighting Republicans. They were involved in rackets, they were involved in criminality and those sorts of things discredited them in front of the ordinary people because their activities in Loyalist areas had the effect in some instances of destroying the quality of life. They had Shebeens, they had protection rackets, they were throwing their weight around locally and just generally upsetting people. And the idea that they would actually fire on and attack police goes against the grain. (Lord Reg Empey, interview with the author, 11 November 2011)

The UDA in particular became heavily absorbed in extensive criminal enterprises, and the difference between it and the Ulster Volunteer Force (UVF) in this regard (as in others) has often been elided by journalistic and academic investigations. From the beginning of its existence it attracted 'gangsters who saw a position in the UDA as an easy way to good cars, thick gold jewellery and winter holidays in Spain' (Bruce, 1992: 17), and a prevalent belief among UVF ex-combatants is that many who joined the UDA were driven by the basic desire for individual aggrandisement. This is seen to persevere in the form of contemporary UDA spokesmen: 'The likes of Frankie Gallagher and Jackie McDonald, I wouldn't in a million years associate them as having a voice that's representative of anything other than themselves. Not only because they're not elected but because their organisation historically has went down that line. You only have to look at anything they're associated with: it's personally and financially beneficial' (William Mitchell, interview with the author, 26 July 2012).

In the context of the Troubles the UVF was a deadlier outfit, while its notorious east Antrim wing was also immersed in criminality from the early 1970s (Cusack and McDonald, 1997: 107–9). But there is much to be said for the view that the UDA's criminal actions were expanded by the power it enjoyed from 1974.[10] Its exertions had begun (as Empey stated) prior to the UWC strike but, unchallenged by security forces, a generation of leaders within the UDA – such as McDonald and John 'Grug' Gregg – cut their teeth in the stoppage (Wood, 2006: 40–1). The manning of barricades, oil and fuel smuggling, extortion and black markets all flourished, generating some of the more unpropitious images associated with Loyalism thereafter. This situation may also be understood, as a recent work on global crime couches it, as a by-product of 'unimaginative politicians who lack either the vision or the interest to address the great structural inequities ... upon which crime and instability thrive' (Glenny, 2008: 394). In *Pentecost*, as the UWC tightens its grip on the province, Peter delineates the atmosphere around the centre of its headquarters in East Belfast, not far from the gates of Stormont:

> PETER: is this what you want? – the apemen in charge, shops without food to sell, garages without petrol ... there's a mile-long queue of doctors and nurses and social workers, and lawyers, up at Hawthornden Road, queuing up to beg for a special pass to get them through the barricades to their patients and clients, and from who? – from the hard men who can barely sign their name to their special bloody passes, from shipyard bible-thumpers, unemployed binmen, petty crooks and extortionists, pig-brain mobsters and thugs, they've seized control over all of us. (Parker, 1989: 184)

In fairness to the UDA, its members tended to own up to these activities to an almost comical degree. One public relations officer, Sammy Duddy, admitted the UDA had originally 'incorporated among many of our companies and brigades gangsters, petty thieves and so on', and that after attempting 'to put forward some sort of political initiative this organisation has been very disappointed at the public response. We deduce from this that the only thing that pays in this country is violence' (quoted in *The Guardian* 15 August 1979: 24). To the dismay of those strike leaders with trade union backgrounds, the UDA discovered it was better at racketeering than socialism.

Republicanism

The literature of Sunningdale's impact on militant Irish Republicanism, like much of the literature on the period, is underwhelming and deserves further expansion. The response of Republicans ranged across a spectrum, though most have hit back at Seamus Mallon's famous dictum. An unlikely ally in the Irish media would retrospectively claim that the Agreement collapsed 'because it did not have mainstream republican or unionist parties on board', so that arguably 'the slow learners were in fact the participants in Sunningdale who thought they could do it without bringing in the political representatives of the mainstream paramilitary groups' (O'Clery, 1998: 5). This comment, made in the somewhat delusive glow of Good Friday 1998, captures a commonly held view even amongst dissenting Republicans. At a conference held to mark the fortieth anniversary of the strike, the former Provisional IRA hunger striker Tommy McKearney lashed the SDLP for sitting down with Faulkner and disputed Mallon's aphorism: 'If there were any slow learners it was the people who coined that phrase, because if Unionism wasn't willing to do the deal, and if the British Government wasn't willing to enforce it, the slow learners were those who thought that it might work'. Nobody appreciates being labelled a slow learner, but other Republicans believe that 1973 actually represented a 'better deal' for Republicans. The North–South/East–West relationships and toothless British–Irish Council enacted by subsequent agreements were arguably inferior to the 'Irish-run' Council of Ireland (Richard O'Rawe, interview with the author, 18 January 2012).

At the time the Provisional IRA was thrown into disarray by the resistance to Sunningdale. As some commanders talked of ratcheting up the bombing campaign, the leadership exhibited a Pearse-esque admiration, Dáithí Ó Conaill describing the strike as 'in the Wolfe Tone tradition' (quoted in Walsh, 1994: 139). There were areas of agreement between the Provisionals and the UWC over opposition to Internment and the Diplock court system, but essentially the Provisional IRA began thinking – as previously had the Official IRA – that working-class Unionists could be 'useful to Republicanism' (Walsh, 1994: 139). As the Troubles wore on, however, and the Protestant working class continued to refuse the 'deluded Irishmen' designation, this strain of thought was completely abandoned by the time the new Northern leadership, i.e. Adams and McGuinness, took over the reins of Sinn Féin (Pollak, 1983: 3). Nevertheless the Provisionals can be seen to have gained much from the UWC strike, including learning about the importance of electric power when thwarting a British Army plan to control Newry's street lighting in the autumn of 1974. For the duration of the stoppage their armed volunteers were posted in shops, churches and the interfaces of Catholic estates, while 'Emergency committees' were set up to distribute food in the Falls and Andersonstown. By the strike's second week the IRA was supervising convivial open-air barbecues (Fisk, 1975: 208–9) in the same areas.

At the same time the street-level competition for control of Catholic districts ensured things were rather more complex than originally thought. Jim McCorry, a chief organiser of the Falls Community Council and the Irish Republican Socialist Party (IRSP), remembered that the Provisional IRA felt threatened by his groups' activities during the UWC strike:

> when we took over a hut at the Glen Road School. Indeed, because we had a van and the contacts for food, we actually took over the provisioning of much of Catholic West Belfast. We took over the running of the petrol stations; people used to have to come to us to get petrol: doctors, priests, whoever. Those of us in the Co op did all that. We'd petrol lorries going down to the South to fill up ... But most of those in the 'army' had no sense of this as a community thing. Especially during the UWC strike they just felt, as they saw it, that I'd taken over. (McCorry, 2005: 15–16)

The Provisionals' solution to this was to propose shooting McCorry, which they never got round to doing. But in a key moment during the strike it was announced within the Sunningdale Executive that the organisation would take over foodstuff distribution in Catholic areas (PRONI, OE/2/31, 'Minutes of Executive Meeting'). This was official recognition of the authority of the Provisional IRA and a harbinger of future political developments.

UDA spokesmen liked to talk up the idea that the Protestant and Catholic working class 'came together' during May 1974, with Loyalist paramilitaries reaching 'an understanding with some Catholic leaders' concerned about the strike's sectarian connotations. On taking over fuel distribution, and with essential services now guaranteed by the Strike Committee, the UWC pointedly directed the first petrol truck to West Belfast. This gesture impressed the Provisionals, though it was actually the order the shop steward Harry Murray and not a decision taken in conjunction with either the UDA or the IRA (Fisk, 1975: 207). Tommy 'Tucker' Lyttle echoed his UDA colleagues in claiming that for the first time since 1969 Loyalists had contact 'with the people who had opposite views to us' (quoted in *Irish Times* 4 July 1974: 12). It spoke volumes that Lyttle himself embodied the UDA's initial political shoots – co-founding the Ulster Political Research Group – before presiding over its 'mafia-style criminal gang' elements when the politics failed (*The Guardian* 21 October 1995: 32). If the UDA retained the power arising from its criminality, the Provisional IRA held on to the power arising from the recognition it received in 1974.

Conclusion

Instructive is the case of Unionists who served as ministers in the Executive who were all, in different ways, utterly scattered following the collapse of

Sunningdale. Basil McIvor, Herbert Kirk and John Baxter retired almost immediately from politics to careers in law and accountancy, while both Leslie Morrell and Roy Bradford lost their seats in the Constitutional Convention election the following year. The modernising guard, the logical culmination of O'Neillism, had been categorically decimated. Duncan Pollock, a Presbyterian who soldiered on in Faulkner's doomed Unionist Party of Northern Ireland (UPNI), believed 'They saw the Executive working and they decided to wreck it. I was hammered in the elections to the Convention (1975). I expected it, but they really hammered me' (quoted in *Irish Times* 12 July 1979: 10). Generated by a 'sense of humiliation' and feeling that 'Catholics had been "winning" consistently since 1968' (Miller, 2007: 163), the consequent euphoria expressed in Protestant working-class areas veiled a relief. As Glen Barr now declares: 'The Loyalist people had taken such a terrible battering over those years from 1968 up to 1974. There was no consultation with them when their government, their institutions, were taken away. 1974 I think was the last time that the Loyalist people held their head up, the last time they had got a lift' (speaking at '40 Years On' conference, held at Queen's University Belfast, 19 May 2014).

At the same time this momentum was destructive rather than creative, as captured – again – by Stewart Parker. Surveying the jubilation which greets the fall of the Executive, Peter in *Pentecost* despairs: 'You'd think they'd given birth, actually created something for once, instead of battering it to death, yet again, the only kind of victory they ever credit, holding the good old fort, stamping the life out of anything that starts to creep forward' (Parker, 1989: 199). Barr himself wished the strike had bequeathed to the Protestant community a 'willingness to cast off the old-style politician who waved the Union Jack every five years' (quoted in *Irish Times* 24 June 1974: 8), but in this and his hopes of Left/Right politics where 'people like Paddy Devlin and myself sit on one side of the House and people like Leslie Morrell and Brian Faulkner sit on the other side' (Interview with the author, 28 November 2012) he was to be sorely disappointed.

Perhaps the first victim of the powerful veto established by the opposition to Sunningdale was another of the strike leaders. Less than two months after its denouement shop steward Harry Murray appeared at a conference in Oxford where he reiterated the UWC's opposition to Internment and urged Loyalists, almost *Pentecost*-like, to engage and talk with the Provisional IRA (on the condition the latter put down their arms). Following vigorous denunciation from Unionist politicians, Murray was forced to resign from the UWC within a matter of days (*Irish Times* July 1974: 6). Ironically Murray was known to have disapproved of paramilitary involvement during May 1974, though the UDA backed him for his Oxford comments. Before the end of the year he had founded a non-sectarian peace group (*The Times* 9 September 1974: 2), appearing on platforms with members of the Corrymeela community and peace activists in Derry. He joined the non-sectarian Alliance Party, which he would later stand for as a candidate in local government elections, and by the time of the hunger strikes had reconvened the UWC as an organisation to promote job creation and 'unity among all Northern Ireland workers' (*The Guardian* 28 February 1981: 24). If indeed the head was beginning to eat the tail, Murray's own example demonstrated that individuals in Northern Ireland could persist in their own engagement and reconciliation, even if they had to circumnavigate their political culture to do so.

Notes

1 Parker died of stomach cancer (aged 47) the following year.
2 Under Faulkner's brief as Minister of Commerce, motor-car manufacturing and the fibres industry were drastically expanded in the mid-1960s (*The Guardian* 19 August 1976: 9).
3 Following the all-party talks chaired by the US Diplomat Richard Haass at the end of 2013, it transpired that politicians from the Democratic Unionist Party had briefed victims and survivors' campaigner William (Willie) Frazer and loyalist activist Jamie Bryson on the final proposals. Both Unionist parties eventually withdrew their support, leading to the talks breaking up without agreement (*Belfast Telegraph* 8 January 2014: 11).
4 The phrase of the SDLP Minister of Health and Social Services, Paddy Devlin. The other man who grasped Faulkner's predicament was the Irish Minister for Posts and Telegraphs, Conor Cruise O'Brien.
5 Two-thirds of the UWC Committee was drawn from the trade unions, the Loyalist paramilitaries providing the other third.
6 Law is a trade unionist from the largely demolished Agnes Street area of the Lower Shankill. For the perspective of one from within the community who defied the strike see the memoir of Baroness May Blood (2007: 80).
7 Speaking at the conference '40 Years On: The Strike Which Brought Down Sunningdale', held at Queen's University Belfast on 19 May 2014.
8 Later Harmon fumes, rather more realistically: 'All your moderates, all your stuck-up fur-coat brigade – they're tucked up nice and snug in their bungalows down in Cultra watchin' the telly! While we're on the streets!' (Bradford, 1981: 101–2).
9 Harry Murray, Glen Barr and Bill Craig – all major players in 1974 – opposed the 1977 strike (*Irish Times* 7 May 1977: 4).
10 Despite the input of the UVF's Ken Gibson, the strike was primarily associated with the UDA (see the comments of David Ervine in Moloney, 2010: 347).

12

'Slow learners'? Comparing the Sunningdale Agreement and the Belfast/Good Friday Agreement

Thomas Hennessey

The 1973 Sunningdale and 1998 Belfast/Good Friday Agreements are, on the face of it, remarkably similar: both involve power sharing (although this was negotiated prior to Sunningdale it remained central to the working of that concord) and an institutional link between Northern Ireland and the Republic of Ireland. The phrase 'Sunningdale for slow learners' (Gillespie, 1998: 100), attributed to Seamus Mallon, captures the apparent prolonging of the Northern Ireland conflict when, to all purposes its 'solution' had already been laid out in principle a quarter of a century earlier; but, as this chapter will show, this masks a misunderstanding of the fundamental differences between the two Agreements.

The consent principle

The consent principle – the right of Northern Ireland to remain within the United Kingdom or become part of a united Ireland – was the key constitutional determinant underlying the political conflict in the 'Troubles'. Consent has been part of British policy since partition: it was formalised, in statute, in the Ireland Act 1949, and then again in the Northern Ireland Constitution Act 1973. The principle was a source of tension between the Irish state and successive UK governments until Sunningdale: indeed Nationalists across the island interpreted 'consent' as a Unionist 'veto' on Irish unity following the artificial partition of the Irish nation.

Bunreacht na hÉireann (the Irish Constitution of 1937) declared, in Article 2, that: 'The national territory consists of the whole island of Ireland, its islands and the territorial seas'. Article 3 stated that, pending the 're-integration of the national territory', the Irish parliament and government had the right to exercise jurisdiction over the whole of the island although it chose, voluntarily, not to apply this to Northern Ireland. This was a territorial claim by successive Irish governments to sovereignty over the entire island of Ireland. According to the Irish Constitution, Northern Ireland was a part of both the Irish nation and the independent Irish state – it was *not* part of the United Kingdom. In contrast, according to the relevant British constitutional points of reference – the British and Irish Acts of Union of 1800 – Northern Ireland *was* part of the United Kingdom. Thus the Irish state formally challenged the right of British sovereignty over Northern Ireland. Consent, constitutional recognition and sovereignty were all bound up.

This constitutional guarantee, in Dublin's opinion, had a 'stultifying effect' on Northern Ireland politics and on British government policies in relation to the North. Prior to Sunningdale it was the Irish government's policy to urge that the guarantee should be reformulated. For example, in 1971, the then Taoiseach, Jack Lynch, argued: 'It would take nothing away from the honour of Britain or the rights of the majority in the North if the British government were to declare their interest in encouraging the unity of Ireland, by agreement, in independence and in a harmonious relationship between the two islands' (NAI, D/T 2004 21/2) – in effect asking Her Majesty's Government (HMG) to become persuaders for Irish unity.

At the Sunningdale negotiations the position of Brian Faulkner, the leader of the Ulster Unionist Party (UUP), was clear: given that his recently agreed power-sharing arrangement with the Social and Democratic Labour Party (SDLP) had met with significant hostility from large sections of the majority community, one thing was vital if the latter's confidence was to be won: the Irish Republic should 'accept the right of the people of Northern Ireland to order their own affairs' (TNA, CJ4/474). The position of the Irish government at Sunningdale, however, was to avoid defining the constitutional position of Northern Ireland as part of the UK: an internal government paper stated that 'in determining our position on the status of Northern Ireland, we should seek to meet the minimal requirements of responsible Northern Protestant opinion; that we should have regard to opinion in the Republic which attaches importance to the claim inherent in Articles 2 and 3 of the Constitution; and that we should not commit ourselves to legal action which would be invalidated by an appeal to these Articles unless we intend to repeal them'. Thus, driven by a fear of public opinion and that a recognition of Northern Ireland's constitutional position within the UK would be deemed unconstitutional in Irish courts, there was to be no written formulation of Dublin's position on the status of Northern Ireland: it was to be enunciated through an *oral* declaration by the Taoiseach, Liam Cosgrave, but only on the occasion of a final agreement covering such matters as a Council of Ireland and the formation of a Northern Ireland power-sharing executive. The oral declaration would recognise the 'different elements' who lived on the island; that political unity should be pursued through reconciliation alone; and, so long as a majority of the people of Northern Ireland wished to maintain its 'present status', the Irish government would work in friendship and co-operation with the 'legitimate' institutions established in Northern Ireland (NAI, D/T 2004/21/627). That 'present status' would remain undefined and therefore there would be no constitutional recognition of Northern Ireland as part of the United Kingdom; all on the island would continue to be regarded as part of the Irish nation; and Dublin would continue to claim sovereignty over the entire island.

In contrast, the UK's position, on the constitutional status of Northern Ireland, at Sunningdale was outlined by two officials, Kelvin White and P.J. Woodfield, in a document containing a phrase that HMG supported the present wishes of the majority to 'stay British'. The significant omission in their text was the phrase 'the present status of Northern Ireland is that it is part of the United Kingdom'. The UUP delegation at the negotiations insisted that this be inserted (TNA, CJ4/474). The Irish, and in particular Dr Conor Cruise O'Brien, pointed out it was constitutionally impossible for the Irish government to commit itself to a public statement that the constitutional status of Northern Ireland was as part of the United Kingdom. It was Woodfield who made the apparent breakthrough by drafting two separate formulas – one for the Republic and one for HMG – and suggested to O'Brien that these two formulas might appear in parallel in a final communiqué. Faulkner accepted this (TNA, CJ4/474).

While both declarations stated that Northern Ireland's status could not be changed without the consent of a majority of its people, only the British declaration defined Northern Ireland as *part of the United Kingdom*. The Irish declaration, in contrast, did not define the 'present status' of Northern Ireland: the Six Counties, Dublin could argue, remained a part of the Republic of Ireland but not a part of the United Kingdom.

This proved costly in terms of Faulkner's credibility within Unionist circles. There was, however, some movement on the part of the Irish as, for the first time, the Fine Gael–Labour coalition government clearly defined that Northern Ireland's consent was necessary for Irish unity: the previous Fianna Fáil government had tended to speak generally of 'unity by consent', the implication being that of the Northern majority, 'but room was left for the possibility that it could mean consent of the British and Irish governments, with perhaps some kind of reluctant acquiescence by the majority in the North' (NAI, D/T 2004/21/627).

In terms of the consent principle the contrast between Sunningdale and the Belfast/Good Friday Agreement (B/GFA) could not have been starker. In the B/GFA the Irish state formally recognised that Northern Ireland was *not* part of the Republic of Ireland but *was* part of the United Kingdom. A new Article 2 recognised the right of persons on the island of Ireland to be part of the Irish nation if they so wished ('It is the entitlement and birth right of every person born on the island of Ireland ... to be part of the Irish nation') (Belfast Agreement: Annex A); unlike the 1937 Constitution's Article 2, which claimed everyone on the island as part of the Irish nation as of right, there was now a choice: the B/GFA also recognised the 'birth right of all the people of Northern Ireland to identify themselves and be accepted as Irish or British, or both, as they may so choose' (Ibid.).

A new Article 3 set out the aspiration of a united Ireland. It recognised, however, that this could be 'brought about only by peaceful means with the consent of a majority of the people, democratically expressed, in both jurisdictions' – thereby recognising two legal state entities on the island of Ireland (Ibid.). Both the British and Irish governments recognised the legitimacy of whatever choice was freely exercised by a majority of the people of Northern Ireland 'with regard to its status, whether they prefer to continue to support the Union with Great Britain or a sovereign united Ireland' (Ibid.). In contrast to the problems that confronted Faulkner, his 1998 successor as UUP leader, David Trimble, could argue that the first paragraph of the B/GFA clearly recognised that it was for the people of Northern Ireland alone, without any outside interference, to determine the destiny of Northern Ireland (Trimble, 1998: 1152–3).

When the Government of Ireland Act 1920 was repealed (Belfast Agreement: Annex A and B (NIO, 1998)) – the Irish government erroneously thought that the 1920 Act was a British territorial claim over Northern Ireland as it contained a declaration that Westminster was sovereign over all matters in Northern Ireland when it was in fact the Act of Union that constituted the title deeds of the Union – a new Northern Ireland Act reasserted the sovereignty of the British Parliament (Northern Ireland Constitution Act: 1998: Clause 43). Unlike Faulkner, who was undermined by the Irish failure to recognise Northern Ireland's constitutional status within the UK,

Trimble's problems within Unionism did not stem from the constitutional aspects of the B/GFA.

Republicans and consent

Another key difference between Sunningdale and the B/GFA was inclusivity: the Republican movement's political wing, Sinn Féin, was absent from the 1973 process while integral to the 1998 settlement. It were joined in the multi-talks process by the Ulster Democratic Party, associated with the Ulster Defence Association (UDA), and the Progressive Unionist Party, associated with the Ulster Volunteer Force (UVF), two Loyalist paramilitary organisations instrumental in bringing down Sunningdale. Although Republicans remained aloof from Sunningdale there was an active engagement with the leadership of the Provisional IRA (PIRA). As in the 1990s, John Hume, of the SDLP, played a key part in pushing the PIRA towards a ceasefire in 1972 (TNA, CJ4/1456). Following a truce in that year William Whitelaw, the Secretary of State for Northern Ireland (SSNI), met with the IRA Chief of Staff, Sean Mac Stiofain, who was accompanied by the future leaders of the Republican movement, Martin McGuinness and Gerry Adams, in London. The meeting laid down the political barriers that were to prohibit an accommodation between the British and the IRA for the following quarter of a century: the IRA demanded that the British government should recognise publicly that it was the right of the whole of the 'People of Ireland acting as a unit' to decide the future of Ireland (all-Ireland self-determination); and that HMG should immediately declare its intention to withdraw all British forces from Irish soil, such withdrawal to be completed on or before the first day of January 1975; and called for a general amnesty for all 'political prisoners' in Irish and British jails (TNA, CJ4/1456). MacStiofain made it clear that the crucial item was the 'Declaration of Intent' – if that was 'got right the rest would follow: so it was only worth talking about that' (TNA, PREM 15/1009). On the question of the Declaration of Intent, Whitelaw pointed out that successive British governments had given a pledge, confirmed in legislation, that the majority of the people of Northern Ireland would not be forced into a united Ireland against their will. Mac Stiofain explained the Republicans' view on Irish unity, their belief that British statutes could be undone by further statutes (TNA, CJ4/1456). Following the meeting the British noted that the timing (though not the principle) relating to the role of the British Army in Northern Ireland was negotiable, and 'no doubt' amnesties were also. But the British concluded it was difficult to see how the IRA leaders could accept any reformulation of the Declaration which preserved the British government's commitment not to alter the status of Northern

Ireland except in accordance with the will of the majority of the people of Northern Ireland (TNA, PREM 15/1009).

When the protagonists engaged once more it was in the wake of the Ulster Workers' Council strike that brought Sunningdale down. In December 1974 a group of senior Protestant clergy had met with IRA leaders in Feakle, Co. Clare. handing over proposals for transmission to the Provisional Army Council (PAC) (TNA, DEFE 24/1933). The PAC's view was: 'It is Sovereignty rather than political or territorial interests, which is the basic issue. Until HMG clearly states it has no claim to sovereignty to any part of Ireland' the clergy's proposals were 'meaningless'. The PAC also wanted the establishment of a Constituent Assembly elected by the people of Ireland through universal adult suffrage and proportional representation. The Assembly would draft a new All-Ireland Constitution which would provide for a Provincial Parliament for Ulster (nine counties) with meaningful powers followed by a public commitment by the British government to withdraw from Ireland within 12 months of the adoption of the new All-Ireland Constitution (Ibid.).

This remained the collective view of the PAC as passed on to the British dovernment which sanctioned initial contacts with the Provisionals – through the Secret Intelligence Service (SIS) whose representative signalled to the Republican movement that HMG wished to discuss 'structures of disengagement' (Taylor, 1997: 177–8) and that 'withdrawal' was on the agenda for any discussions (Ibid.: 178–9). The subsequent talks between Republican representatives and British officials worried the Irish government, which feared a total British withdrawal from Northern Ireland and the prospect of civil war. Dublin's position was of 'no negotiation' and advised the British that 'it would be as damaging to negotiate with Provisional Sinn Fein as with the PIRA: this was a fundamental point for the Irish government: The Provisional Movement could not be divided into respectable and terrorist wings' (TNA, DEFE 24/1933). The British, in turn, reassured the Irish that 'We recognised that a principal aim of the PIRA in present circumstances is to try to manoeuvre us into a position in which they could claim that they were negotiating with us: we were very alive to this danger, and equally determined to avoid it' (TNA, PREM 16/515). 'Withdrawal' was a flexible concept for the British, indicating a withdrawal of the British Army to barracks and a gradual disengagement from the North in the longer term – it did not mean the British were relinquishing sovereignty. As Merlyn Rees, the Secretary of State for Northern Ireland, put it to colleagues:

> The Provisionals will no doubt try to bring us quickly to discuss a declaration of British intent to withdraw. We must try to make them realise that this is in a sense an irrelevancy; it is their Protestant fellow-Irishmen with whom they must come to terms. But

> if the Provisionals are looking for a face-saving formula, I do not rule out the possibility that we could find a form of words which would be consistent with previous ministerial statements and not inflame the Loyalists. (TNA, CAB 134/3921)

There was to be no break from the consent principle. And the contacts with Republicans in the ensuing ceasefire demonstrated the incompatibility of the two positions when HMG claims of a British economic withdrawal from Northern Ireland were regarded by the Provisionals as 'an academic red herring and puts the cart before the horse, ie economic disengagement before military and political withdrawal'. The IRA 'visualised declaration of intent first, all-Ireland convention then, 32-county government follows'. The latter would decide economic priorities (NUIG, POL28; Ruairí Ó Brádaigh Papers: Instructions 5.6.75). The HMG representatives in the talks assured the Provisionals that the British 'were going and it would be a tragedy if anything happened. Two roads were leading in the same direction, only [the] RM was travelling faster on its road than the Brits were on theirs' (Ibid.). But, despite Republican pressure for a private British declaration of intent to withdraw (Ó Dochartaigh, 2011: 82), the British patted this away with the fallback position that they wished to avoid the 'danger of a Congo-type situation resulting' (NUIG, POL28 Ó Brádaigh Papers). As Rees confirmed, the usurping of the consent principle for a Declaration of Intent was never a serious proposition:

> To give the Provisionals what they seek, namely a private assurance that we intend to withdraw, would no doubt buy their quiescence. Although we think they would endeavour to preserve the confidentiality of such an assurance it would be impossible for them to do so. Everyone in Northern Ireland would assume from the sudden end of the Provisional campaign that we had given some such undertaking. There could be no other explanation. We should then face massive confrontation with the Protestant population in Northern Ireland and conflict with the Government of the Republic. (TNA, PREM 16/958)

The talks, and the accompanying truce, unsurprisingly collapsed, and subsequent British-PIRA contacts in the 1990s faltered once more on the Republican refusal to accept the consent principle: while the latter's demand for a Declaration of Intent to withdraw was dropped, consent was to be circumvented by the British recognising all-Ireland national self-determination and becoming 'persuaders' (to the Unionist community) for a united Ireland. The British refused point blank to adopt the position of persuaders and instead re-emphasised the principle of consent – the self-determination of the people of Northern Ireland. They also demanded a permanent end to PIRA violence.[1] The subsequent Downing Street Declaration represented a common set of principles agreed by the British and Irish governments which formed the bedrock of the peace process. The British formally announced that they had no selfish strategic or economic interest in Northern Ireland (although the absence of a comma after 'selfish' suggested that they might have an *unselfish* strategic interest in Northern Ireland) and that they would legislate for a united Ireland if that was the wish of a majority of people in Northern Ireland. But this would rest on the consent of the people of Northern Ireland. The Declaration recognised the right of the Irish people to self-determination – a nationalist concept – but only on the basis of concurrent agreement between North and South. thereby preserving the principle of Northern Irish self-determination – the consent principle.[2]

The Declaration determined the basic unnegotiable principles of the multi-party talks Sinn Féin joined in 1997. By engaging in them the Republican leadership had been forced to accept that the outcome would be based on the consent principle. And, in a *volte face* of seismic proportions, following their acceptance of the B/GFA, the position of Sinn Féin on how to achieve a united Ireland was now based on the principle of consent (*An Phoblacht* 18 August 2011).

Governance

Although the first power-sharing Executive was a separate negotiation from the North-South aspects of the Sunningdale Agreement, the interdependency of the institutions agreed meant that both parts were as integral to one another as they were in the B/GFA. The starting point in both negotiations was Unionist opposition to consociation government. Throughout his tenure as Prime Minister of Northern Ireland, and in the year after the suspension of Stormont, Faulkner's stance was for a return of government 'without general power sharing'. He felt that it was not possible to share power between, on the one hand, a majority party in favour of a continuance of Northern Ireland and, on the other, representatives of parties who would want to destroy that state. In Faulkner's opinion in any new elections the opposition members of a new Assembly would consist of such 'extremists' as this (PRONI, CAB/9/J/90/10). By this he clearly meant the SDLP.

Once, however, the British government had issued a White Paper, in 1973, endorsing power sharing, Faulkner was boxed in: if he wanted Unionists to have any control over their political destiny he would have to abandon his insistence on a return to majority rule. After he conceded the principle of power sharing – despite heavy opposition within his party – the main obstacle to overcome was the distribution of ministerial positions among the pro-White Paper participants in the talks chaired by Whitelaw. The main and continuing problem had been the weakness of Faulkner's position within the Unionist Party; his leadership was repeatedly being called into question at party meetings because of his acceptance of power sharing. 'There is no doubt that he must be kept afloat if an Executive is to be formed' determined Whitelaw as he chaired the inter-party talks. The SSNI concluded that any power-sharing executive must have an absolute Unionist majority if Faulkner was able to survive. But the problem was that the SDLP and the Alliance Party had set their faces against a Unionist majority in the Executive (TNA, FCO 87/225 GEN 79(73)).

Ultimately, Whitelaw's persistence and cajoling delivered the Unionist majority Faulkner needed to survive: the Executive would consist of six Ulster Unionists, four SDLP members and one Alliance Party member. After Parliamentary approval was sought for another four positions that were not to be Heads of Departments the final tally gave the following distribution amongst the parties: seven Ulster Unionists, six SDLP members and two Alliance Party members. The entire arrangement was subject to agreement on issues such as the Council of Ireland.[3]

At Sunningdale, Faulkner warned the other participants that 'Power sharing is not yet widely accepted by our fellow citizens'. Thus, even to conceive of a Council of Ireland was '100 times more difficult for unionists (with a small u) to accept than a power sharing executive. All unionists (with a small u) fear that in a Council of Ireland there may be hidden a half-way house to a united Ireland' (TNA, CJ4/474). From the beginning Faulkner had no objection to the formation of a Council of Ireland consisting of elected representatives from both sides of the border provided the Irish government 'recognised Northern Ireland's right to run its own affairs' (PRONI, CAB/9/J/90/10). The initial assessment, in Dublin, of the UUP position was that it envisaged a '*weak* Council of Ireland which would be little more than a "talking shop"' (NAI, D/T 2004 21/2). In contrast the Irish insisted that a 'meaningful' list of 'executive' functions be undertaken by a Council in its own right and not by recommendation to the governments in the North and South. Despite, at Sunningdale, the Unionist representatives stressing that it was politically difficult for them to agree to such a list – and they received some support from the representatives of the SDLP (TNA, CJ4/474) – Prime Minister Heath (effectively chairing the conference) was able to announce he understood that broad agreement had been reached on the question of executive functions (TNA, CJ4/474).

Faulkner's early acquiescence to a Council with executive powers proved a fatal mistake in terms of his position within the wider Unionist community. He claimed that the appendages of the Council – a North–South Consultative Assembly, a Permanent Secretariat, the executive functions of the Council of Ministers – 'fell in my mind into the "necessary nonsense" category'. They were necessary to get the co-operation of the SDLP and the Irish government. 'But nothing agreed at Sunningdale infringed on the powers of Northern Ireland Assembly by which everything would have to be approved and delegated. Given the overwhelmingly Unionist composition of that body and the unanimity rule in the Council of Ministers we were satisfied that the constitutional integrity of Northern Ireland was secure' declared Faulkner (1978: 236–7). His Unionist critics, however, focused on the very fact that the Council would have executive powers, which meant it was an embryonic all-Ireland government. It was a powerful argument in the Unionist–Loyalist alliance that toppled Faulkner, power sharing and the Sunningdale Agreement in 1974.

In contrast, despite a brief flirtation with a North–South body possessing executive powers in the guise of the British–Irish Frameworks Documents (1995) which once more sparked Unionist opposition,[4] the B/GFA resulted in a completely different form of cross-border institution. In a reversal of the sequencing of 1973, agreement in 1998 on a power-sharing government (known in the multi-party talks as Strand One and referring to the internal governance of Northern Ireland) emerged as a consequence of North–South agreement (known as Strand Two and referring to relations between Northern Ireland and the Irish Republic).

Unlike Faulkner, Trimble resisted any executive powers being given to any North–South body that might emerge from the 1998 talks. As the negotiations reached their climax they were turned into crisis as the 'Mitchell Document' (named after the American chair of the talks) envisaged a North–South Ministerial Council (NSMC) with a long list of areas in which the body would decide common policies, specific areas where decisions would be taken on action for implementation and a series of implementation bodies. Effectively, the proposed Northern Ireland Assembly (NIA) – where Unionists would have an input and veto – was completely by-passed. It was not Belfast, but London and Dublin which determined the remit of the Council. This meant, from a Unionist perspective, that the people of Northern Ireland – by which they meant the majority Unionist community – had no control over the degree and pace of North–South co-operation.[5] The Council was to take decisions on action at an all-island and cross-border level across its long list of competence through implementation bodies.[6] Where 'it is agreed that new implementation bodies are to be established' the two governments were to 'make all necessary legislative and other preparations to ensure the establishment of these bodies at the inception of the British/Irish Agreement or as soon as feasible thereafter, such that these bodies function effectively as rapidly as possible'.[7] Only *further* bodies, in addition to the long list already specified, would be by agreement in the Council and with the specific endorsement of the NIA and the Oireachtas.[8] The transfer of functions, by

London and Dublin, to the NSMC made it the source of authority for North–South co-operation and therefore it would, in Unionist eyes, be acting as a third level of government in Ireland.

Surprisingly, Strand Two issues were agreed along the UUP model relatively quickly, with a plan developed by one of the UUP's negotiators, Reg Empey, dropping the implementation bodies, although the NIA would be bound to agree at least six matters for future co-operation and implementation. This was the compromise: Nationalists were guaranteed that the NSMC would not be merely an 'empty house' and that there would be at least six areas of co-operation; Unionists were secure that any implementation bodies would be agreed and established by the Assembly. Authority would thus flow from the NIA and not the North–South Council.

As far as Trimble was concerned he had secured a consultative body that was the antithesis of the proposed Framework Document which had executive powers. He argued that the NSMC, unlike the 1973 proposed Council of Ireland, had 'no supra-national characteristics' (Trimble, 1998: 1155–6). For Trimble it was essential that it should clearly draw its authority from the NIA and Dáil Éireann and be accountable to these democratic institutions.

A crucial difference in deciding the outcome of the 1973 and 1998 Agreements was the attitude of the respective British Prime Ministers: unlike Heath at Sunningdale, Tony Blair, in effect, backed the Unionist position on an institutional North–South body; and the Taoiseach Bertie Ahern, unlike Cosgrave who stood firm on an executive Council of Ireland, decided to renegotiate on the NSMC, after contemplating the implications of a refusal to do so – the potential collapse of the negotiations. This was in defiance of the advice of his aides who felt that Dublin had negotiated in good faith with London and urged that the efforts of the two governments be devoted to persuading the political parties to accept that agreement (Mitchell, 1999: 170–1).

The diplomatic background to the B/GFA was also very different from that of Sunningdale. Unionists needed agreement to halt any slide towards greater Dublin input into the internal affairs of Northern Ireland. Consultation with the Irish Republic had already been institutionalised in the Anglo-Irish Intergovernmental Conference (granting Dublin a permanent civil service presence in the North) as part of the Anglo-Irish Agreement (AIA) of 1985; in the B/GFA a British–Irish Intergovernmental Conference replaced the body set up by the AIA. British and Irish ministers and officials would be unable to discuss matters devolved to the Assembly while Northern Irish ministers would be allowed to attend Conference meetings as observers (Belfast Agreement: Strand Three, Paras 1–10), thus removing the Unionists' fear of secret deals behind their backs. The inclusive nature of the B/GFA, unlike Sunningdale, extended beyond the island of Ireland: Strand Three (covering relations between the United Kingdom and the Republic) saw a British–Irish Council (BIC) established. This was the 'British dimension', absent from Sunningdale, which matched the Irish dimension in both Agreements. The BIC was to be made up of all devolved administrations within the United Kingdom, Crown dependencies within the British Isles and the sovereign governments in London and Dublin; both the BIC and the NSMC were consultative bodies with no executive power (Belfast Agreement: Strand Three, British–Irish Council: Paras 1–12).

The successful conclusion of Strand Two to the satisfaction of Unionists opened the door for movement on their part in Strand One where the impasse was the SDLP's proposed maximum executive, legislative and administrative power for the NIA, with a cabinet open to all parties to participate in it, subject to an electoral threshold which would be a matter for clarification and negotiation, in contrast to the Unionist Party's proportional committee model which envisaged no collective responsibility – no cabinet. This basically summed up unionism's traditional aversion to institutional power sharing. Instead a Chief Executive would have a co-ordinating and representational role between the committees and a negotiating role with bodies outside Northern Ireland. The role of the Chief Executive and his co-ordinating role would be the nearest thing to an executive.[9] The impasse was broken with the Unionists accepting the SDLP's model for a power-sharing executive following the former's success in securing their constitutional and North–South objectives.

While both Agreements contained an assembly and a power-sharing executive at their heart, a significant difference between Sunningdale and the B/GA was where the latter saw the NIA governed by 'sufficient consensus' or a double veto. This meant that for a decision to be ratified by the Assembly there would have to be a majority of Unionists and Nationalists separately. Although there was a First Minister (Unionist) and a Deputy First Minister (Nationalist), they were co-equal and neither was subordinate to the other (Belfast Agreement: Strand One, Paras 1–33). Both Unionists and Nationalists had a veto over one another.

Security, policing and rights

One thing both Agreements had in common was the apparent intractability of issues revolving around security, policing and criminal justice. At Sunningdale the British and Unionist concern was focused on the inability to extradite terrorist suspects from the Republic to the North as Southern courts refused to do so if the defendant claimed the alleged offence was 'political'. The UK Attorney General, Sir Peter Rawlinson, had considered the simple solution to this problem to be an amendment of the extradition law in the Republic so that offences involving firearms and explosives were excluded from the definition of a political offence. The Irish remedy, on the other hand, was to suggest a special court, to be set up under the Council of Ireland, having jurisdiction over a limited schedule of offences. The court would have the power to sit in the North or the South and to try an accused person for committing a scheduled offence in any part of the island. A person would be tried in the place where he or she was arrested. Such a court would deal effectively with terrorists wherever they were caught and would thus get round the present difficulty in the extradition law (TNA, CJ4/474). The absence of consensus on this led to the British and Irish governments jointly setting up a commission to consider all the proposals put forward at the Conference (Sunningdale Communiqué: Para. 10). But, by the time the Anglo-Irish commission reported, the Sunningdale Agreement was effectively dead in the water.

In terms of policing, both the Irish government and the SDLP argued at Sunningdale that the North's minority community had difficulty in identifying with the Royal Ulster Constabulary (RUC) and that this difficulty could be solved if a police authority there was appointed by the Council of Ireland. The Irish government would reciprocate by creating a police authority in the Republic the membership of which would also be appointed by the Council. There should be a common procedure for examining complaints against the two police forces, and this should be the responsibility of the Council. John Hume further argued that HMG had been mistaken in refusing to alter the name of the RUC but the only way left of making the police force acceptable to the minority was in some way to associate it with the Council of Ireland. Only by doing this could the Catholic minority identify with the police force and give it their support against criminals and extremists. Faulkner commented that the Unionist Party would have great difficulty in agreeing to a Northern Ireland police authority being appointed by the Council in the way suggested; he also opposed the altering of the RUC's name (TNA, CJ4/474). The compromise, brokered by Heath, was for the Irish government to set up a police authority, appointments to which would be made after consultation with the Council of Ministers on the Council of Ireland. In the case of the Northern Ireland police authority, appointments would be made after consultation with the Northern Ireland Executive which would consult with the Council of Ministers of the Council of Ireland (Sunningdale Communiqué: Para. 15). The British ruled out any change in the name of the RUC.

In 1998 there was little debate on these issues as the talks were dominated by debate on constitutional issues. While it was envisaged that there would

be an end of Emergency Powers legislation, combined with a reform of policing and the criminal justice system, these would be based upon the proposals
of new commissions (Belfast Agreement: Security: Paras 1–5; Policing and
Justice: Paras 1–5) separate from the final Agreement. The outcome of the
policing commission would, to the consternation of Unionists, witness the
demise of the RUC – as Hume had desired at Sunningdale – and the creation
of the Police Service of Northern Ireland (PSNI), thereby ending the debate
of Nationalist alienation from the police's association with the symbols of
Britishness. The B/GFA, as with Sunningdale (Sunningdale Communiqué:
Para. 11), aspired to the incorporation of the European Convention on
Human Rights in domestic legislation in each part of Ireland (Belfast Agreement: Rights, Safeguards and Equality of Opportunity: Paras 1–10). Two of
the most controversial aspects of the B/GFA were those of decommissioning
and prisoners. All paramilitary prisoners were to be released on licence within
two years, provided their organisation remained on ceasefire (Ibid.: Prisoners: Paras 1–2). As for decommissioning, the Agreement stated merely that
parties to the Agreement were to use their 'influence' with paramilitaries to
achieve disarmament (Ibid.: Decommissioning: Paras 1–6).

Conclusion

The Sunningdale and Belfast/Good Friday Agreements both witnessed a
split in Unionism: this, however, is a superficial commonality, for the sources
of division were radically different. With Sunningdale, Unionist opposition
centred on power sharing (coming so soon after the loss of their majority-rule
parliament), the absence of constitutional recognition from Dublin and the
powers of the Council of Ireland. With the B/GFA it was much more of an
emotional response within the Unionist community that energised resistance. While, on both occasions, anti-Agreement Unionists claimed that the
institutions established were a threat to Northern Ireland's place in the
Union, in 1998 it was the release of paramilitary prisoners that was too much
for many of the Protestant community, for whom this represented the freeing
of murderers back on to the streets. This affect was accentuated by Sinn Féin's
automatic participation, by right of votes cast, in a power-sharing executive
without the PRIA decommissioning its arsenal of weapons first. Power
sharing with Nationalists, *per se*, was no longer unacceptable.

The Sunningdale Agreement looked to establish a Council of Ireland
with executive powers that had the potential to evolve into an embryonic
all-Ireland government; the Belfast/Good Friday Agreement established a
consultative North–South Ministerial Council with no executive powers
that could not evolve into a united Ireland by incremental moves. This was

the key to Unionist acceptance of the latter Agreement in comparison to Unionist rejection of Sunningdale. In constitutional terms the B/GFA was a Unionist settlement that secured Northern Ireland's position within the United Kingdom, recognised British sovereignty in Northern Ireland and established that a united Ireland could be achieved only on the basis of the principle of consent – there was no 'constructive ambiguity' despite Sinn Féin's claims to the contrary. In contrast the Sunningdale Agreement was, in constitutional terms, a Nationalist settlement that did not recognise Northern Ireland as part of the UK and attempted to bypass the principle of consent by establishing a Council of Ireland with executive powers that was, in essence, an embryonic all-Ireland government.

The Good Friday Agreement succeeded, in the longer term, despite the psychological turmoil Unionism experienced in terms of prisoner releases, the absence of immediate decommissioning and the reform of policing, because the fundamental constitutional foundations of the accord were Unionist – as demonstrated by the fact that the St Andrews Agreement, championed by the Democratic Unionist Party (DUP) as a 'renegotiation' of the 1998 accord, did not remove any of the institutions established by it. Both Agreements saw power-sharing arrangements which represented a considerable gain for Nationalists; in one respect, though, even the prospect of a power-sharing executive represented some gain for Unionists in 1998 given that it involved the creation of an NIA and a degree of control over decision-making in Northern Ireland that had been, effectively, absent since 1972 and heightened by the signing of the AIA. This made power sharing in the B/GFA more palatable than it seemed in 1973 following the recent loss of majority rule when the Stormont Parliament had been prorogued. The fundamental element of slow learning from 1973 to 1998 was that if Unionists wished to secure Northern Ireland's position within the Union then Nationalists had to be given an equal share in its governance; and if Nationalists wished to persuade Unionists that their future ultimately lay in a united Ireland then the constitutional position of Northern Ireland within the United Kingdom had to be unambiguous and rest solely on the principle of consent.

Notes

1 Linen Hall Library Northern Ireland Political Collection (LHL, NIPC) Messages Between the IRA and the Government: British Message sent 26 February 1993; Message from the Leadership of the Provisional Movement 5 March 1993; British Message sent 11 March 1993; British 9-Paragraph Note sent 19 March 1993; Message from the Leadership of the Republican Movement 22 March 1993. Setting

the Record Straight: Sinn Féin's 'April' Document – Sinn Fin's Basis for Entering Dialogue.
2 LHL, NIPC Joint Declaration by An Taoiseach, Mr Albert Reynolds TD and the British Prime Minister, the Rt Hon John Major MP 15 December 1993 (Government of Ireland: Dublin 1993).
3 TNA, FCO Continuation Minutes of Inter-Party Talks held at Stormont Castle on 21 November 1973.
4 LHL, NIPC Frameworks for the Future Cmmd.2964; We Reject the Governments' 'Frameworks' Proposals as the Basis for Negotiations (Ulster Unionist Party 1995); Response to 'Frameworks for the Future (Ulster Unionist Party n.d.).
5 LHL, NIPC The Independent Chairmen. Draft Paper for Discussion. Strand 2: Para. 5 (ii).
6 Ibid., Para. 5 (iv).
7 Ibid., Para. 7.
8 Ibid., Para. 8.
9 LHL, NIPC Strand One, Twelfth Meeting, 4 March 1998.

The Sunningdale Agreement (December 1973)

Tripartite agreement on the Council of Ireland – the communiqué issued following the Sunningdale Conference

1. The Conference between the British and Irish Governments and the parties involved in the Northern Ireland Executive (designate) met at Sunningdale on 6, 7, 8 and 9 December 1973.

2. During the Conference, each delegation stated their position on the status of Northern Ireland.

3. The Taoiseach said that the basic principle of the Conference was that the participants had tried to see what measure of agreement of benefit to all the people concerned could be secured. In doing so, all had reached accommodation with one another on practical arrangements. But none had compromised, and none had asked others to compromise, in relation to basic aspirations. The people of the Republic, together with a minority in Northern Ireland as represented by the SDLP delegation, continued to uphold the aspiration towards a united Ireland. The only unity they wanted to see was a unity established by consent.

4. Mr Brian Faulkner said that delegates from Northern Ireland came to the Conference as representatives of apparently incompatible sets of political aspirations who had found it possible to reach agreement to join together in government because each accepted that in doing so they were not sacrificing principles or aspirations. The desire of the majority of the people of Northern Ireland to remain part of the United Kingdom, as represented by the Unionist and Alliance delegations, remained firm.

5. The Irish Government fully accepted and solemnly declared that there could be no change in the status of Northern Ireland until a majority of the people of Northern Ireland desired a change in that status. The British Government solemnly declared that it was, and would remain, their policy to support the wishes of the majority of the people of Northern Ireland. The present status of Northern Ireland is that it is part of the United Kingdom. If in the future the majority of the people of Northern Ireland should indicate a wish to become part of a united Ireland, the British Government would support that wish.

6. The Conference agreed that a formal agreement incorporating the declarations of the British and Irish Governments would be signed at the formal stage of the Conference and registered at the United Nations.

7. The Conference agreed that a Council of Ireland would be set up. It would be confined to representatives of the two parts of Ireland, with appropriate safeguards for the British Government's financial and other interests. It would comprise a Council of Ministers with executive and harmonising functions and a consultative role, and a Consultative Assembly with advisory and review functions. The Council of Ministers would act by unanimity, and would comprise a core of seven members of the Irish Government and an equal number of members of the Northern Ireland Executive with provision for the participation of other non-voting members of the Irish Government and the Northern Ireland Executive or Administration when matters within their departmental competence were discussed. The Council of Ministers would control the functions of the Council. The Chairmanship would rotate on an agreed basis between representatives of the Irish Government and of the Northern Ireland Executive. Arrangements would be made for the location of the first meeting, and the location of subsequent meetings would be determined by the Council of Ministers. The Consultative Assembly would consist of 60 members, 30 members from Dail Eireann chosen by the Dail on the basis of proportional representation by the single transferable vote, and 30 members from the Northern Ireland Assembly

chosen by that Assembly and also on that basis. The members of the Consultative Assembly would be paid allowances. There would be a Secretariat to the Council, which would be kept as small as might be commensurate with efficiency in the operation of the Council. The Secretariat would service the institutions of the Council and would, under the Council of Ministers, supervise the carrying out of the executive and harmonising functions and the consultative role of the Council. The Secretariat would be headed by a Secretary-General. Following the appointment of a Northern Ireland Executive, the Irish Government and the Northern Ireland Executive would nominate their representatives to a Council of Ministers. The Council of Ministers would then appoint a Secretary-General and decide upon the location of its permanent headquarters. The Secretary-General would be directed to proceed with the drawing up of plans for such headquarters. The Council of Ministers would also make arrangements for the recruitment of the staff of the Secretariat in a manner and on conditions which would, as far as is practicable, be consistent with those applying to public servants in the two administrations.

8. In the context of its harmonising functions and consultative role, the Council of Ireland would undertake important work relating, for instance, to the impact of EEC membership. As for executive functions, the first step would be to define and agree these in detail. The Conference therefore decided that, in view of the administrative complexities involved, studies would at once be set in hand to identify and, prior to the formal stage of the conference, report on areas of common interest in relation to which a Council of Ireland would take executive decisions and, in appropriate cases, be responsible for carrying those decisions into effect. In carrying out these studies, and also in determining what should be done by the Council in terms of harmonisation. the objectives to be borne in mind would include the following:
(1) to achieve the best utilisation of scarce skills, expertise and resources;
(2) to avoid in the interests of economy and efficiency, unnecessary duplication of effort; and
(3) to ensure complementary rather than competitive effort where this is to the advantage of agriculture, commerce and industry.
In particular, these studies would be directed to identifying, for the purposes of executive action by the Council of Ireland, suitable aspects of activities in the following broad fields:
(a) exploitation, conservation and development of natural resources and the environment;

(b) agricultural matters (including agricultural research, animal health and operational aspects of the Common Agriculture Policy), forestry and fisheries;

(c) co-operative ventures in the fields of trade and industry;

(d) electricity generation;

(e) tourism;

(f) roads and transport;

(g) advisory services in the field of public health;

(h) sport, culture and the arts.

It would be for the Oireachtas and the Northern Ireland Assembly to legislate from time to time as to the extent of functions to be devolved to the Council of Ireland. Where necessary, the British Government will cooperate in this devolution of functions. Initially, the functions to be vested would be those identified in accordance with the procedures set out above and decided, at the formal stage of the conference. to be transferred.

9. (i) During the initial period following the establishment of the Council, the revenue of the Council would be provided by means of grants from the two administrations in Ireland towards agreed projects and budgets, according to the nature of the service involved.

(ii) It was also agreed that further studies would be put in hand forthwith and completed as soon as possible of methods of financing the Council after the initial period which would be consonant with the responsibilities and functions assigned to it.

(iii) It was agreed that the cost of the Secretariat of the Council of Ireland would be shared equally, and other services would he financed broadly in proportion to where expenditure or benefit accrues.

(iv) The amount of money required to finance the Council's activities will depend upon the functions assigned to it from time to time.

(v) While Britain continues to pay subsidies to Northern Ireland, such payments would not involve Britain participating in the Council, it being accepted nevertheless that it would be legitimate for Britain to safe-guard in an appropriate way her financial involvement in Northern Ireland.

10. It was agreed by all parties that persons committing crimes of violence, however motivated, in any part of Ireland should be brought to trial irrespective of the part of Ireland in which they are located. The concern which large sections of the people of Northern Ireland felt about this problem was in particular forcefully expressed by the representatives of the Unionist and Alliance parties. The representatives of the Irish Government stated that they understood and fully shared this concern. Different ways of solving

this problem were discussed; among them were the amendment of legislation operating in the two jurisdictions on extradition, the creation of a common law enforcement area in which an all-Ireland court would have jurisdiction, and the extension of the jurisdiction of domestic courts so as to enable them to try offences committed outside the jurisdiction. It was agreed that problems of considerable legal complexity were involved, and that the British and Irish Governments would jointly set up a commission to consider all the proposals put forward at the Conference and to recommend as a matter of extreme urgency the most effective means of dealing with those who commit these crimes. The Irish Government undertook to take immediate and effective legal steps so that persons coming within their jurisdiction and accused of murder, however motivated, committed in Northern Ireland will be brought to trial, and it was agreed that any similar reciprocal action that may be needed in Northern Ireland be taken by the appropriate authorities.

11. It was agreed that the Council would be invited to consider in what way the principles of the European Convention on Human Rights and Fundamental Freedoms would be expressed in domestic legislation in each part of Ireland. It would recommend whether further legislation or the creation of other institutions, administrative or judicial, is required in either part or embracing the whole island to provide additional protection in the field of human rights. Such recommendations could include the functions of an Ombudsman or Commissioner for Complaints, or other arrangements of a similar nature which the Council of Ireland might think appropriate.

12. The Conference also discussed the question of policing and the need to ensure public support for and identification with the police service throughout the whole community. It was agreed that no single set of proposals would achieve these aims overnight, and that time would be necessary. The Conference expressed the hope that the wide range of agreement that had been reached, and the consequent formation of a power-sharing Executive, would make a major contribution to the creation of an atmosphere throughout the community where there would be widespread support for and identification with all the institutions of Northern Ireland.

13. It was broadly accepted that the two parts of Ireland are to a considerable extent inter-dependent in the whole field of law and order, and that the problems of political violence and identification with the police service cannot be solved without taking account of that fact.

14. Accordingly, the British Government stated that, as soon as the security problems were resolved and the new institutions were seen to be working effectively, they would wish to discuss the devolution of responsibility for normal policing and how this might be achieved with the Northern Ireland Executive and the Police.

15. With a view to improving policing throughout the island and developing community identification with and support for the police services, the governments concerned will cooperate under the auspices of a Council of Ireland through their respective police authorities. To this end, the Irish Government would set up a Police Authority, appointments to which would be made after consultation with the Council of Ministers of the Council of Ireland. In the case of the Northern Ireland Police Authority, appointments would be made after consultation with the Northern Ireland Executive which would consult with the Council of Ministers of the Council of Ireland. When the two Police Authorities are constituted, they will make their own arrangements to achieve the objectives set out above.

16. An independent complaints procedure for dealing with complaints against the police will be set up.

17. The Secretary of State for Northern Ireland will set up an all-party committee from the Assembly to examine how best to introduce effective policing throughout Northern Ireland with particular reference to the need to achieve public identification with the police.

18. The Conference took note of a reaffirmation by the British Government of their firm commitment to bring detention to an end in Northern Ireland for all sections of the community as soon as the security situation permits, and noted also that the Secretary of State for Northern Ireland hopes to be able to bring into use his statutory powers of selective release in time for a number of detainees to be released before Christmas.

19. The British Government stated that, in the light of the decisions reached at the Conference, they would now seek the authority of Parliament to devolve full powers to the Northern Ireland Executive and Northern Ireland Assembly as soon as possible. The formal appointment of the Northern Ireland Executive would then be made.

20. The Conference agreed that a formal conference would be held early in the New Year at which the British and Irish Governments and the Northern

Ireland Executive would meet together to consider reports on the studies which have been commissioned and to sign the agreement reached.

Source: Conflict Archive on the Internet (CAIN), University of Ulster (http://cain.ulst.ac.uk/events/sunningdale/agreement.htm, accessed on 7 March 2016)

References

Books and journal articles

Adams, G. (1986) *The Politics of Irish Freedom* (Dingle: Brandon Books).

Aguilar, P. (2002) *Memory and Amnesia: The Role of the Spanish Civil War in the Transition to Democracy*, translated by Mark Oakley (Oxford: Berghahn Books).

Akenson, D. (1994) *Conor: A Biography of Conor Cruise O'Brien* (Montreal: McGill-Queen's University Press).

All-Party Anti-Partition Conference (1949) *Ireland's Right to Unity: The Case Stated by the All-Party Anti-Partition Conference, Mansion House, Dublin, Ireland,* 2nd ed. (Dublin: Mansion House Committee).

Andrews, E. (1987) Stewart Parker, *Pentecost* Theatre Programme (Derry: Field Day).

Ascherson, N. (1974) 'The Republic of Hawthornden Road', *The Observer*, 2 June, 11.

Aughey, A. and Barnes, C.A. (2006) 'Fantasy Echo' in J. Wilson and K. Stapleton (eds) *Devolution and Identity* (London: Sage), 127–42.

Aughey, A. and Gormley-Heenan, C. (2011) *The Anglo-Irish Agreement: Rethinking Its Legacy* (Manchester: Manchester University Press).

Aveyard, S. (2012) 'The "English Disease" Is to Look for a "Solution of the Irish Problem": British Constitutional Policy in Northern Ireland after Sunningdale 1974–1976', *Contemporary British History*, 26 (4), 529–49.

Aveyard, S. (2014), ' "We Couldn't Do a Prague": British Government Responses to Loyalist Strikes in Northern Ireland, 1974–77', *Irish Historical Studies*, 39 (153), 91–111.

Bardon, J. (2005) *A History of Ulster*, updated ed. (Belfast: Blackstaff).

Bell, G. (1976) *The Protestants of Ulster* (London: Pluto Press).

Bennett, H. (2010) 'From Direct Rule to Motorman: Adjusting British Military Strategy for Northern Ireland in 1972', *Studies in Conflict & Terrorism*, 33 (6), 511–32.

Bermeo, N. (1992), 'Democracy and the Lessons of Dictatorship', *Comparative Politics*, 24 (3), 273–91.

Bew, J. and Frampton, M. (2012) 'Debating the "Stalemate": A Response to Dr Dixon', *The Political Quarterly*, 83 (2), 277–82.

Bew, J., Frampton, M. and Gurruchaga, I. (2009) *Talking to Terrorists: Making Peace in Northern Ireland and the Basque Country* (London: Hurst).

Bew, P. (2007) *Ireland: The Politics of Enmity 1789–2006* (Oxford: Oxford University Press).

Bew, P. and Gillespie, G. (1999) *Northern Ireland: A Chronology of the Troubles 1968–1999* (Dublin: Gill and Macmillan).

Bew, P. and Patterson, H. (1984) *The British State and the Ulster Crisis from Wilson to Thatcher* (London: Verso).

Blair, T. (2011) *A Journey* (London: Penguin).

Bleakley, D. (1975) 'Prospects for the Ulster Convention', *Socialist Commentary*, May, 8–9.

Blood, M. (2007) *Watch My Lips, I'm Speaking!* (Dublin: Gill and Macmillan).

Bloomfield, K. (1994) *Stormont in Crisis: A Memoir* (Belfast: Blackstaff Press).

Bloomfield, K. (2007) *A Tragedy of Errors: The Government and Misgovernment of Northern Ireland* (Liverpool: Liverpool University Press).

Bourke, R. (2003) *Peace in Ireland: The War of Ideas* (London: Pimlico).

Bowman, J. (1982) *De Valera and the Ulster Question, 1917–1973* (Oxford: Clarendon Press).

Boyle, K., Hadden, T. and Hillyard, P. (1975) *Law and the State: The Case of Northern Ireland* (London: Martin Robinson).

Bradford, R. (1981) *The Last Ditch* (Belfast: Blackstaff Press).

Brett, C.E.B. (1978) *Long Shadows Cast Before: Nine Lives in Ulster* (Edinburgh: John Bartholomew and Son).

Briggs, A. (1998) *Chartism* (Stroud: Sutton).

Bruce, S. (1992) 'It's Terrorism as Usual', *The Guardian*, 12 August, 17.

Bruce, S. (1994) *The Edge of the Union: The Ulster Loyalist Political Vision* (Oxford: University Press).

Bruce, S. (2007) *Paisley: Religion and Politics in Northern Ireland* (Oxford: Oxford University Press).

Butterfield, H. (1931) *The Whig Interpretation of History* (London: Bell and Sons).

Callaghan, J. (1973) *A House Divided: The Dilemma of Northern Ireland* (London: Collins).

Callaghan, J. (1990) *Socialism in Britain since 1884* (Oxford: Blackwell).

Campbell, A. (2014) *The Irish Diaries, 1994–2004* (Dublin: The Lilliput Press).

Campbell, S. (2015) *Gerry Fitt and the SDLP: 'In a Minority of One'* (Manchester: Manchester University Press).

Chalfont, Lord (1972) 'The Balance of Military Forces' in J.C. Beckett (ed.) *The Ulster Debate: Report of a Study Group of the Institute for the Study of Conflict* (London: The Bodley Head).

Chesterton, G.K. (1917) *A Short History of England* (London: Chatto and Windus).

Clancy, M. (2010) *Peace without Consensus* (Farnham: Ashgate).

Clarke, L. and Johnston, K. (2001) *Martin McGuinness: From Guns to Government* (Edinburgh and London: Mainstream).

Coakley, J. (2002) 'Conclusion: New Strains of Nationalism and Unionism' in J. Coakley (ed.) *Changing Shades of Orange and Green: Redefining the Union and the Nation in Contemporary Ireland* (Dublin: UCD Press), 132–54.

Coakley, J. (2009) 'Voting for Unity or Union? The Complexities of Public Opinion on the Border Issue', *Journal of Cross-Border Studies in Ireland*, 4, 79–90.

Corthorn, P. (2012) 'Enoch Powell, Ulster Unionism, and the British Nation', *The Journal of British Studies*, 51 (4), 967–97.

Craig, T. (2010) *Crisis of Confidence: Anglo-Irish Relations in the Early Troubles* (Dublin: Irish Academic Press).

Craig, T. (2012) 'From Backdoors and Back Lanes to Backchannels: Reappraising British Talks with the Provisional IRA, 1970–1974', *Contemporary British History*, 26 (1), 97–117.

Craig, T. (2014) 'Monitoring the Peace?: Northern Ireland's 1975 Ceasefire Incident Centres and the Politicisation of Sinn Féin,' *Terrorism and Political Violence*, 26 (2), 307–19.

Cunningham, M. (2001) *British Government Policy in Northern Ireland 1969–2000* (Manchester: Manchester University Press).

Currie, A. (2004), *All Hell Will Break Loose* (Dublin: O'Brien Press).

Cusack, J. and McDonald, H. (1997) *UVF* (Dublin: Poolbeg).

Devine, F. (2009) *Organizing History: A Centenary of SIPTU, 1909–2009* (Dublin: Gill and Macmillan).

Devlin, P. (1975) *The Fall of the Northern Ireland Executive* (Tralee: Paddy Devlin).

Dixon, P. (1997) 'Paths to Peace in Northern Ireland (II): The Peace Processes 1973–74 and 1994–96', *Democratization*, 4 (3), 1–25.

Dixon, P. (2001/2008) *Northern Ireland: The Politics of War and Peace* (Basingstoke: Palgrave).

Dixon, P. (2012) 'Bew and Frampton: Recognisably Neoconservative', *The Political Quarterly*, 83 (2), 283–6.

Donoughue, B. (1987) *Prime Minister: Conduct of Policy under Harold Wilson and James Callaghan, 1974–79* (London: Jonathan Cape).

Donoughue, B. (2004) *Downing Street Diary: With Harold Wilson in No. 10* (London: Jonathan Cape).

Edwards, A. (2014) ' "A Whipping Boy if Ever There Was One"? The British Army and the Politics of Civil–Military Relations in Northern Ireland, 1969–79', *Contemporary British History*, 28 (2), 166–89.

English, R. (2003) *Armed Struggle: A History of the IRA* (London: Pan Macmillan).

Evelegh, R. (1978) *Peace-Keeping in a Democratic Society: The Lessons of Northern Ireland* (London: Hurst and Company).

Farrel, M. (1976) *Northern Ireland The Orange State* (London: Pluto Press).

Farren, S. (2007) *Sunningdale: An Agreement Too Soon?* IBIS Working Papers: 80 (Dublin: University College Dublin: Institute for British–Irish Studies).

Farren, S. (2010) *The SDLP: The Struggle for Agreement in Northern Ireland, 1970–2000* (Dublin: Four Courts Press).

Farrington, C. (2007) 'Reconciliation or Irredentism? The Irish Government and the Sunningdale Communiqué of 1973', *Contemporary European History*, 16 (1), 98–107.

Faulkner, B. (1978) *Memoirs of a Statesman* (London: Weidenfeld and Nicolson).

Fisk, R. (1975) *The Point of No Return: The Strike Which Broke the British in Ulster* (London: André Deutsch).

FitzGerald, G. (1972) *Towards a New Ireland* (London: C. Knight).

FitzGerald, G. (1991) *All in a Life* (Dublin: Gill and Macmillan).

Gillespie, G. (1994) 'Loyalist Politics and the Ulster Workers' Council strike of 1974'. Unpublished PhD thesis (Belfast: Queen's University).

Gillespie, G. (1998) 'The Sunningdale Agreement: Lost Opportunity or an Agreement too far?', *Irish Political Studies*, 13, 100–14.

Gillespie, G. (2004) 'The Origins of the Ulster Workers' Council Strike: Structure and Tactics', *Études Irlandaises*, 29 (1), 129–44.

Glenny, M. (2008) *McMafia: Crime Without Frontiers* (London: The Bodley Head).

Godson, D. (2004) *Himself Alone: David Trimble and the Ordeal of Unionism* (London: Harper Collins).

Gordon, M. (2010) *Theatre and the Mind* (London: Oberon Books).

Gray, C.S. (1999) *Modern Strategy* (Oxford: Oxford University Press).

Haas, E.B. (1958) *The Uniting of Europe: Political, Economic and Social Forces, 1950–1957* (London: Stevens and Sons).

Haas, E.B. (1967) 'The Uniting of Europe and the Uniting of Latin America', *Journal of Common Market Studies*, 5 (4), 315–43.

Haas, E.B. (1970) 'The Study of Regional Integration: Reflections on the Joy and Anguish of Pretheorizing', *International Organization*, 24 (4), 606–46.

Haines, J. (1977) *The Politics of Power* (London: Jonathan Cape).

Hamill, D. (1986) *Pig in the Middle: The Army in Northern Ireland 1969–1985* (London: Methuen)

Hayes, M. (1995) *Minority Verdict: Experiences of a Catholic Public Servant* (Belfast: Blackstaff).

Hayward, K. (2009) *Irish Nationalism and European Integration: The Official Redefinition of the Island of Ireland* (Manchester: Manchester University Press).

Hennessey, T. (2007) *The Evolution of the Troubles 1970–72* (Dublin: Irish Academic Press).

Hirschman, A.O. (1970) *Exit, Voice and Loyalty: Responses to Decline in Firms, Organisations, and States* (Cambridge, MA: Harvard University Press).

Hobsbawm, E. (2000; 1st edition 1969) *Bandits* (London: Abacus).

Hoffman, B. (1998) *Inside Terrorism* (New York: Columbia University Press).

Hoffmann, S. (1966) 'Obstinate or Obsolete? The Fate of the Nation-State and the Case of Western Europe', *Daedalus*, 95 (3), 862–915.

Hooghe, L. and Marks, G. (2009) 'A Postfunctionalist Theory of European Integration: From Permissive Consensus to Constraining Dissensus', *British Journal of Political Science*, 39 (1), 1–23.

Howe, G. (1994) *Conflict of Loyalty* (London: Macmillan).

Hume, D. (1986) 'Days of Action: Loyalism on Strike', *Fortnight*, 236, 24 March–20 April, 6–7.

Hume, J. (1979) 'The Irish Question: A British Problem', *Foreign Affairs*, 58 (2) (Winter), 308.

Hume, J. (1997) *A New Ireland: Politics, Peace, and Reconciliation* (Boulder, CO: Robert Rinehart Publishers).

Hurd, D. (2003) *Memoirs* (London: Little Brown).

Ivory, G. (1999) 'Revisions in Nationalist Discourse among Irish Political Parties', *Irish Political Studies* 14 (1), 84–103.

Jackson, A. (2003) *Home Rule: An Irish History, 1800–2000* (London: Weidenfeld and Nicolson).

Johnstone, R. (1989) 'Playing for Ireland', *Honest Ulsterman*, 86 (Spring/Summer), 59–64.

Kelly, S. (2013) *Fianna Fáil, Partition and Northern Ireland, 1926–1971* (Dublin: Irish Academic Press).

Kerr, M. (2011) *The Destructors: The Story of Northern Ireland's Lost Peace Process* (Dublin: Irish Academic Press).

Krosigk, F. (1971) 'A Reconsideration of Federalism in the Scope of the Present Discussion on European Integration', *Journal of Common Market Studies*, 9 (3), 197–223.

Kyle, K. (1975) 'Sunningdale and After: Britain, Ireland, and Ulster', *World Today*, 31 (11), 439–50.

Laird, J. (2010) *A Struggle to Be Heard* (Exeter: Global and Western Publishing).

Lamb, P. (2010) 'Guild Socialism' in Mark Bevir (ed.) *Encylopedia of Political Theory* (London: Sage).

Lynch, J. M. (1972) 'Anglo-Irish Problem', *Foreign Affairs*, 50 (4), 601–17.

Maguire, M. (2008) *The Civil Service and the Revolution in Ireland, 1912–1938: 'Shaking the Blood-Stained Hand of Mr Collins'* (Manchester: Manchester University Press).

McAllister, I. (1977) 'The Legitimacy of Opposition: The Collapse of the 1974 Northern Ireland Executive', *Éire-Ireland*, 12 (4), 25–42.

McAuley, J.W. (2010) *Ulster's Last Stand? Reconstructing Unionism after the Peace Process* (Dublin: Irish Academic Press).

McCluskie, T. (2013) *The Rise and Fall of Harland and Wolff* (Stroud: The History Press).

McCorry, J. (2005) 'Recollections' in *Grassroots Leadership*, 3 (Newtownabbey: Island Publications).

McDaid, S. (2012) 'The Irish Government and the Sunningdale Council of Ireland: A Vehicle for Unity?', *Irish Historical Studies*, 38 (150), 283–303.

McDaid, S. (2013) *Template for Peace: Northern Ireland, 1972–75* (Manchester: Manchester University Press).

McDermott, S. (2014) 'The Dimensions of Irish Government Involvement in the Pursuit of a Settlement of the Northern Ireland Conflict', *Irish Political Studies*, 29 (1), 98–115.

McGrattan, C. (2009) 'Dublin, the SDLP and the Sunningdale Agreement: Maximalist Nationalism and Path-Dependency', *Contemporary British History*, 23 (1), 61–78.

McGrattan, C. (2010) *Northern Ireland 1968–2008: The Politics of Entrenchment* (Houndmills, Basingstoke: Palgrave Macmillan)

McIvor, B. (1998) *Hope Deferred: Experiences of an Irish Unionist* (Belfast: Blackstaff Press).

McKittrick, D. and McVea, D. (2001) *Making Sense of the Troubles* (Belfast: Blackstaff Press).

McKittrick, D., Kelters, S., Feeney, B. and Thornton, C. (1999/2004), *Lost Lives: The Stories of the Men, Women and Children Who Died as a Result of the Northern Ireland Troubles* (Edinburgh: Mainstream).

McLoughlin, P.J. (2007) *'Dublin Is Just a Sunningdale Away'?: The SDLP, the Irish Government and the Sunningdale Agreement*, IBIS Working Paper No. 82 (Dublin: University College, Dublin, Institute for British–Irish Studies).

McLoughlin, P.J. (2010) *John Hume and the Revision of Irish Nationalism* (Manchester: Manchester University Press).

McLoughlin, P.J. (2011) ' "Humespeak": the SDLP, Political Discourse and the Peace Process' in K. Hayward and C. O'Donnell (eds) *Political Discourse and Conflict Resolution: Debating Peace in Northern Ireland* (London: Routledge).

Millar, F. (2008) *David Trimble: The Price of Peace* (Dublin: The Liffey Press).

Miller, D.W. (2007; 1st edition 1978) *Queen's Rebels: Ulster Loyalism in Historical Perspective* (Dublin: University College Dublin Press).

Mitchell, G. (1999) *Making Peace: The Inside Story of the Making of the Good Friday Agreement* (London: William Heinemann).

Mitchell, S. (2014) 'The Permanent Crisis of 21st Century Unionism', *Irish Marxist Review*, 3 (9), 27–42.

Mitrany, D. (1965) 'The Prospect of Integration: Federal or Functional', *Journal of Common Market Studies*, 4 (2),119–49.

Moloney, E. (2002) *A Secret History of the IRA* (London: Penguin).

Moloney, E. (2010) *Voices from the Grave: Two Men's War in Ireland* (London: Faber and Faber).

Moloney, E. and Pollak, A. (1986) *Paisley* (Dublin: Poolbeg).

Moore, C (2013) *Margaret Thatcher* (London: Penguin Books).

Mulholland, M. (2000) *Northern Ireland and the Crossroads: Ulster Unionism in the O'Neill Years, 1960–9* (Basingstoke: Palgrave Macmillan).

Mulholland, M. (2013) *Terence O'Neill* (Dublin: University College Dublin Press).

Murphy, D. (1979) *A Place Apart* (Harmondsworth: Penguin).

Murphy, M. (2007) *Gerry Fitt: A Political Chameleon* (Cork: Mercier Press).

Murray, G. (1998) *John Hume and the SDLP: Impact and Survival in Northern Ireland* (Dublin: Irish Academic Press).

Nelson, S. (1977) 'A Criminal Lack of Politics', *Fortnight*, 140 (14 January), 13.

Nelson, S. (1984) *Ulster's Uncertain Defenders* (Belfast: Appletree Press).

Neumann, P. (2003) *Britain's Long War: British Strategy in the Northern Ireland Conflict, 1969–98* (Basingstoke: Palgrave Macmillan).

Newsinger, J. (1995) 'From Counter-Insurgency to Internal Security: Northern Ireland, 1969–1992', *Small Wars and Insurgencies*, 6 (1), 88–111.

Ó Beacháin, D. (2010) *The Destiny of the Soldiers: Fianna Fail, Irish Republicianism and the IRA 1926–1973* (Dublin: Gill and Macmillan).

O'Brien, C. (1972) *States of Ireland* (London: Hutchinson).

O'Brien, C. (1998) *Memoir: My Life and Themes* (Dublin: Poolbeg Press).

O'Clery, C. (1998) 'Sunningdale Failed Partly Because Mainstream Republicans and Unionists Were Not on Board', *Irish Times* (6 April), 5.

O'Clery, C. (1999) *Ireland in Quotes* (Dublin: The O'Brien Press).

Ó Dochartaigh, N. (2011) ' "Everyone Trying", the IRA Ceasefire, 1975: A Missed Opportunity for Peace? *Field Day Review*, 7, 1 January.

O'Donnell, C. (2007a) *Fianna Fáil, Irish Republicanism and the Northern Ireland Troubles, 1968–2005* (Dublin: Irish Academic Press).

O'Donnell, C. (2007b) *The Sunningdale Communiqué, 1973, and Bipartisanship in the Republic of Ireland.* Working Papers in British–Irish Studies No. 81 (Dublin: Institute for British–Irish Studies, University College Dublin).

O'Duffy, B. (1999) 'British and Irish Conflict Regulation from Sunningdale to Belfast Part I: Tracing the Status of Contesting Sovereigns, 1968–1974', *Nations and Nationalism*, 5 (4), 523–42.

O'Kane, E. (2006) 'When Can Conflicts Be Resolved? A Critique of Ripeness', *Civil Wars*, 8 (3–4), 268–84.

O'Kane E. (2007) *Britain, Ireland and Northern Ireland Since 1980* (Abingdon: Routledge).

O'Kane E. (2015) 'Talking to the Enemy? The Role of the Back-Channel in the Development of the Northern Ireland Peace Process', *Contemporary British History*, 29 (3), 401–20.

O'Leary, B. (1989) 'The Limits of Coercive Consociationalism in Northern Ireland', *Political Studies*, 37 (4), 569–70.

O'Leary, B. (1997) 'The Conservative Stewardship of Northern Ireland 1979–97: Sound-Bottomed Contradictions or Slow Learning?', *Political Studies*, XLV (4).

Ó Murchú, N. (2005) 'Ethnic Politics and Labour Market Closure: Shipbuilding and Industrial Decline in Northern Ireland', *Ethnic and Racial Studies*, 28 (5), 859–79.

O'Toole, F. (1995) 'You Never Step into the Same Play Twice', *Irish Times*, 31 October, 10.

Oakeshott, M. (1991) *Rationalism in Politics and Other Essays*, revised and expanded edition (Indianapolis: The Liberty Press).

Papadopoulos, Y. (2013) *Democracy in Crisis? Politics, Governance and Policy* (Basingstoke: Palgrave Macmillan).

Parker, S. (1989) *Pentecost*, in *Three Plays for Ireland* (Birmingham: Oberon Books).

Patterson, H. (1997) *The Politics of Illusion: A Political History of the IRA* (London: Serif).

Patterson, H. (2006) *Ireland since 1939: The Persistence of Conflict* (Dublin: Gill and Macmillan).

Patterson, H. (2010) 'Sectarianism Revisited: The Provisional IRA Campaign in a Border Region of Northern Ireland', *Terrorism and Political Violence*, 22 (3), 57.

Patterson, H. (2013) *Ireland's Violent Frontier: The Border and Anglo-Irish Relations during the Troubles* (Basingstoke: Palgrave).

Patterson, H. and Kaufmann, E. (2007) *Unionism and Orangeism in Northern Ireland since 1945: The Decline of the Loyal Family* (Manchester: Manchester University Press).

Pollak, A. (1983) 'The Left that Never Was', *Fortnight*, 196 (July–August), 3–4.

Powell, J. (2009) *Great Hatred Little Room: Making Peace in Northern Ireland* (London: The Bodley Head).

Power, P. (1977) 'Sunningdale Strategy and Northern Majority Consent Doctrine in Anglo-Irish Relations', *Eire-Ireland*, 12 (1), 35–67.

Prior, J. (1986) *A Balance of Power* (London: Hamish Hamilton).

Pruitt, D. (2006) 'Negotiation with Terrorists', *International Negotiation*, 11 (2006), 371–94.

Purvis, D. (2014) *Picking Up Worms* (Unpublished). Privately held archive.

Ramsay, R. (2009) *Ringside Seats: An Insider's View of the Crisis in Northern Ireland* (Dublin: Irish Academic Press).

Rees, M. (1985) *Northern Ireland: A Personal Perspective* (London: Methuen).

Reid, C. (1989) *The Belle of the Belfast City; Did You Hear the One About the Irishman?: Two Plays* (London: Methuen).

Rolleston, T.W. (1975) 'Introduction' to P.B. Shelley, *An Address to the Irish People* (New York: AMS Press).

Rose, A. (1999) 'From Sunningdale to Peace?', *Peace Review*, 11 (1), 139–46.

Rose, R. (1971) *Governing Without Consensus* (London: Faber and Faber).

Ryder, C. (2006) *Fighting Fitt* (Belfast: The Brehon Press).

Scott, J.W. (2001) 'Fantasy Echo: History and the Construction of Identity', *Critical Inquiry*, 27 (Winter), 284–304.

Shirlow, P. (2012) *The End of Ulster Loyalism?* (Manchester: Manchester University Press).

Smith, W.B. (2011) *The British State and the Northern Ireland Crisis, 1969–1973: From Violence to Power-Sharing* (Washington, DC: US Institute of Peace).

Snyder, R. (2013) 'The Decline of Revolutionary Nationalism and the Beginning of the Peace Process in Northern Ireland and the Middle East', in T. White (ed.) *Lessons from the Northern Ireland Peace Process* (Madison, WI: The University of Wisconsin Press)

Spencer, G. (2008) *The State of Loyalism in Northern Ireland* (Basingstoke: Palgrave Macmillan).

Staunton, E. (2001) *The Nationalists of Northern Ireland: 1918–1973* (Dublin: Columba Press).

Stewart, A.T.Q. (2001) *The Shape of Irish History* (Belfast: Blackstaff Press).

Stoker, G. (2006) *Why Politics Matters: Making Democracy Work* (Basingstoke: Palgrave Macmillan).

Tannam, E. (1999) *Cross-border Cooperation in the Republic of Ireland and Northern Ireland* (Basingstoke: Macmillan).

Tannam, E. (2001) 'Explaining the Good Friday Agreement: A Learning Process', *Government and Opposition*, 36 (4), 493–518.

Taylor, P. (1997) *Provos: The IRA & Sinn Fein* (London: Bloomsbury Publishing).

Thatcher, M. (1993) *The Downing Street Years* (London: Harper Collins, 1993).

Thompson, E.P. (1991) *The Making of the English Working Class* (Harmondsworth: Penguin Books).

Todd, J. (2013) 'Thresholds of State Change: Changing British State Institutions and Practices in Northern Ireland after Direct Rule', *Political Studies*, i-First publication.

Tonge, J. (2000) 'From Sunningdale to the Good Friday Agreement: Creating Devolved Government in Northern Ireland', *Contemporary British History*, 14 (3), 39–60.

Tonge, J. (2003) 'Victims of Their Own Success? Post-Agreement Dilemmas of Political Moderates in Northern Ireland', *The Global Review of Ethnopolitics*, 3 (1), 47–53.

Tonge, J., Shirlow, P. and McAuley, J.W. (2011) 'So Why Did the Guns Fall Silent? How Interplay, Not Stalemate, Explains the Northern Ireland Peace Process', *Irish Political Studies*, 26 (1), 1–18.

Tonge, J., Braniff, M., Hennessey, T., McAuley, J.W. and Whiting, S. (2014) *The Democratic Unionist Party: From Protest to Power* (Oxford: Oxford University Press).

Trimble, D. (1975) Review of *The Point of No Return* by Robert Fisk, *Fortnight* 115 (21 November), 13–14.

Trimble, D. (1998) '*The Belfast Agreement*', *Fordham International Law Journal*, 22, 1145.

Walker, G. (2004) *A History of the Ulster Unionist Party: Protest, Pragmatism and Pessimism* (Manchester: Manchester University Press).

Walsh, P. (1994) *Irish Republicanism and Socialism: The Politics of the Republican Movement 1905 to 1994* (Belfast: Athol Books).

Webber, D. (2014) 'How Likely Is It that the European Union Will Disintegrate? A Critical Analysis of Competing Theoretical Perspectives', *European Journal of International Relations*, 20 (2), 341–65.

White, R. (2006) *Ruairí Ó Brádaigh: The Life and Politics of an Irish Revolutionary* (Bloomington and Indianapolis: Indiana University Press).

Wilson, H. (1979) *Final Term: The Labour Government 1974–1976* (London: Weidenfeld and Nicolson).

Wolff, S. (2001) 'Context and Content: Sunningdale and Belfast Compared' in R. Wilford (ed.) *Aspects of the Belfast Agreement* (Oxford: Oxford University Press), pp. 11–27.

Wolff, S. (2003) 'Introduction: From Sunningdale to Belfast, 1973–98' in J. Neuheiser and S. Wolff (eds), *Peace at Last? The Impact of the Good Friday Agreement on Northern Ireland* (Oxford: Berghahn Books).

Wood, I.S. (2006) *Crimes of Loyalty: A History of the UDA* (Edinburgh: Edinburgh University Press).

Wright, F. (1973) 'Protestant Ideology and Politics in Ulster', *European Journal of Sociology*, 14 (2), 212–80.

Ziegler, P. (2011) *Edward Heath* (London: Harper Collins).

Newspapers

Belfast Telegraph
Daily Express
Daily Mail
The Evening News
Fortnight
The Gadsden Times
Irish Independent
Irish News
Irish Times
News Letter
Republican News
Salford City Reporter
Sunday Independent
Sunday Press

Organisation newsheets

An Phoblacht
Ulster Vanguard (1973a) *Community of the British Isles* (Belfast: Ulster Vanguard)
Ulster Vanguard (1973b) *Government Without Right* (Belfast: Ulster Vanguard)
Ulster Workers' Council (UWC) *News Sheet*
Workers Association (1974) 'Strike Bulletin Number 1', The Ulster General Strike: Strike Bulletins of the Workers Association Belfast: Workers Association. Phrased in the document as 'The National Senate of Ireland'

Reports

Bullock Report (1977) *The Report of the Committee of Inquiry on Industrial Democracy* [The Bullock Report] (London: HMSO).
Chief Constable's Report for 1974 (1975) (Belfast: Police Authority for Northern Ireland).
Garry, J. (2011) Report for the Electoral Reform Society: Northern Ireland 2011 Assembly election and AV Referendum, available at www.qub.ac.uk/schools/ SchoolofPoliticsInternationalStudiesandPhilosophy/FileStorStafffiles/ JGarry/Filetoupload,281998,en.pdf (accessed 29 January 2014).
Green Paper (1972), *Northern Ireland: A Paper for Discussion* (London: HMSO).
HMSO (1974) *The Northern Ireland Constitution*, Cmnd. 5675 (London: HMSO).
HMSO (1975) *Report, together with the Proceedings of the Convention and Other Appendices: Northern Ireland Constitutional Convention* (London: HMSO).

HMSO (1976) *The Northern Ireland Constitutional Convention*, Cmnd. 6387 (London: HMSO).

Irish Reports (1974) Kevin Boland, Plantiff v. An Taoiseach and others, Defendants (1973 No. 3289).

New Ireland Forum Report (1984) (Dublin: The Stationery Office).

NIO (1972) *The Future of Northern Ireland: A Paper for Discussion* (London: HMSO).

NIO (1973) *The Northern Ireland Constitutional Proposals* (Belfast: HMSO).

NIO (1998) *The Belfast Agreement* (Belfast: HMSO).

SDLP (1972) *Towards a New Ireland* (Belfast: SDLP, 1972).

Sunningdale Communiqué (1973) available at http://cain.ulst.ac.uk/events/sunningdale/agreement.htm (accessed 26 November 2014).

Archives

CAIN website, PRONI Records on CAIN: 1974 http://cain.ulst.ac.uk/proni/list-year.html#1974 (accessed 1 July 2014).

Glen Barr Papers

Imperial War Museum, London, Department of Documents (IWM), Private Papers of General Sir Ian Freeland

Liddell Hart Centre For Military Archives, (LHCMA) King's College, London

Linen Hall Library

London School of Economics, Papers of Stanley Orme (LSE)

The National Archives of the United Kingdom (TNA)

National Archives of Ireland (NAI)

National University of Ireland, Galway (NUIG), The Ruairi Ó Brádaigh Papers

Public Records Office of Northern Ireland (PRONI)

Index

Lightning Source UK Ltd.
Milton Keynes UK
UKHW021124100520
363019UK00005B/366